Learning and
Learning Difficulties

Other titles of interest:

Spelling
Peter Westwood
1 84312 193 X

Reading and Learning Difficulties
Peter Westwood
1 84312 196 4

Numeracy and Learning Difficulties
Peter Westwood
1 84312 194 8

Learning and Learning Difficulties

Approaches to teaching and assessment

Peter Westwood

David Fulton Publishers

David Fulton Publishers Ltd
The Chiswick Centre, 414 Chiswick High Road, London W4 5TF

www.fultonpublishers.co.uk

First published in Australia in 2004 by ACER Press
Australian Council for Educational Research Ltd
19 Prospect Hill Road, Camberwell, Victoria, 3124
Copyright © Peter Westwood 2004

First published in Great Britain in 2004 by David Fulton Publishers

Note: The right of the author to be identified as the author of this
work has been asserted by him in accordance with the Copyright,
Designs and Patents Act 1988.

David Fulton Publishers is a division of Granada Learning, part of ITV plc.

Copyright © Peter Westwood 2004

British Library Cataloguing in Publication Data
A catalogue record for this book is available from the Britsh Library.

ISBN 1 84312 195 6

Typeset by RefineCatch Ltd, Bungay, Suffolk
Printed and bound in Great Britain

Contents

For my dear friend Chan Wing Yan (Carol).
An excellent student and teacher.

Preface

In writing this book I have attempted to place the phenomenon of learning difficulty within a much wider context than is usual by exploring a variety of learning processes, learning theories, and concepts about learning. An understanding of the way in which learning occurs is fundamental to an understanding of how and when problems in learning may arise. By painting this broader canvas I hope to help teachers and others appreciate that problems in learning are not all due to weaknesses within students or to lack of motivation on their part. Indeed, many learning difficulties are created or exacerbated not by factors within the students but by influences within the environment in which they live and learn. Many such factors in the learning environment are amenable to modification and improvement, whereas deficits within learners are not so easily changed.

Two of the most powerful influences in the learning environment are the school curriculum and the approaches to teaching. It is argued here that teaching methods and materials must be selected carefully to suit the types of learning involved in specific lessons, and to accommodate the learning characteristics of the students. Many learning problems are prevented or minimised by matching teaching methods and lesson content to learners' current aptitude and prior experience.

Of course, some learning problems are indeed due to deficits or impairments within students themselves and discussion focuses on such causes in later chapters of the book. However, the point is made that some commonly observed weaknesses or 'deficits' (for example, poor attention to task, limited concentration, poor retention and recall of information) are often the outcome of learning failure, not the cause. The impact of inappropriate curriculum, insufficient teaching, and persistent failure is discussed, with particular reference to the detrimental effects they can have on students' affective development and motivation.

Readers will identify a number of recurring themes running through the chapters — including the need to catch and maintain students' attention, the importance of explicit teaching and guided practice, and the value of teaching students effective task-approach strategies. Also emphasised in many chapters is the importance of addressing students' personal and emotional needs, as well as working toward cognitive and academic goals.

I have drawn widely on international literature to support my arguments and to present contemporary perspectives on learning and learning difficulty. There is universal agreement that early prevention of learning failure is much more effective than later attempted cures.

PETER WESTWOOD
FACULTY OF EDUCATION
UNIVERSITY OF HONG KONG

1 Perspectives on learning

When people are asked what schools are for, a common reply is: 'To help children learn'. (Santrock, 2001, p. 238)

Many experts suggest that children are born with intrinsic motivation – a natural desire to make sense of the world and become competent (for example, Seligman, 1995; Smilkstein, 2003; West, 2002). The mastery orientation displayed by young children in the preschool years suggests that they enjoy informal learning for its own sake, and they gain satisfaction from completing tasks they have set themselves. Even when faced with difficulties, they will still persist rather than give up, and will constantly tackle new challenges (Hauser-Cram, 1998). Children exhibit such mastery orientation in almost every facet of their exploratory play in the preschool years.

Slavin (1994) indicates that almost all children, regardless of social class or other factors, enter school for the first time full of enthusiasm, motivation and self-confidence, expecting to succeed. But before the end of Year 1 some of them lose that confidence because they are not experiencing success. Lack of success reduces mastery orientation, weakens a child's feelings of self-efficacy, lowers self-esteem and diminishes motivation (Neal and Kelly, 2002; Rosner, 1993). Linden (2002, p. 76) states, 'Already in their first year in school some pupils will have had traumatic experiences of not being able to cope [and] the loss of a feeling of competence can create unhappiness, fear and disappointment.'

Why does this situation arise? Do the children suddenly become incapable of effective learning once they enter the school environment? Does the fault lie with the children, or is it related to the nature of the educational programme and the manner in which it is implemented?

To answer these questions, teachers need to know much more about human learning and the factors that can enhance or impede it. It is hoped that this book will help increase teachers' understanding of learners, learning processes, and learning difficulties.

Teaching should be based on a knowledge of learning

Understanding *how* children learn is of fundamental importance for teaching and for effective curriculum planning. An understanding of theories and principles of learning can help teachers select the most appropriate methods of instruction to suit different types of subject matter, different types of learning, different educational outcomes, and different characteristics of learners (Gagne and Wager, 2002). A thorough knowledge of curriculum content, together with an appreciation of the steps and processes involved in learning that type of content, can help teachers implement sound educational programmes.

Knowledge of learning processes can also help teachers anticipate the difficulties some students may encounter in certain school subjects. Teachers can then consider how best to prevent or minimise learning problems and how to motivate their students to learn (Brophy, 2001; Penso, 2002; Sasson, 2001).

Teachers' deep understanding of these issues is often referred to as *pedagogical content knowledge* (Shulman, 1987; Tan *et al.*, 2003) and the most effective teachers in our schools are usually those equipped with a great deal of this professional know-how. The other essential element of pedagogical knowledge is an awareness of the learning characteristics of the students they teach, including those with special educational needs. Learners have many common characteristics at various ages and stages, but individual learners also differ in many educationally significant ways. Teachers need to understand both the commonalities and the differences in order to meet students' needs.

Learning defined and described

It appears to be a simple task to define what we mean by the term 'learning' – after all, we have spent our entire lives learning new things. When asked to provide a definition of 'learning' teachers usually offer such responses as:

- Knowing something you didn't know before.
- Gaining knowledge and skills.
- Acquiring information that you can use in new situations.
- Benefiting from instruction.
- Developing your intelligence.
- Acquiring a different perspective on the world.

There is, of course, a great deal of truth and value in all these suggested definitions. But how do psychologists define the phenomenon of learning? Some of the common (and a few less common) definitions of learning from the field of psychology include the following.

Key concepts embodied in some of these definitions will be discussed and applied in this and later chapters.

- Learning is the process whereby an organism changes its behaviour as a result of experience (Driscoll, 2000).
- Learning is a relatively permanent change in capacity for performance, acquired through experience (Good and Brophy, 1990).

- Learning is a relatively permanent change in mental associations due to experience (Ormrod, 2003).

- Learning is a potential change in behaviour resulting from experience in processing information (Walker, 1996).

- Learning is the way that human beings acquire new skills, knowledge, attitudes and values. The outcomes of learning are the new capabilities possessed by the learner (Gredler, 2001).

- Learning consists of the acquisition of increasingly automated schemata held in long-term memory (Sweller, 1999).

- Neuroscientists define learning as two neurons communicating with each other (Sprenger, 1999).

Types of learning

Many years ago the psychologist David Ausubel (1968) argued that it must not be assumed that all types of learning involve the learner in precisely the same set of mental, emotional or physical processes – in other words, different types of learning may well involve quite different psychological processes and require different methods of teaching. Any false assumption that all learning is in some way 'the same' can lead to the erroneous notion that one general method of teaching will serve all educational purposes and will suit all learners (Gregory and Chapman, 2002). It has become popular to say of teaching methods, 'one size does not fit all'.

Ausubel (1968) suggested that if instructional programming for different curriculum areas is to be truly effective, teachers need to identify the different types of learning involved in each area, and then select teaching methods that are most likely to facilitate that type of learning. As Galton *et al.* (1999) have indicated, a theory of pedagogy requires that teachers identify the nature of what it is the child is expected to learn, and then decide on the most effective instructional principles for bringing about the required learning processes.

Categories of learning

There have been many and varied attempts to categorise examples of learning. The most obvious categories that appeal to common sense comprise:

- Knowledge
- Skills
- Attitudes and values.

These three broad categories or domains have provided the basic framework for planning a wide variety of learning objectives within school curricula, as reflected in the vast literature on educational programming and curriculum design (for example, Gunter *et al.*, 2003). Most schools would readily acknowledge their responsibility to facilitate learning in the three domains.

There are other more detailed ways of analysing learning that subdivide the three broad domains into specific categories of learning. For example, Robert Gagne (1984 *et al.*, 1992; Gagne and Wager, 2002) developed a taxonomy for categorising different forms of learning. His early model was complex and contained a variety of sub-types such as *signal learning, stimulus-response learning, discrimination learning, chaining, verbal association, rule learning* and *concept learning*. These categories served a useful purpose in contexts where psychologists were

carrying out controlled experiments in human learning, but the categories were more difficult to apply in school contexts where most episodes of learning involve simultaneous and integrated use of several subtypes of learning within one task or lesson. However, Mastropieri and Scruggs (2002) still advocate a very similar taxonomy of learning for use when designing effective instruction for students with special needs. Their taxonomy comprises: *discrimination learning, factual learning, rule learning, procedural learning, conceptual learning,* and *problem solving and thinking*. Some of these categories will be discussed in more detail in this and other chapters.

In a later analysis, Gagne, Briggs and Wager (1992) moved toward a much broader system of classification using five main categories of learning – physical skills, information, intellectual skills, cognitive strategies, and attitudes. The writers also gave a brief indication of the type of instruction required for facilitating each type of learning and the conditions that must be established if optimal learning is to occur. Gagne used the term 'capabilities' to describe each of these categories; and it will be noted in the definitions of learning quoted above that other writers also favour the word 'capabilities'. Gredler (2001, p. 405) defines a human capability as 'the outcome of learning'. Robert Gagne's (1992) categories of human capability are summarised below.

Learning physical (psychomotor) skills

Psychomotor skills are learned capabilities that involve the coordination of brain, muscles, hand and eye. Psychomotor skills include such diverse activities as cutting with a pair of scissors, getting dressed, swimming, walking, eating with a spoon, using a computer keyboard, writing, riding a bicycle, and driving a car. Children, without direct teaching, acquire very many physical skills through imitation and trial and error, but most of the physical skills associated with performance in school need to be directly taught and frequently practised. It is generally accepted that very large amounts of practice are needed in order that motor skills can eventually be performed with a high degree of automaticity (Howe, 1999).

In the early stages of teaching a new motor skill, modelling, imitation, and precise verbal instruction are extremely important. Sometimes direct physical guidance of the learner's movements is required, when helping a young child or a child with a physical disability to form the numeral 7, for example; or an older child to experience the movement for a backhand stroke in tennis. It is also clear that corrective feedback is necessary to help learners improve their motor skill performance. Some of this feedback comes from the instructor, but an even more essential component of feedback must come from the learner's own internal self-monitoring of performance, resulting in self-correction.

Acquiring information

This type of learning involves the acquisition of factual information (knowledge) that the learner is able to state and use. Examples include factual knowledge such as, 'Bus number 91 will take me to Aberdeen'; 'The shops in my street open at 8.00am'; 'Paris is the capital of France'; '7 + 2 = 9'. This type of knowledge is known as *'declarative knowledge'* to differentiate it from *'procedural knowledge'* which involves knowing the steps in carrying out a procedure (see below).

A sound knowledge-base of information provides much of the raw material utilised in the performance of intellectual skills – for example, thinking and reasoning usually require the retrieval and application of some factual information (Hirsch, 2000). When used in combination with cognitive strategies and intellectual skills, information enables an individual to reason, reflect, solve problems, explain, and generate new ideas.

Information is of most value (and is most easily accessed) when it links with related information also stored in the learner's memory. This issue will be discussed more fully later in the section describing the formation of *schemata* and the role of *working memory*. Isolated fragments of information are often easily forgotten or are difficult to access. Information is more readily remembered when it is linked directly to prior learning and when students are encouraged to process it actively.

Students acquire huge amounts of factual information incidentally in daily life, particularly in this era of communication technology. In school, teachers still need to set high priority on making sure students are building a deep and relevant knowledge base. A teacher's task is to make key information available to students and to help them make appropriate connections with prior knowledge and experience. Sometimes, important curriculum information needs to be conveyed to students by direct teaching and through use of appropriate texts and computer programs. At other times, information is readily acquired through students' independent study, group work, and discussion. The currently popular *constructivist* theory of learning suggests that the acquisition of information occurs best when learners actively engage in exploratory modes of learning. Constructivist theory will be discussed fully in Chapter 2.

Some instances of learning difficulty can be traced to lack of automaticity in the retrieval of essential declarative knowledge, or in the application of procedural knowledge. A learner who lacks automaticity has to expend inappropriately large amounts of concentrated effort in recalling information or remembering the simple lower-order steps in a cognitive process. He or she is therefore hampered in engaging in higher-order thinking. An example might be difficulty in comprehension when reading due to lack of automaticity in word recognition and phonics. The reader's efforts have to be focused on basic decoding of the print on the page rather than reading for meaning. Similarly in mathematics, poor automaticity with recall of simple number facts, or a weakness in recalling steps in a multiplication algorithm, will distract the student from reflecting logically upon the features of a contextual problem. Gage and Berliner (1998, p. 262) suggest that, 'A student's failure to perform well, or a teacher's failure to teach well, may be due to inadequate declarative knowledge, inadequate procedural knowledge, or both.'

Developing intellectual skills

Intellectual skills represent the cognitive abilities that enable individuals to interact successfully with their environment and tackle new tasks effectively. Intellectual skill development involves the acquisition of concepts, rules, routines, and symbol systems. Learning an intellectual skill usually means learning how to perform the cognitive processes involved in thinking, reasoning and problem solving.

Robert Gagne (1984) indicates that much human behaviour is 'rule-governed'. Basic rules include principles such as understanding that printed language in English is sequenced from left to right, that in oral language words must be produced in a particular sequence to obey the rules of grammar, that traffic lights operate in set sequence, and that birds and animals can be classified into species according to their specific characteristics. Learners create higher-order rules as they attempt to work out solutions to problems. They draw upon concepts and basic rules already known and combine them in new ways. For example, a preschool child solves the problem of how to assemble the track for a new toy train by combining prior knowledge about the ways in which some objects can be linked together with prior knowledge that the tracks provided for other moving toys often form a circle. In carrying out this task the child has combined fragments of prior knowledge and utilised previous experience in a unique way to solve a new problem. In doing so the child has acquired a set of principles that might be used again in similar circumstances (in other words, can be *generalised* or *transferred*).

Teaching lower-level intellectual skills (discriminations, simple concepts, symbol recognition) usually involves direct explanation, demonstration, and guided practice. Basic rules are also best taught through direct instruction, followed by application. However, higher-order rules have to be constructed by the learner, who therefore needs to be given opportunity to solve problems and apply accumulated knowledge to new situations. This level and type of learning suggest the need for an enquiry or problem-solving classroom approach. Robert Gagne *et al.* (1992) indicate that what is learned in this domain of intellectual skills is mainly *procedural skills* – knowing *how*, rather than knowing *that*.

Learning cognitive and metacognitive strategies

Cognitive strategies can be regarded as mental plans of action that learners develop to help them approach any learning task or problem. An effective cognitive strategy enables learners to plan what they will do, and then monitor and modify their own thoughts and actions as they proceed. We refer to this ability to 'think about our own thinking' as *metacognition* (Kershner, 2000). For example, a student trying to solve a problem may think, 'This isn't working out correctly – I had better try a different way.' This student is effectively monitoring and adapting his or her own performance. The child who thinks, 'I need to write this down to help me remember it', is also illustrating a metacognitive *self-regulating strategy*.

Metacognitive processes that supervise and control our cognition are sometimes termed *internal executive processes* (Gourgey, 2001). These executive processes enable us to plan, monitor and evaluate performance throughout the execution of a task. It is now believed that all academic and intellectual tasks, like writing an essay, reading with comprehension, solving a mathematical problem, analysing data for a project, are most easily and effectively accomplished through the application of cognitive and metacognitive strategies. It is also believed that many learning difficulties are caused by students' lack of appropriate cognitive strategies and relative absence of metacognition (Bradshaw, 1995; Chan, 1991; Smith, 1998).

Practical methods for improving a learner's ability to use cognitive and metacognitive strategies are currently receiving much attention from educational researchers (for example, Hartman, 2001; Pressley and McCormick, 1995; Taylor, 2002). It is proving to be possible to teach students to use cognitive strategies more efficiently, thus resulting in an improved rate of success (for example, Graham and Harris, 2000a; Pressley, 1999; Swanson, 2000a; Xin and Jitendra, 1999). In general, cognitive strategies are taught by direct explanation and modelling, with the teacher 'thinking aloud' as he or she demonstrates an effective strategy for a given task. The learners are encouraged to observe and develop similar 'self-talk' to help them apply the new strategy effectively. Guided practice is then provided, with feedback from the teacher. Deliberate efforts are made to help the learner recognise other contexts in which a particular strategy can be used (the principle of training for transfer and generalisation of learning). The learners are also encouraged to monitor and reflect upon the effectiveness of their own use of specific strategies.

Developing attitudes, beliefs and values

Robert Gagne *et al.* (1992) define an attitude as an internal state that affects an individual's choice of personal action toward some object, person, or event. Many of the most important goals of education deal with the development of positive and productive attitudes, beliefs and values in students. The methods of instruction to be employed in establishing desired attitudes differ considerably from those applicable to the learning of intellectual skills, information, or cognitive strategies

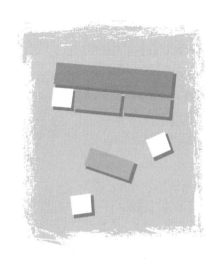

because attitudes cannot be taught directly. They may be acquired through a combination of observing a model displaying the particular attitude, reflecting upon the outcomes from the actions of self and others, from peer group pressure, and to some degree through active persuasion and the use of incentives (rewards). Once they are acquired, attitudes tend to be reinforced when others agree with and support them.

Some of the most significant beliefs and attitudes learners develop are associated with their own competence and efficacy as learners; and these beliefs are shaped by the extent to which they succeed or fail in school (Eccles *et al.*, 1998; Galloway *et al.*, 1995). This important issue of self-efficacy will be discussed fully in Chapter 2.

While the five categories of learning identified by Robert Gagne *et al.* (1992) are extremely useful for analysing learning in a school context and for identifying appropriate methods to facilitate learning in the five domains, there are other ways of classifying human learning.

Intentional learning and incidental learning

Good and Brophy (2002) make an important distinction between two broad categories of learning, *intentional* and *incidental* learning. Intentional learning operates in a situation where the learner is deliberately setting out to acquire some particular knowledge, skill or strategy, and is putting focused effort into the task. Incidental learning, on the other hand, occurs when an individual is not making any conscious effort to acquire information or skill but is merely exposed by chance to some experience – such as passively observing the actions of another person, watching a film, or over-hearing a conversation. It is believed that many of the attitudes, beliefs, and values we hold are acquired mainly through incidental learning rather than from deliberate instruction.

Some contemporary classroom approaches rely fairly heavily on children's incidental learning capacity to acquire basic skills and concepts. Advocates of these approaches regard incidental learning as preferable to direct instruction because it is considered to be a more 'natural' way of acquiring information and skills. For example, in many English-speaking countries in the 1980s and 1990s teachers employed the 'whole language approach' to the teaching of reading and writing, believing firmly that children would all acquire word recognition, phonic knowledge, spelling skills and the rules of grammar through incidental learning by engaging in reading and writing activities each day (Goodman, 1986). Similarly, it has been argued that basic number skills and concepts will be discovered effectively through activity-based, problem-solving methods, rather than from direct teaching, drill and practice.

In recent years these views have been challenged and the current belief is that indirect methods used exclusively are inappropriate for the types of learning involved in the initial acquisition of basic literacy and numeracy skills (Birsh, 1999; Hirsch, 2000; Pressley, 1998; Sasson, 2001). Many psychologists and educators now believe that important facts and skills are taught most effectively in the early stages by direct instruction (for example, Kauffman, 2002). The current view is that effective teaching of basic academic skills requires a careful combination of student-centred activity and direct teaching. It is also believed that certain students make significantly more progress when directly taught than when left to discover important concepts for themselves (Graham and Harris, 1994; Mastropieri and Scruggs, 2002). One potential cause of learning difficulty for some students is lack of direct instruction in curriculum areas where and when it is most needed.

Observational learning

Observational learning, as the term implies, is learning that occurs when a person observes and imitates someone else's responses or behaviour, or when information and concepts are acquired without active participation. In many instances, learning by observation and imitation is a quick and effective process, and many typical lessons in classrooms rely on some degree of observation and modelling by the learners.

Learning by observation requires the activation of four processes (Santrock, 2001):

- *Attention*: the learner must obviously be attending to the actions of the model and taking in the information presented.
- *Retention*: the learner must store the observed actions or information in memory.
- *Reproduction*: the learner can recall and imitate (albeit imperfectly) what they have seen.
- *Reinforcement or incentive*: the learner needs to be motivated to want to reproduce and carry out the observed behaviour or recall the information.

Observational learning can be intentional or incidental. When modelling and imitation are used as teaching strategy – for example, when teaching a new skill to students with intellectual disability – the behaviour to be learned may need to be broken down into several smaller steps with each step demonstrated and rehearsed many times to facilitate the eventual development of the complex skill or behaviour.

Observational learning is a major component of *social learning theory* or *social cognitive theory*. The word 'social' in this context emphasises the fact that desirable behaviours or responses that are observed and imitated are usually also reinforced by factors in the social environment. In terms of social behaviour, it appears that very many behaviours are learned incidentally through observation of the behaviour of others, with powerful or respected models being more readily imitated than weaker models (Gagne *et al.*, 1993; Long, 2000). Vicarious learning occurs by observing others and becoming aware of the reinforcement or punishment they receive for their actions (Schunk, 2000). Social learning theory covers very much more, however, than merely the learning of social behaviours. Many cognitive skills and processes are also shaped by social learning principles, including language competencies, problem-solving strategies, and work habits.

The way that individuals think about themselves and others in social contexts (*self-understanding*, *self-efficacy* and *social cognition*) is also accounted for by social learning theory (Henson and Eller, 1999). In many ways, social learning theory bridges the gap between behavioural perspectives on learning and cognitive theories. For this reason, some writers suggest that social learning theory should be classed under a new category, 'neobehaviourism' (for example, Tan *et al.*, 2003). Neobehaviourism is discussed in Chapter 2.

For more detailed coverage of social cognitive theories of learning, see Ormrod (2003) and McInerney and McInerney (2002).

Rote learning versus meaningful learning

Most psychologists and educators differentiate between rote learning and meaningful learning. In recent years it has become popular to criticise the use of rote learning methods, partly because the learner may commit to memory information which is not understood and is therefore of no functional value. Material that is forced into memory by drill-type repetition without understanding tends to remain isolated within the learner's long-term memory, rather than being connected with prior knowledge (Rosenshine, 1995). For this reason, information stored by rote is not easily retrieved when needed. Rote-memorised material is also easily forgotten unless rehearsed frequently, and is unlikely to generalise to new contexts. Students who lack effective learning strategies frequently resort to rote learning, even when its use is not appropriate.

There is an important difference between rote learning and memorisation. It should be mentioned that in some cultures (for example, Chinese) memorising important information that is understood by the learner is regarded as a necessary and effective way of mastering subject matter and of eventually deepening understanding (Watkins and Biggs, 2001). Such use of memorisation is not strictly speaking learning by *rote* but rather is an example of appropriate *overlearning*. Some authorities do support the place of a certain degree of memorisation within our classrooms. This is particularly the case in the initial stages of learning important factual information or processes which need to be mastered to a high level of automaticity for use when performing higher-order cognitive tasks (Bourke, 1989; Gage and Berliner, 1998). Such material might include definitions of important terms and concepts, mathematical or other symbols and notation, basic number facts, foreign language vocabulary, the correct spelling of frequently used irregular words, and safety checks on equipment. Having this information instantly retrievable from long-term memory reduces the cognitive load placed upon working memory when planning a strategy, solving a problem or carrying out a task (Tuovinen and Sweller, 1999).

Bourke (1989) relates the issue of memorisation to teaching by saying that, although the procedure may have been over-emphasised in the past, assisting students to memorise core material should still have a place in the repertoire of instructional methods used by any teacher at appropriate times. Whenever students are required to memorise information, it should always be linked with meaningful content. The learner should always appreciate why it is important to commit the given information to memory and how the knowledge thus acquired will be useful (Ormrod, 2003). As Pound (1999) points out, all effective learning depends on making connections and seeing relationships.

In meaningful learning, new information and new concepts are connected with the learner's prior knowledge. Meaningful learning thus contributes in a major way to the development of what Gagne, Briggs and Wager (1992) refer to as 'intellectual skills' and 'cognitive strategies'. As discussed above, intellectual skills and strategies build upon each other to form increasingly elaborate mental structures that permit the operation of higher-order cognitive processing required in problem solving, planning and decision-making (Gredler, 2001).

More will be said about meaningful learning in Chapter 2.

Learning hierarchies

Another major contribution of Robert Gagne (1984) was the notion that each new stage or level in learning is dependent upon the possession of prerequisite knowledge, skills and strategies at lower levels. When a student fails to learn something it is often because he or she lacks adequate proficiency in prerequisite learning (*entry capabilities*) necessary for the task. For example, in arithmetic the ability to carry out the written algorithm for long division is built upon the ability to carry out the simple division process. Ability to perform simple division is built upon an understanding of the concept of sharing or sub-dividing groups of real objects, together with the skill of counting objects, and the ability to recognise and write numerals. Gagne described these identifiable steps in acquiring the skill as forming a *learning hierarchy* for any particular task. Gredler (2001, p. 409) defines a learning hierarchy as, 'an organized set of intellectual skills from simple to complex that indicates the set of prerequisites for each capability to be learned'.

Such hierarchies are frequently represented on paper as flow-charts, with the learning outcome or goal identified at the top and the essential prior learning stages sequenced in descending order of complexity to the most basic at the bottom. To construct a learning hierarchy for any particular task, teachers or other curriculum designers work back from the final goal. At each step they ask themselves, 'In order to do that, what did I need to know?' until they reach the most basic prior knowledge. The flow chart produced when we analyse tasks in this way can also serve as a useful tool for diagnosing points of difficulty a certain student may be experiencing.

Determining the learning hierarchy for particular tasks (*task analysis*) can help teachers sequence instruction effectively. Task analysis is extremely useful and is very widely used by teachers working in special education settings. In the wider context, it is reported in studies of teacher effectiveness that a key characteristic of highly effective teachers is that they do sequence the learning of a new topic into easy steps (Kauchak and Eggen, 2003).

The process and sequence of learning

Having identified qualitatively different types of learning, it is also necessary to point out that in many instances learning occurs over a period of time, and moves through different stages, rather than occurring as a result of a single moment of experience. Most types of learning take more time to accomplish if the learner has an intellectual impairment (see Chapter 9). In many ways, the key difference between students who learn easily and those with difficulties is the amount of time needed to reach a level of mastery in a given subject or skill. A leading advocate of *mastery learning* stated many years ago that IQ might cease to be a powerful predictor of academic success if the quality of instruction and time available for learning could be made optimum (Block, 1971).

The stages through which a learner progresses when acquiring new knowledge, skills and strategies can be summarised as follows:

1   Attention to task
2   Acquisition
3   Application
4   Fluency (automaticity)
5   Maintenance
6   Generalisation
7   Adaptation

During the time when learners move from no knowledge or skill in a particular area to complete mastery in that area they pass through the various stages of proficiency identified above (Mastropieri and Scruggs, 2002). An important individual difference among learners is the time they need to take at each stage. The list of seven stages is valuable when attempting to determine the underlying cause of a student's failure to learn and how far he or she has progressed toward mastery.

Attention to task: Underpinning all stages of learning is *attention*. Many (perhaps most) learning problems begin at the point of attention (Naparstek, 2002; Rooney, 2002). Howse *et al.* (2003) report that at-risk children tend to display much poorer ability to regulate their own attention, are easily distracted, and do not stay cognitively alert during a task. Failing to give attention to the task or to the content of a lesson makes it virtually impossible for the student to acquire and store the related knowledge, skills and strategies. This vital point will be discussed fully in Chapter 4.

Acquisition, application and fluency: To facilitate learning of knowledge, skills and strategies at the acquisition stage, direct teaching that combines demonstration, modelling, prompting and error correction can be effective. The methods used must gain and hold attention. It is, of course, possible to acquire knowledge and skills without direct instruction, through student-centred activity methods. However, using informal methods often puts students with learning difficulties at risk (see Chapters 2 and 4).

The first stage in acquiring a new skill may reflect a high error rate until the learner has had adequate successful practice. For example, a very young child using the 'mouse' to move the cursor carefully on the computer screen may at first have very great difficulty in coordinating hand and eye (*acquisition phase*). After sufficient practice, the actions become more controlled, and eventually the child can move the cursor automatically without deliberate thought (*fluency phase*). A second example might be a student learning the operation for adding tens and units. At first the student may perform the procedure slowly and somewhat laboriously, making frequent errors and needing corrective feedback (*acquisition phase*). Later, after practice, the student will perform the same process rapidly and accurately (*fluency*), sometimes even shortcutting the written procedure by solving the problem mentally. Teaching strategies involving frequent practice, application and reinforcement are necessary to ensure *fluency* and *automaticity*. Many learning difficulties can be traced to lack of practice, or to inappropriate practice in the form of decontextualised exercises.

The acquisition phase in learning frequently takes much longer than many teachers realise, and some learning problems are the direct result of students being moved too rapidly through the acquisition and application stages. Consider the teacher who says of Nancy's reading, 'She knew those words yesterday but she doesn't know them now!' The teacher may well have devoted too little time to getting Nancy to practise matching, reading, writing and saying the words before requiring her to retrieve them unaided from long-term memory. The teaching method and activities used may also have lacked interest for Nancy, so her attention to task was therefore less than optimal.

Maintenance: Forgetting (*decay*) occurs if the learner does not make use of the stored information or skill for any purpose or if the learner is required to learn more material of a very similar nature (*interference*) (Henson and Eller, 1999; Snowman and Biehler, 2003). Constant practice through application and regular rehearsal and review ensures that the skill is maintained over time.

Generalisation: Generalisation occurs when the student recognises any situation or problem where the same information, skill or strategy can be applied. This is the most difficult level of learning, and it requires that teaching must occur across different contexts and with frequent reviews and revision (Gresham, 2002). Students with learning difficulties, particularly those with intellectual disability, have great trouble in generalising new knowledge and skills. With this in mind, teachers need to spend more time helping students connect new knowledge, skills and strategies to different contexts rather than expecting that

transfer will occur spontaneously. For example, students will need to be shown how to apply a measurement technique taught in mathematics to tasks set in geography lessons. They will need help in recognising that a reading comprehension strategy taught in English can be applied equally well to the textbook used in science lessons. To aid transfer of learning teachers should first ensure that the learner is really fluent in applying the knowledge, skill or strategy in one context before introducing different problems or tasks. It is helpful to discuss openly with the students the similarity between the demands of any new type of problem and the appropriate knowledge and skills

previously acquired. Carefully selecting new learning tasks to ensure that there is a gradual increase in difficulty or difference can also facilitate generalisation. Teaching for generalisation is an essential feature of effective instruction, particularly for students with intellectual disability or learning difficulty.

Adaptation: Adaptation occurs when the learner has fully mastered the concept, skill, or strategy and can modify it to suit the changing demands of different situations and new contexts. It represents the highest level of mastery and is essential for independence in learning.

The role of practice

It must be evident from the material already presented that practice is an essential aspect of learning. While a few learning experiences are so full of impact that they do not require repetition, most types of learning in school require practice if the knowledge, skill or strategy is to be retained over time and applied with ease. Periods of practice that are spaced or *distributed over time* appear more effective than a large amount of practice massed over a single period (Gredler 2001).

One of the main benefits resulting from practice is the development of automaticity. When recall of a procedure or item of information becomes automatic, less effort is required on this aspect of a task and it becomes much easier to do two things simultaneously (Kameenui and Carnine, 2002; Westen, 2002). For example, the child whose handwriting or keyboard skills have become highly automatic through practice is much better able to give attention to the ideas he or she is including in the piece of writing.

Two forms of practice are usually referred to in the classroom context, *guided practice* and *independent practice*. During guided practice the learners' performance is very closely monitored by the teacher, who provides feedback to the learners on the quality of the performance. Frequently the feedback will be corrective. Immediate feedback appears to be far more powerful than delayed feedback. During independent practice, learners are continuing to work on the same concepts or tasks, or extensions of these, without close monitoring and without frequent feedback from the teacher.

Review and *revision* are also important for effective learning within the school curriculum. Teachers who appear to foster the highest levels of achievement are reported to include in their lessons frequent reviews of previously taught material. Appropriate use of such reviews and regular revision by students can dramatically improve the retention of classroom learning (Dempster, 1991). In the same way that spaced practice achieves more than massed practice, so too spaced revision achieves more than massed and infrequent revision. Regular, spaced revision appears to result in a firmer and more elaborate understanding of a topic. It also helps students to experience a personal feeling of competence and mastery: 'I have proved to myself that I can do this'.

Further reading

Gredler, M.E. (2001) *Learning and Instruction: Theory and Practice* (4th edn). Upper Saddle River, NJ: Merrill-Prentice Hall.

Hill, W. (2002) *Learning: A Survey of Psychological Interpretations* (7th edn). Boston: Allyn & Bacon.

McInerney, D. and McInerney, V. (2002) *Educational Psychology: Constructing Learning* (3rd edn). Sydney: Prentice Hall.

Minke, K.M. and Bear, G.G. (2000) *Preventing School Problems: Promoting School Success.* Bethesda, MD: National Association of School Psychologists.

Newton, D.P. (2000) *Teaching for Understanding: What It Is and How to Do It.* London: Routledge-Falmer.

Slavin, R. (2003) *Educational Psychology* (7th edn). Boston: Allyn & Bacon.

2 Theories of learning and motivation

A characteristic of learning theories is that they provide a mechanism for understanding the implications of events related to learning in both formal and informal settings. (Gredler, 2001, p. 15)

There is no single comprehensive theory that covers all types of learning — and no learning theory has yet been able to provide a definitive answer to the fundamental question, 'What is learning?' (Henson and Eller, 1999). However, existing theories are useful in helping teachers understand how specific instances of learning occur, and each theory adds something to our overall appreciation of the factors influencing learning.

According to Driscoll (2000, p. 11), a learning theory '… comprises a set of constructs linking observed changes in performance with what is thought to bring about those changes'. Such constructs might include variables such as memory, reinforcement, attention, and motivation. Gredler (2001) points out that theories of learning deal with general principles and are independent of subject matter and learner characteristics.

Theories of learning are usually categorised as *behavioural*, *cognitive*, or *neo-behavioural*. It should not be assumed that theories are mutually exclusive or incompatible one with another. Rather, each theory takes the main account of specific types or examples of learning as will become clear in the following overview.

Behavioural theory

Behavioural learning theorists consider that all behaviour is learned and that learning occurs as a result of the effect of one's behaviour on the environment. A learner's actions and responses are in some way either rewarded or punished, and thereby strengthened or weakened. One underlying principle within behavioural theory is that when an action or response produces a pleasant or rewarding outcome that behaviour is likely to be repeated (Thorndike's *Law of Effect*) and the more the response is repeated, the more it is strengthened (Thorndike's *Law of Exercise*) (Tan *et al.*, 2003; Thorndike, 1927). In contrast, responses that bring displeasure or pain are likely to weaken and fade. These simple but powerful principles govern much of what goes on in various ways in typical classrooms.

Teaching approaches and behaviour management methods based on behavioural theory (*applied behaviour analysis*) make extensive use of precise goal setting, modelling, prompting, cueing, rehearsal, reinforcement and shaping. Prompts and cues refer to the hints or guidance given to the learner to increase the likelihood that a desired response will occur and can be rewarded. The prompts are gradually faded (reduced and then removed) as the learner approaches independent functioning. 'Shaping' is the term applied to procedures that reinforce approximations to the desired response until the correct response is fully established. Santrock (2001, p. 251) states, 'Shaping can be an important tool for the classroom teacher because most students need reinforcement along the way to reaching a learning goal.'

Operant conditioning (also known as *instrumental conditioning*) involves a learner's self-initiated response or behaviour being strengthened through reinforcement or weakened by neutral or negative consequences. Reinforcement is provided by any factor (for example, praise, token reward, or simply succeeding in a task) that increases the probability that a response will be repeated. The delivery of the reinforcer is contingent on the learner making the correct or near correct response, and to that degree the reinforcing process is in the learner's own hands (Mazur, 2001).

When operant conditioning principles are applied to teaching situations, the schedule of rewards can be engineered to bring about learning toward the objectives of the lesson. Instructional computer programs, for example, make full use of operant conditioning principles by providing various forms of demonstration, modelling, prompting, cueing, fading of cues, and giving immediate rewards for correct responses (Gredler, 2001). Everyday 'rewards' in the classroom (smiles, praise, tokens, privileges) are also examples of

extrinsic reinforcement, strengthening and shaping desired responses and behaviours. To maximise the effects of reinforcement in the classroom, teachers should identify what students find personally rewarding and use this information systematically to enhance learning (Arthur *et al.*, 2003). Sometimes the reward given in the classroom situation can be time on a favourite activity: for example, 'When you finish your mathematics problems you can play the computer game.' Using a favourite activity to reinforce a student's engagement in a less popular activity is termed the *Premack Principle* (Premack, 1959).

Of course, punishment and other negative consequences also shape behaviour but should be regarded as the least favoured option. The principal objection to punishment or aversive control is that while it may temporarily suppress certain responses, it may evoke a variety of undesirable outcomes (fear, alienation, resentment, an association between school and punishment, a breakdown in the relationship between student and teacher). Punishment may also suppress a child's general responsiveness in school.

Operant conditioning principles are embodied to some extent in direct instruction methods, particularly highly structured teaching programmes such as *Reading Mastery* (Engelmann and Bruner, 1988) and *Corrective Spelling through Morphographs* (Dixon and Engelmann, 1979). These, and similar programmes, rely on detailed task analysis of content, clear demonstrations, modelling, guided practice, immediate correction of student errors, cueing of correct responses, high active participation and success rates, and frequent reinforcement. There is a large body of research evidence indicating that direct instruction methods of this type are very successful in teaching a range of basic academic skills to a wide variety of students (McInerney and McInerney, 2002; Swanson, 2000a). However, in teaching environments where child-centred education is strongly favoured, such direct methods of instruction and behavioural techniques are regarded with deep suspicion.

Another form of learning covered by behavioural theory relates to *classical conditioning*. Classical or reflex conditioning relates to situations where a physiological or emotional reaction becomes paired with, and later evoked by, a particular stimulus — for example, increased heart rate at the thought of a visit to the dentist; or perhaps Pavlov's famous dog salivating at the sound of a bell. The way children feel about school and certain school subjects is often associated closely with good or bad experiences they have had. As Ormrod (2003, p. 304) states, '… when they encounter unpleasant stimuli — negative comments, public humiliation, or constant frustration and failure — they may eventually learn to fear or dislike a particular activity, subject area, teacher, or (perhaps) school in general'. Much of the anxiety and avoidance behaviour observed in students with learning difficulties is due in part to classical conditioning (Santrock, 2001).

Teachers wishing to find out more about applied behaviour analysis and the application of behavioural principles to everyday teaching are referred to titles in the further reading section at the end of the chapter.

Cognitive theories of learning

In contrast to behavioural psychologists who are concerned with observable behaviour change as evidence of learning, cognitive psychologists are interested in studying learning as an internal mental phenomenon. Eggen and Kauchak (2003) state that from a cognitive perspective, learning is a change in 'mental structures'. Cognitive learning theories deal with the issue of how people process and store information to gain an understanding of themselves and the environment, and how their thinking and reasoning influence their actions and reactions (Henson and Eller, 1999). Cognitive psychology explores interrelationships among variables involved in learning, such as perception, attention, memory, language, motivation, concept development, reasoning and problem solving (Eysenck and Keane, 2000). Some of these variables will be discussed more fully in later chapters.

Many separate theories and perspectives contribute to the cognitive school of thought, including information processing theory, metacognition, schema theory, social learning theory, and higher-order thinking. Cognitive theories underpin the currently popular *constructivist approach* to learning and are influencing classroom practice to a very significant degree. Constructivist theory sees learners as active participants in the process of learning, seeking to interpret and make meaning from multiple sources of information by linking them with what is already known.

Information processing

The processing of information begins at the level of *sensation*, in the so-called *sensory register*. The individual is bombarded constantly by stimuli in the environment (sounds, colours, textures, aromas) and these are either attended to or ignored. An individual can only attend to limited amounts of information at one time, so many sensations are not actively processed. Information in the sensory register stays very briefly — less than a second for visual stimuli; perhaps two or three seconds for auditory information (Ormrod, 2003). Information that is *attended to* and thus *perceived* then moves into short-term or working memory for processing.

If the information is relevant to the learner at that moment, and particularly if it links with what the learner already knows, it will pass in some encoded form (for example, visual images, words) into longer-term memory. Cognitive psychologists usually refer to the information 'stores' involved at various stages in processing information as *sensory register, short-term memory, working memory,* and *long-term memory*. Attention and memory are intimately involved in all deliberate acts of learning; and weaknesses in attention and memory are implicated in many cases of learning failure (see Chapters 3 and 4).

Representing information in long-term memory

It has been mentioned previously that stored information is often categorised as *declarative knowledge* (facts, definitions, propositions, rules, etc.) or *procedural knowledge* (knowing how to perform a cognitive task or action). Declarative knowledge may be encoded in memory in verbal form and can be retrieved when necessary. It can also be stored as images and patterns of linked information (such as ordered lists; figures; models; etc.), or as *schemata*. Mental schemata (or schemas) are organised bodies of knowledge we build up about particular objects, situations or phenomena (Ormrod, 2003). Sweller (1999) suggests that schemata are essential to cognitive functioning because they permit us to store multiple elements of information as a single, easily accessed whole. Long-term memory holds huge numbers of automated schemata for indefinite periods, perhaps represented in specific neural networks within the brain. One definition of learning presented in Chapter 1 was that learning consists of the acquisition of *increasingly automated schemata held in long-term memory.* Sweller (1999) further indicates that schemata not only allow us to hold a great deal of material in long-term memory, they massively reduce the burden on working memory, allowing us to accomplish intellectual tasks that otherwise would be impossible.

Schemata can be thought of as the highly functional 'cognitive networks' or 'mental representations' that are acquired as a result of experience. Santrock (2001) defines a schema as comprising linked concepts, knowledge, and information about what already exists in a person's mind. When a learner is making sense of a learning experience, separate units of information or concepts become closely interconnected and form the raw material used in thinking, reasoning and imagining. Well-developed schemata contain knowledge that can be used to interpret new experiences (Eggen and Kauchak, 2003; McInerney and McInerney, 2002).

Children have been acquiring schemata since birth because the ability to do so is part of our basic cognitive architecture (Sweller, 1999). Schemata constantly change as learners make sense of a wider and wider range of experiences and as they link new information with prior knowledge. It is believed that a learner establishes highly effective schemata as new relationships are recognised between previously disconnected information (Nuthall, 1999). The taking in of new information (the process of *assimilation*) usually results in some restructuring of the existing schema (the process of *accommodation*).

The notion of schemata owes most to the early work of Piaget (for example, 1929; 1952) who was a pioneer in the study of children's cognitive development. His perspective, often described as 'cognitive structuralism', has exerted a tremendous influence on educational theory and practice, particularly in the early childhood and primary years. The notion of child-centred, activity-based programmes with an emphasis on 'process' rather than product, and exploration rather than direct 'transmission' teaching, reflects basic Piagetian principles. Schema theory is important for all teachers since it stresses the importance of facilitating new learning by making strong connections with the learner's prior knowledge.

A simple example of the expansion of a schema is that which occurs when you move to live in a new town. At first you may know only one route from your flat to the bus station. Gradually, through exploration your knowledge of the area increases and you add to your 'route-to-the-bus schema' routes from the flat to the shops and from the bus station to the shops. You then discover a quicker route to the bus station via the park; and in doing so you recognise that a tower you have previously only seen from your window actually belongs to a building that shares a boundary with the park. You also find a bus stop that allows you to walk through the park when you return from work, and so on. You have literally created a mental 'map' that has steadily expanded and become refined with experience, and has become increasingly functional. According to schema theory, during our lifetime we develop an infinite number of such schemata connected with all our meaningful learning. For example, we develop schemata connected with particular objects, with the number system, with the grammar of our language, with interpreting text, with codes of social behaviour, with the classification of types of animals, and so on.

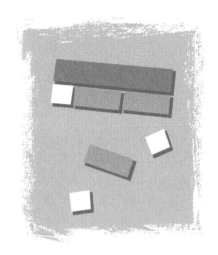

Schemata associated with particular events are often called *scripts*. An example of a script might be one's memory (knowledge) of what it is like to take part in a school sports day — expectations, codes of behaviour, ways of participating, events, routines, etc. Scripts are schemata that provide us with background knowledge and plans of action applicable to certain situations.

Schemata are not confined to the cognitive domain; in the affective domain they also represent the way in which individuals have constructed their perceptions and experiences to create their personal belief systems and values (Ayers *et al.*, 2000). Schemata in the affective domain influence how we perceive others and ourselves. For example, our self-concept and feelings of self-efficacy are two very important affective schemata that impact upon our motivation and engagement in learning tasks.

Constructivist perspective

Constructivist theory builds on the earlier work of Piaget, Bruner and Vygotsky (see Daniels, 2001); and Sasson (2001, p. 189) describes constructivism as '… a mixture of Piagetian stage theory with postmodernist ideology'. The constructivist viewpoint on human learning suggests that true understanding cannot be directly passed from one individual to another, but rather has to be constructed anew by each learner in his or her own mind as a result of experience and reflection (Waite-Stupiansky, 1997).

Adoption of a constructivist approach in the classroom requires a shift from a teacher-directed method to a student-centred, active learning approach (Phillips, 1995). It is also argued by *social*-constructivists that knowledge is socially constructed and thus requires inter-personal collaborative effort among learners. Constructivist approaches therefore place great importance on cooperative group work and discussion focused on authentic investigations and problem solving (Gagnon and Collay, 2001; Selley, 1999). Many constructivists believe that classrooms should become 'communities of learners' where teachers and children are motivated to learn together (Eggen and Kauchak, 2003).

If one subscribes to a constructivist philosophy, the teacher's task is no longer one of developing instructional strategies to present information to students directly, but rather to discover ways of creating exploratory activities in which students may engage. The constructivist theory of learning leads to a process-centred teaching approach, with the role of the teacher changing from instructor to facilitator of children's own explorations and discoveries. Learning occurs as students make connections between new insights they obtain and their existing foundation of knowledge.

Constructivist practices draw heavily on the principles espoused by Vygotsky (1962) and Bruner (1966) – for example, the social nature of the learning process, the role of language in learning and concept formation, and the pedagogical strategy of 'scaffolding'. Scaffolding refers to the variety of ways in which teachers and others help or support learners to move beyond their current level of understanding by giving them cues, suggestions or even direct guidance at appropriate moments in their investigations or activities. These '… social acts of assistance are gradually internalized by the child to become the basis of self-regulated thinking and learning' (Kershner, 2000, p. 292). Learning that builds effectively on the child's current capabilities is said to be within the learner's *zone of proximal development* (ZPD). The ZPD defines those things a learner can do if given some small amount of assistance by the teacher or peer. After such assistance the individual will from then on be able to do the tasks independently. Teaching, it is argued, should be designed to take learners smoothly from their current zone of development into the next.

Constructivist theory has gained much popularity in recent years and has significantly influenced our thinking about teaching methods (De Vries, 2002; Gabler and Schroeder, 2003). Constructivist principles now underpin many of the curriculum guidelines created by education departments around the world. Originally associated with contemporary approaches to mathematics, science and social studies teaching, constructivism has now permeated almost all areas of the curriculum, and regularly emerges under titles such as problem-based learning or the enquiry approach (Marlowe, 1998).

Criticisms of the constructivist viewpoint

The constructivist viewpoint is not without its critics when it comes to practical implementation in classrooms (for example, Hirsch, 2000; Westwood, 1996). Cobb (1994) for example refers to the fact that the justification for constructivism is often reduced to the mantra-like slogan 'students must construct their own knowledge'; but no hard evidence is provided to support the claim that all students are effective in learning and 'making meaning' for themselves. Nor is much specific practical advice given to teachers, beyond the need to use child-centred activities and discussion, perhaps leaving teachers to assume that student engagement in an activity always equals learning (Eggen and Kauchak, 2003). This brave assumption is sometimes very far from reality.

The use of child-centred, process-type approaches to the total exclusion of direct teaching is unwise, particularly in the teaching and learning of basic skills such as reading, writing and mathematics (Stanovich, 1994). Pressley and Harris (1997) point out that two previous 'great reforms' in education based on principles of child-centredness have failed this century because they were too extreme and too difficult to sustain. Activity-based and problem-solving curricula are not easy to implement, particularly where there are large classes or when behaviour management is a problem.

The case that purely constructivist approaches to learning are sometimes inefficient or inadequate comes from Sweller (1999, p. 156) who writes:

> We all must actively engage with information and construct a knowledge base, whether the information is directly presented to us or whether we must search … The major difference between direct and indirect presentation of information is that it is more difficult to construct schemas if we must unnecessarily discover aspects of the material ourselves rather than being told.

It also seems likely that rather than being generally applicable to all types of learning, constructivist strategies are actually important at particular *stages* of learning. For example, Jonassen (1992) presents a three-stage model of knowledge acquisition in which 'initial knowledge acquisition' is stage one, followed by 'advanced knowledge', and finally 'expertise'. He strongly supports the view that initial knowledge acquisition is served best by direct teaching, while advanced knowledge and expertise develop best through a practical application of constructivist principles. Pressley and Harris (1997) argue that excellent teaching often begins with explanation and modelling, and continues with teacher scaffolding of students' more independent efforts. Stanovich (1994) has applied an identical argument to the teaching of early reading skills, with word identification skills and decoding being taught explicitly, and higher-order skills being developed under the control of the learner as he or she seeks to construct meaning from text. According to Creemers (1994), direct teaching is often the most efficient method for first imparting new information and skills; and this view is certainly supported by the research evidence from work with students with learning difficulties (for example, Kavale and Forness, 2000b; Swanson, 2000a).

Perhaps the most serious problem associated with an exclusive use of constructivist principles in the classroom is that some children do not cope particularly well with unstructured tasks. They experience failure and frustration when the demands of learning tasks are not made clear to them and when they are not taught appropriate strategies to use (Graham and Harris, 1994; Westwood, 1993). Not all children discover for themselves the many strategies they need to use when coping with the academic demands of the school curriculum. For some students, discovery methods are inefficient at best – requiring far longer time than it would take to teach the same strategies to children using direct explanation. Problem-based learning and discovery methods may increase the cognitive load and misdirect the use of available learning time to a detrimental level for lower ability students. On the other hand, many children are capable of making new ideas their own quite quickly when these ideas are transmitted clearly to them.

Pressley and McCormick (1995) believe that good quality instruction from a teacher, including the key components of modelling, direct explanation and guided practice actually stimulates rather than restricts constructive mental activity in students. Presenting knowledge directly to a learner does not prevent the individual from making meaning. Being told something by a teacher might be just what learners require at a particular moment in order to help them construct meaning. Actively presenting information to students in a way that helps them organise their network of knowledge (schemata) has been shown by research to be a key component of effective teaching (Rosenshine, 1995).

The most effective lessons are likely to contain an appropriate balance between teacher direction and student activity. The balance must be achieved in the planning stage when the teacher takes account of the types of learning involved in the particular lesson and the characteristics of the students. The two viewpoints on learning and teaching — direct instruction vs. student-centred, constructivist learning models — are not mutually exclusive.

Neobehaviourism

Neobehavioural (or *cognitive-behavioural*) theories of learning are positioned somewhere between behaviourial and cognitivist explanations, combining essential elements of both. Tan *et al.* (2003) state that the term *neobehaviourism* covers theories and models based on the belief that changes in behaviour (learning) are the net result of environmental influences interacting with innate predispositions and processes within the learner. It is believed that learners do not passively respond to reinforcement and other environmental feedback, as extreme behaviourists assume; and nor do they simply process information without involvement of feelings, beliefs and emotions as perhaps the cognitivists assume. Environmental influences on learning are mediated by many different internal factors. Emotions evoked during learning affect both the ways people learn, their memories of events, their perceptions of their own ability, and their future attitude toward engaging in similar activities (Howe, 1998).

Social cognitive theory (Bandura, 1977) can be classed as an example of neobehavioural theory. The theory was discussed in the previous chapter in relation to observational learning. Social cognitive theory places emphasis on the important role of modelling and imitation in the learning of complex social behaviours and language. Schunk (2000, p. 78) states, 'By observing others, people acquire knowledge, rules, skills, strategies, beliefs, and attitudes.' Social cognitive theory holds that direct and immediate reinforcement is not necessary in some forms of learning because people can and do learn vicariously through observing others (Ayers *et al.*, 2000). It is not necessary to imitate immediately the behaviours they have seen. The observer may note, for example, that when an individual exhibited helpful behaviour toward another person, he or she was rewarded in some way. This evokes a positive emotional reaction in the observer (*vicarious reinforcement*) who may then act in the same way at some future time. Often, any direct reinforcement for the learner comes much later, when he or she actually exhibits the behaviour. Obviously observing another person being punished for some action (*vicarious punishment*) can also evoke emotional reactions in the observer, and these can exert a restraining influence deterring him or her from imitating that behaviour.

Social cognitive theory is also concerned with how individuals develop beliefs about their own ability to cope effectively in a variety of situations (*self-efficacy*) and how they learn to monitor and manage their own learning processes (*self-regulation*) (Gredler, 2001; Schunk, 2000). Self-regulation will be discussed later in relation to metacognition. Attention here will be devoted to self-efficacy, since its development is closely connected with successful and unsuccessful learning experiences, and with future motivation.

Self-efficacy

The development of personal awareness of self-efficacy is influenced to a large extent by one's successes and failures, and by the actions, reactions and comments of others concerning one's capabilities. Positive perceived self-efficacy in any domain arises mainly out of experiencing successful performance in that domain. Achieving good results, being praised and admired by others, enjoying your successes, and knowing that you are doing well all contribute to the development of one's beliefs about one's own competence (Bandura, 1997; Chan, 1994). Conversely, poor results and too much criticism from others reduce perceived self-efficacy and lower a learner's aspirations (Biggs, 1995). As Porter (2000) remarks, perceived self-efficacy is vulnerable to repeated failures and to criticism. Some students appear to be particularly vulnerable to negative comments from teachers, and quickly lose confidence in their own capabilities (Weinstein, 2002).

A lowering of self-efficacy is likely to have a detrimental effect on motivation and on willingness to persist with challenging tasks. Individuals low in self-efficacy tend to shy away from difficult tasks because they are seen as personally threatening and likely to result in some loss of self-worth (Long, 2000). Such students focus on their own weaknesses rather than on their abilities, and they tend to view any new learning situation as more difficult than it is in reality (Martin and Marsh, 2003).

Studies have indicated that students with learning disabilities (see Chapter 5) may have unrealistically high self-efficacy beliefs in some situations because they have a problem gauging their own capabilities and predicting the difficulty level of the task. They may for example, believe they can carry out a particular written assignment easily only to find later that they cannot attempt it (Klassen, 2002). Such inability to judge one's competence can lead to frequent failures and frustrations.

Positive beliefs concerning self-efficacy appear to reduce stress and frustration, maximise a learner's effort, and sustain interest and involvement in challenging situations (Silverman and Casazza, 2000). In contrast, low self-efficacy beliefs result in reduced effort, anxiety, stress, avoidance behaviour, and a tendency to give up very easily. Persistent failure and criticism can take low self-efficacy beliefs to the state known as *learned helplessness* (Craske, 1988; Dweck and Licht, 1980; Eisner and Seligman, 1996; Valas, 2001). Howe (1998, p. 90) remarks that:

> … people who repeatedly experience failures and events that are outside their control often do develop an expectation, which may not be entirely unrealistic, that they are powerless and cannot influence the important events in their lives. Not surprisingly, these people may become apathetic and fatalistic, and they are likely to suffer from low self-esteem and depression.

It is known that frequent punishment and criticism contribute to the development of learned helplessness (Lieberman, 2000) and to chronic states of anxiety and stress (Tarpy, 1997). Many students with a long history of learning difficulties have often experienced punishment and other negative consequences for their efforts. It is therefore fairly common for these students to be under stress in learning situations. Unfortunately, effective learning does not occur when the learner is under stress, so their problems are exacerbated (Pound, 2002).

It is believed that many students with learning difficulties will develop learned helplessness unless they can be shown that through their own efforts and actions they can improve. To do so they need help in developing a more *internal locus of control*. The locus of control construct relates to the individual's personal perception of the causes of their successes and failures (Rotter, 1966; Weiner, 1972; Weiner, 1995).

Locus of control and attribution theory

We can readily appreciate that frequent failure undermines a child's self-esteem and feelings of self-worth, but does this mean that all activities should be so simple that students never fail? Definitely not — accepting occasional failure and *attributing that failure to the correct cause* is an essential part of learning. It is not feasible or desirable that a child never experiences failure (Seligman, 1995). For teachers, particularly in the early school years, the problem is how to limit the amount of failure that any child encounters. When natural failures do occur, children need help in attributing that failure to the correct cause. Studies have indicated that young children do not necessarily attribute failure to the correct factor (for example, completing a task too quickly, not putting in sufficient effort, not really listening to the instructions). They are more inclined to blame external and uncontrollable factors such as bad luck or the teacher's mood on that day — both examples of an *external locus of control* (Boekaerts, 1996; Eccles *et al.*, 1998; Eisner and Seligman, 1996).

In particular, young children may not appreciate the connection between making greater effort and achieving more frequent success (Butler, 1994). Even secondary-age students may not fully recognise the direct relationship between effort ('working hard') and quality of outcome, instead attributing achievement almost entirely to innate ability and to the difficulty level of the task – two factors beyond their personal control (Bissaker, 2001). Wearmouth (2002, p. 218) reminds us that, '… when students find a task difficult, those who attribute their difficulties to controllable factors such as insufficient effort, are more likely to persist than are students who attribute their difficulties to uncontrollable factors, such as lack of ability'. When students believe that effort will not result in mastery, they refrain from putting in effort, and instead will settle for the belief that the subject matter is too difficult and that their personal resources are inadequate.

Explanatory style

The issues above are directly related to another important concept in educational psychology – *explanatory style*. Explanatory style can be defined as the tendency to explain events, particularly one's own failures, as due either to internal, global, and stable factors or to external, specific and unstable factors (Hill, 2002).

Weiner (1985) has addressed the same issue regarding learners' attributions for success and failure, agreeing with the dimensions of stability and internality/externality but calling the third dimension *controllability* – the extent to which the learner perceives that poor outcomes can be changed by his or her action.

Examples of *internal factors* are feelings of lack of aptitude, lack of personal interest in the topic, and poor concentration. *External factors* include blaming the teacher for setting a difficult test, or the textbook for containing too few diagrams. Examples of *global explanations* include believing that no textbook is ever helpful and that all examinations are impossibly difficult. In contrast, *specific explanations* might include a belief that this particular textbook is too complex, or that today's examination had unfair questions. *Stable factors* include a firm belief that one always lacks ability or has no talent. *Unstable factors* might be that one explains a poor result by saying one was not feeling well that day.

If failures are attributed to internal, stable and global causes the learner is likely to feel pessimistic about changing the situation, and therefore will anticipate continuing problems. Feelings of low self-efficacy grow out of these same causes and have a detrimental impact on motivation. Students with learning difficulties often have very negative self-efficacy beliefs and consider their failures are due to internal, stable, and uncontrollable causes (Santrock, 2001).

Attribution retraining

Attribution retraining is an intervention strategy that attempts to give students a more internal locus of control and thus prevent or reduce learned helplessness. In particular, attribution retraining seeks to establish a much clearer understanding in the student of the possible causes of his or her failures. Strategies are used to help overcome the student's false beliefs about lack of ability or schoolwork being too difficult. Tasks are set to demonstrate that achievement improves when careful and sustained effort is expended. Usually the students are given reasonably challenging tasks to attempt but are helped and encouraged to complete the tasks successfully. The teacher uses descriptive praise that highlights the controllable aspects of the situation where the student performed well. The student may also be taught a self-reinforcing internal script to apply: for example, 'I copied the diagram carefully. I took my time. It looks very good.'

Metacognition and self-regulation

Metacognition, as explained briefly in Chapter 1, is the ability to think about one's own thought processes, self-monitor, and modify one's learning strategies as necessary. Children who have metacognitive awareness are able to plan how best to tackle tasks and monitor their efforts. It is considered that metacognition helps a learner recognise that he or she is either doing well or is having difficulty learning or understanding something. A learner who is monitoring his or her own on-going performance will detect the need to pause, to double-check, perhaps begin again before moving on, to weigh up possible alternatives, or to seek outside help (Kershner, 2000; Tan *et al.*, 2003). For children who are developing normally, metacognitive awareness and the intentional use of task-approach strategies improve steadily throughout the school years (McDevitt and Ormrod, 2002). Metacognition is obviously closely associated with the notion of using 'cognitive strategies' – mental plans of action that allow us to tackle particular learning tasks in the most effective ways.

Metacognition often involves inner verbal self-instruction and self-questioning – talking to one's self in order to focus, reflect, control or review. Training in self-regulation involves teaching students to tell themselves specifically what they need to do and how they need to monitor and self-correct during the task.

One example is the scaffolding that effective teachers provide for students through the modelling of 'thinking aloud' that later influences students' own use of inner language. The teaching of verbal self-instruction is considered very important in helping all students become better self-regulated and metacognitive. Studies over many years have yielded data indicating that self-regulated students (those who use metacognition in relation to school tasks) tend to do well in school (Chan, 1991). They are more confident, resourceful and motivated.

One of the common observations concerning students with learning problems is that they have little confidence in their own ability to control learning or bring about improvement through their own effort or initiative. Teaching students how to regulate and monitor their performance in the classroom must be a major focus in any intervention programme.

Motivation

Most of the topics discussed above really fall within the general domain of *motivation*. Motivation plays a central role in human learning, and the study of motivation has generated a vast research literature of its own. Motivation theory focuses on an individual's reasons for learning and the conditions under which motivation is maximised (Covington and Mueller, 2001). Recent investigations in the field have stressed the need to study motivation within specific learning situations, rather than as a decontextualised general phenomenon (Volet, 2001). In this chapter only brief coverage of the topic will be provided, with particular reference to the impact that success and failure in the classroom can have on students' level of motivation to learn. Santrock (2001) suggests that the current socio-cognitive perspective regards students' emotional reactions to their own failures as very strong determinants of their future motivation. The challenge for the teacher is to understand students' eagerness or reluctance to learn.

Teachers often blame a student's learning problems on his or her so-called *lack of motivation*. According to Driscoll (2000), teachers believe that this lack of motivation is the underlying reason students avoid class work, refuse to become fully engaged in a learning task, fail to complete work they could easily do, or are willing to complete a task only for some tangible reward it may bring. It is almost as if teachers believe motivation to be an innate trait of learners rather than a variable that is significantly shaped and influenced by outside factors (Paris and Turner, 1994). On this issue Galloway *et al.* (1998, p. 17) have remarked:

> Too often, motivation is seen as a characteristic of pupils, perhaps not quite as unchanging as age or eye colour, but nevertheless firmly embedded in their make-up. We have argued that it can be seen as the product of an interaction between pupils and the varying situations in which they find themselves at school.

Schunk (2000, p. 300) defines motivation as '… the process of instigating and sustaining goal-directed behaviour'. In layman's terms being motivated is commonly taken to mean being 'energised' to work willingly toward some valued goal, and having the desire to put in sufficient effort to succeed. Westen (2002, p. 335) says that motivation is '… the driving force behind behavior that leads us to pursue some things and avoid others'. Both internal factors (beliefs, values, expectations, and goals) and external factors (rewards, support, and feedback or approval from others) play important roles in defining the nature of motivation and how to enhance its effect (McCombs and Pope, 1994).

Humans are motivated by many different factors, and motivational psychologists study the variables that make people act and think in certain ways. They explore possible reasons or forces behind an individual's choice of activity, the persistence with which the person will engage in the activity, their reactions when faced with difficulties, and their thoughts about themselves as learners (Eccles *et al.*, 1998; Howe, 1998; Wall, 2003). Young children, for example, appear to be driven by a strong innate need or desire to learn, to acquire knowledge, and to become competent. They are confident in their own capabilities and seem reasonably resilient to occasional failures (Stipek and Greene, 2001). The period up to age 6 years is critical for developing positive attitudes toward learning. Later, in the secondary school years, some students appear to lose this desire to learn, usually because of negative outcomes from their previous learning experiences (McCombs and Pope, 1994; Ryan and Deci, 2000).

Extrinsic and intrinsic motivation

Two main categories of motivation are recognised — *extrinsic* and *intrinsic* motivation. Intrinsic motivation is seen when learners willingly engage in an activity purely for the personal satisfaction it brings. It is the kind of motivation displayed by young children in the preschool years and students of any age when they study for the pure joy and satisfaction of learning. Intrinsic motivation is almost entirely absent in students with a history of learning difficulty in school. Extrinsic motivation, on the other hand, is seen at work when an individual tries hard to learn in order to gain some reward or to avoid negative consequences of not learning. Both forms of motivation are extremely important. The motivation available in any given learning situation is the sum total of intrinsic plus extrinsic influences (Ryan and Deci, 2000; Thorkildsen and Nicholls, 2002).

Teachers readily understand that not all students are intrinsically motivated in certain lessons, and therefore giving some form of reward for task-engagement is one way of motivating students to do work they would otherwise avoid; so gold stars, tokens, praise and privileges are frequently used in primary classrooms.

Rewarding good effort is also believed by teachers to strengthen the likelihood that the student will maintain effort in a similar manner on future occasions. There are arguments for and against the use of extrinsic reward systems in the classroom, with one argument against the system being that persistent use of extrinsic motivators reduces the possibility that students will become intrinsically motivated (McInerney and McInerney, 2002; Ryan and Deci, 2000). However, the relationship between the two types of motivation is not necessarily antagonistic and can be mutually supportive, as Schunk (2000, p. 349) suggests:

> Motivation is conceptualized as a continuum, intrinsic and extrinsic motivation anchor the ends and in the middle are behaviours that originally were extrinsically motivated but have become internalized and are now self-determined. For instance, students may want to avoid some academic activities but they work on them to obtain rewards and avoid teacher punishment. As skills develop and students believe they are becoming more competent they perceive a sense of control and self-determination over learning. The activities become more intrinsically motivating, and positive social reinforcers (e.g. praise, feedback) assist the process.

Expectancy-value theory

What are the factors that determine whether students will work willingly toward a goal or will have to be rewarded for making the effort? In the 1960s the motivational psychologist Atkinson (1966) developed what is now termed the 'Expectancy-Value Theory'. This theory suggests that for students to be willing to expend personal effort on a task the activity and the outcome have to be seen as valuable to the learners, *and* the learners have to believe they will be successful if they attempt the task (Wigfield and Eccles, 2000). If learners do not feel confident about success, or if the task is not valued, very little effort will be expended and low achievement can be anticipated.

Lack of confidence in one's ability obviously relates to self-efficacy, as discussed above, and to feelings of *self-worth* and *fear of failure*. To protect feelings of self-worth some students would rather their failures be attributed to the fact they had not made an effort rather than that they lacked ability (Covington and Teel, 1996). Urdan and Midgley (2001, p. 115) refer to this as the individual's 'struggle to escape looking stupid'. This phenomenon accounts for many of the incidents of task refusal and confrontation that can occur with adolescents who doubt their own capabilities. Some students may seek to protect their feelings of self-worth by refusing to attempt tasks, rather than trying and being seen to fail. O'Brien and Guiney (2001, p. 17) remark that for some students, '… not trying to learn can be emotionally safer than trying and then failing'. Howe (1999) has suggested that lack of confidence in one's capacity to do well and fear of failure impede a learner just as effectively as an absence of knowledge or skill. For some students, fear of failure causes high anxiety, underachievement, reduced resilience, and learned helplessness (Martin and Marsh, 2003).

Reducing effort and task avoidance are sometimes referred to as examples of *self-handicapping* (Covington, 1992; Ormrod, 2003). Another form of self-handicapping is seen in students who avoid seeking help even when they perceive themselves to be needing it because they do not want others to judge them as lacking in ability. Seeking help from others when necessary is an essential component of eventual independence in learning, so students who do not seek help disadvantage themselves and tend to remain passive learners and with low achievement (Ryan *et al.*, 2001). Fear of failure, self-handicapping, learned helplessness and task avoidance are all forms of *maladaptive motivational style* (Leo and Galloway, 1994).

Motivation in the classroom

Studies have tended to confirm the following general principles for maximising students' motivation in the classroom (Martin and Marsh, 2003; Naparstek, 2002; Ryan and Deci, 2000; Santrock, 2001; Schunk, 2000).

Motivation is likely to be highest when:

- Learners do not experience frequent failure and harsh criticism.

- The curriculum material is interesting and relevant; topics are sufficiently challenging, but not overwhelming.

- Learners are encouraged to set their own goals and are then supported in achieving them.

- Learners are given the opportunity to make choices and exercise some control over what they do in class and the manner in which they do it (greater autonomy).

- Collaborative group work is used frequently.

- Teachers reverse students' negative thinking about their own capabilities, and enhance positive self-belief by encouraging open discussion about learning, learning strategies, effort, and ability.

- Teachers remember to apply the principle that learners' motivation and confidence are enhanced by respect and approval from others.

- If a reward system is used in the classroom, it should ensure that all students attain rewards if they put in sufficient effort.

Additional suggestions can be found in the text *Motivating your Students* (McCarty and Siccone, 2001) and *Motivating Students to Learn* (Brophy, 2001).

Further reading

Alberto, P.A. and Troutman, A.C. (2003) *Applied Behavior Analysis for Teachers* (6th edn). Upper Saddle River, NJ: Merrill-Prentice Hall.

Brophy, J. (2001) *Motivating Students to Learn*. Boston: McGraw Hill.

Frieman, J. (2002) *Learning and Adaptive Behavior*. Belmont, CA: Wadsworth.

Gredler, M.E. (2001) *Learning and Instruction: Theory and Practice* (4th edn). Upper Saddle River, NJ: Merrill Prentice Hall.

McCarty, H. and Siccone, F. (2001) *Motivating Your Students*. Boston: Allyn & Bacon.

Schunk, D.H. (2003) *Learning Theories: An Educational Perspective* (4th edn). Upper Saddle River, NJ: Prentice Hall.

Thorkildsen, T.A. and Nicholls, J.G. (2002) *Motivation and the Struggle to Learn: Responding to Fractured Experience*. Boston: Allyn & Bacon.

3 Brain, memory and intelligence

> Teachers are entrusted with a noble profession — educating minds. It is ironic, therefore, that teachers are given no professional preparation about the brain. The mind is the brain at work. (Berninger and Richards, 2002, p. 3)

Healy (1994) suggested that understanding a child's brain and the way it develops is the key to understanding learning. In recent years, many advances in the fields of neuroscience and neuropsychology have helped us view learning from a new perspective. In the past decade a great deal has been discovered about the nature and location of the many electrophysiological and neurochemical changes that occur in the human brain when individuals engage in physical and cognitive activities (Baddeley, 1999). Grant and Ceci (2000) indicate that various forms of neural activity represent every mental process. They suggest that specific neural networks actively process our experiences and store our memories. Meade (2001, p. 16) writes:

> The brain's ability to process information – to capture, store and retrieve records of information in circuits of connected brain cells – is what makes learning possible.

Some writers are already beginning to translate what has been discovered about brain function into practical implications for the classroom (for example, Berninger and Richards, 2002; Jones, 2002; Sousa, 2001a; Sylwester, 2003; Tate, 2003). However, Bruer (2001) wisely warns teachers that information from brain research so far has often been over-interpreted or even misinterpreted by some writers. The suggested connections between specific teaching methods and differentiated and localised brain functioning are at best speculative. However, a basic understanding of the neurology of learning can help teachers select methods that are at least compatible with what we know of how the brain processes, stores and retrieves information and how learners' attention is gained and held.

This chapter will not attempt to provide a comprehensive treatment of brain research but will serve as a brief introduction. Readers are referred to titles in the general references and further reading list for texts covering the subject in depth.

Brain development

The human brain weighs about two to three pounds. Christison (2002) suggests that if you make a fist with each hand and hold them next to each other you can get an accurate idea of how large the human brain is. The brain comprises 100 billion or more nerve cells (*neurons*), each capable of connecting in a functional way with other nerve cells. There are different types of neurons, but basically they share a common characteristic of having a cell body with one main connecting fibre called an *axon*. An axon is the part of a neuron that sends signals to another neuron (Figure 1). To be fully functional, the axon develops a covering sheath of a fatty substance called *myelin*. Myelin seems to serve much the same purpose as the insulating coat of plastic or rubber around an electrical wire. Speed and efficiency in transfer of signals from one cell to another are greatly facilitated by this myelin sheath. Many axons are not myelinated at the time of birth and considerable additional myelination occurs throughout childhood and into adolescence. Sprenger (1999) reports that the final area of the brain to be myelinated is the prefrontal cortex behind the forehead, the main area activated most during decision-making and higher-order thinking (Figure 2).

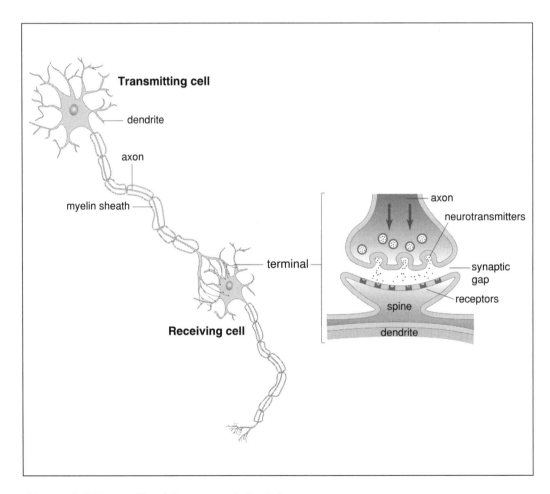

Figure 1: Nerve cells with axon and dendrites

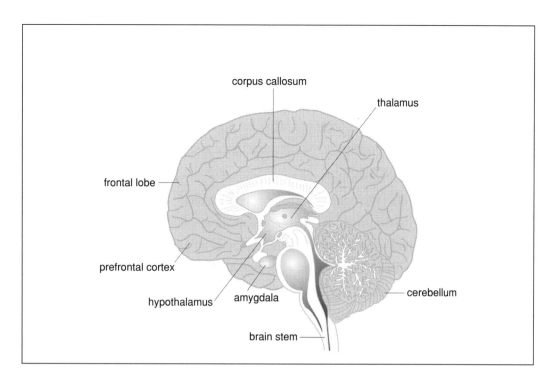

Figure 2: The human brain

A neuron has the ability to grow other branch-like fibres (*dendrites*) that also connect with the axons or cell bodies of adjacent neurons. Dendrites are neuronal structures that receive signals from sending neurons (see Figure 1). At the end of each axon there are additional tiny fibres leading to what are termed *synaptic terminals*. These terminals allow links to be made with adjacent dendrites or cell bodies. Two nerve cells do not actually make physical contact because there is a microscopic gap (*synapse*) between the adjoining surfaces of dendrites and axons. The synaptic terminal contains chemicals used in the transmission of signals between cells across the synaptic junction or cleft. The communication process between brain cells is electro-chemical in nature. Eric Jensen (1995) indicates that our brain's ability to pay attention is regulated by complex variations in the efficacy of chemical neurotransmitter molecules.

There are infinite ways in which networks of brain cells can connect with each other. The average neuron connects with about 1000 others (Westen, 2002). Even before birth, very many synaptic connections are already formed and fully functional so that reflex actions, basic motor responses, and very rudimentary information processing are possible. These earliest connections are almost entirely genetically determined (Perutz, 2001, citing Lewontin, 2000). As learning proceeds through life, additional complex functional linkages among networks of brain cells continue.

It is believed that all the main synapses are formed within the first ten years of life, and those that are used most frequently remain and strengthen while those that are not used disappear (Bruer, 1999; Sprenger, 1999). It is known that dendritic development continues throughout adolescence into young adulthood (Meade, 2001). The specific connections neurons make with other neurons, and the strength and maintenance of these connections, seem to depend on both external stimuli and nutrition.

The way in which the brain 'wires' and 'rewires' itself depends on the experiences the individual has over time (Gopnik *et al.*, 1999; Marschark *et al.*, 2002). The brain development of children deprived of a stimulating environment is reported to be far below optimum (Begley, 1999; Nash, 2001). It is believed that a stimulating physical and social environment, together with active involvement and exploration by the child, are necessary for optimum dendritic growth. Educational programmes and home environments must stimulate children and challenge them appropriately if brain development is to be optimised (Christison, 2002). Perhaps the tongue-in-cheek title of Tate's (2003) book *Worksheets Don't Grow Dendrites*, might remind us that not all school programmes are particularly effective in stimulating cognitive development and brain growth.

Malnutrition before birth or during the formative years can limit neurological development and thus have longer-term consequences for cognitive development (Meade, 2001; Ricciuti, 1993). Poor nutrition in the early years is associated with lower IQ, poorer attention, poorer memory, and lower school achievement (Eysenck and Schoenthaler, 1997). An individual's nutritional status can influence mood, responsiveness, concentration, and general readiness for learning. Some substances found in foods can help with alertness, memory and recall (for example, lecithin, sugars). Even an adequate intake of water is known to be important for the efficient functioning of the brain and for reducing levels of stress in the body. Lack of sufficient water leads to poor attention and often to headaches. Eric Jensen (1995) states that lack of protein in the diet can have negative repercussions on memory processing.

Useful additional information about the relationship between brain function and diet can be found in the text by Carper (2000).

Learning and the brain

Synaptic junctions appear to undergo physical changes as a result of constant use (Greenough and Black, 2000) and neuroscientists view the synapses through which nerve cells communicate as the likely sites of learning and memory. Learning takes place by making existing synaptic connections more effective (Anderson, 2000; E. Jensen, 1998; Roediger and Meade, 2000). Smilkstein (2003, p. 90) confirms that, 'Our dendrites, synapses and neural networks which grow as a result of our personal experiences, are our knowledge; they are the eyes with which we see.'

Hebb (1949) was one early theorist to suggest that learning is probably represented in unique connections that become established among specific assemblies of nerve cells in the brain. It was further conjectured that these neuronal networks or 'cell assemblies' strengthen and become more efficient with frequent use. The phenomenon of increased efficiency within neural networks is referred to as *long-term potentiation* (LTP). Ratey (2001, p. 191) states:

> When a stimulus is received, long-term potentiality blazes a new trail along a series of neurons, making it easier for subsequent messages to fire along the same path. The more the path is re-fired the more permanent the message becomes.

Sousa (2001b, p. 11) explains the process in these terms:

> Learning occurs when the synapses make physical and chemical changes so that the influence of one neuron on another also changes. For instance, a set of neurons 'learns' to fire together. Repeated firings make successive firings easier and, eventually, automatic under certain conditions. Thus, a memory is formed.

Exploring brain function and structure

In recent years technological advances have made it possible for neuroscientists to study aspects of brain structure and function in totally new ways. Procedures such as functional magnetic resonance imaging (fMRI) and positron emission tomography (PET) have revealed much more than we knew previously about the brain (Berninger and Richards, 2002; Rumsey, 1996). PET scans clearly show how blood flow to different parts of the brain varies during different types of activity and different emotional states. The new fMRI approach is a noninvasive technique that permits detection of alterations in blood flow, blood volume and glucose utilisation within the brain while an individual engages in various tasks. It has been possible to identify specific areas of the brain that are involved when, for example, a subject performs an activity such as reading single words, giving meanings of words, or reading continuous text (Grigorenko, 2001; Krasuski, Horwitz and Rumsey, 1996). Neuro-imaging studies are now being extended into the brain activity of individuals when carrying out mathematical calculations. More will be said later on imaging and brain function in later chapters on learning disability.

Although many components of human capability (for example, language) appear to be at least partly localised in specific areas of the brain, it is also clear that, even into adulthood, if specific areas are damaged, other areas and neural networks can eventually take over some of these functions. Evidence of this plasticity or adaptability in brain function can be seen, for example, in cases of partial or full recovery from stroke or cerebral injury. However, certain forms of brain damage do seriously impair physical, sensory and cognitive functioning, as in the case of cerebral palsy, for example.

Memory

One particularly important brain-based human attribute is memory. Memory can be defined as the persistence of learning in a state that can be retrieved at a later time (Silver and Hagin, 2002). Most memories are not just mechanical recollections of information or events but rather constructs built on a whole body of relevant prior experience (Hirsch, 1996). According to Eric Jensen (1998, p. 14):

> Learning and memory are like two sides of a coin to neuroscientists. You can't talk about one without the other. After all, if you have learned something, the only evidence of the learning is memory.

A 'failure to remember' is such an obvious characteristic of students with learning difficulties that the topic merits more detailed discussion here. What do we mean by memory? How do we store and retrieve information? Why do we forget?

The scientific study of memory goes back to the nineteenth century and the topic has generated a vast literature of its own. Many of the first serious experiments in learning were actually experiments involving memory. See Schneider and Bjorkland (2003) for an excellent overview of studies of memory.

One acknowledged expert on human memory, Baddeley (1999, p. 19), states:

> Memory does not comprise a single unitary system, but rather an array of interacting systems, each capable of encoding or registering information, storing it, and making it available for retrieval.

The physiological bases of memory are extremely complex and are not yet well understood (Purdy *et al.*, 2001). It appears that memory involves a persistent change in relationship among neurons through a combination of structural change and the development of biochemical links (Silver and Hagin, 2002). It also seems that memories are not stored in just one specific area of the brain – although damage to a specific area can impair recall of certain types of information. It is generally accepted that memory can involve different processes and different neural systems in different spatial relationships (Bachevalies, 2001; Byrnes, 2001; Sprenger, 1999). LeDoux (2002) states that memories are distributed across many brain systems, and are not always available to you consciously.

For the psychologist, memory is seen to operate as various systems. These systems are described as short-term memory, working memory and long-term memory. Long-term memory can be further subdivided into semantic memory, procedural memory, and episodic memory. Each of these systems will be briefly explained.

Short-term memory

Taylor (2002, p. 237) says that short-term memory '... defines our immediate consciousness'. It can be conceptualised as the system that allows information to be held in mind for only a few seconds. A typical example is looking up a telephone number in a directory and remembering it just long enough to dial the number correctly. Short-term memory is often assessed in intelligence tests by using digit span items that require the individual to repeat progressively longer strings of numbers. It is commonly believed that most individuals can hold between five and nine items of information in short-term memory span at one time (Miller, 1956). In most models of memory, short-term storage is represented as a necessary first step toward long-term storage; but a vast amount of information that enters short-term memory does not need to be transferred to long-term storage and is very rapidly forgotten.

Short-term memory can be impaired by anxiety and stress, and either facilitated or disrupted by certain drugs. Sprenger (1999) reports that short-term memory processes seem to be located in the frontal lobes (see Figure 2) and do not reach capacity until approximately the age of 15 years.

Many writers treat short-term memory as synonymous with 'working memory' but the two concepts are not identical. Short-term memory processes do not necessarily imply any manipulation or transformation of the information during the very brief time it is stored — for example, in a digit span test the numbers are simply repeated back in the same sequence. Working memory goes well beyond this, and allows active processing and modification to the information, as the next section indicates.

Working memory

Leahey and Harris (2001) suggest that working memory processes appear to function mainly in the prefrontal cortex of the brain. Working memory is sometimes conceptualised as 'mental working space for thinking'. It involves those perceptual and cognitive processes that enable a person to hold visual and verbal information in an active state while processing it for a particular purpose or integrating it with other information (Demetriou *et al.*, 2002). In relation to learning, Sweller (1999, p. 23) says, 'The major, perhaps the only, factor determining ease or difficulty of understanding may be the working memory load imposed by the material.' The cognitive load on working memory increases when the elements of a problem or task interact and need to be processed simultaneously.

Working memory, where all conscious cognitive processing occurs, is involved in all acts of thinking, reasoning and problem solving (Paas *et al.*, 2003). For example, working memory is a key factor involved in reading comprehension and in understanding and communicating through spoken language. Ratey (2001) suggests that working memory enables us to maintain continuity in our attention and thoughts from one moment to the next in our daily lives. Ratey also indicates that some individuals have deficiencies in working memory that can cause major problems in learning – as, for example, in genuine cases of attention deficit disorder (ADD). Limitations in working memory are often implicated in difficulties in reading, writing, mathematics and problem solving (Gathercole and Pickering, 2000; Riding, 2002; Swanson, 2002; Swanson and Siegel, 2001). Working memory capacity is also known to be restricted in persons with intellectual disability (Numminen *et al.*, 2002). These points will be covered in more detail in later chapters.

Working memory is conceptualised as having a central 'executive' component that controls the individual's attention and focuses it on the relevant information being processed or rehearsed. Working memory is also thought to involve two 'slave systems' that temporarily store and make available visual or phonological (linguistic) information (Baddeley, 1999). According to Swanson and Saez (2003), students with learning disabilities appear to have weaknesses in executive processes and in the phonological aspects of working memory.

Sweller (1999) suggests there are working memories for different sensory modalities. The overall capacity of working memory is limited and it can handle no more than possibly three interacting elements at one time. Most human intellectual activity (for example, planning, analysing, reflecting, and problem solving) involves many more interacting elements than this; so to carry out these mental activities we supplement the limited information stored in working memory by drawing on our long-term memory store containing vast numbers of associated cognitive schemata (Paas *et al.*, 2003). As described previously, schemata incorporate multiple elements of information into one functional unit, and their automated use in working memory reduces the cognitive load of intellectual tasks. Long-term memory is thus much more than just a passive store of information — it interacts with working-memory to provide the relevant schemata needed in all types of thinking and reasoning.

Long-term memory

Long-term memory represents information that is stored for considerable periods of time. Psychologists usually distinguish between different types of long-term stored information, for example by describing it as *episodic memory*, *semantic memory* or *procedural memory* (Baddeley, 1999). *Episodic memory* refers to the memories we have for times, events and places. Such information is often stored as images that can be recalled quite easily. Even before the age of 2 years children demonstrate ability to store and retrieve memories of events (Bauer *et al.*, 2000). *Procedural memory* refers to our ability to recall the steps in a particular process, skill or strategy. The part of the brain storing this type of memory is believed to be the cerebellum. *Semantic memory* refers to our memories of meaningful facts, rules, definitions, concepts and principles. Most learning within the school curriculum involves semantic and procedural memory.

Most procedural and semantic information becomes stored in long-term memory as a result of repetition (practice). The practice may occur as deliberate rehearsal, but is more likely to occur through natural repetition when information, skills or strategies are applied in everyday situations. According to Roediger and Meade (2000), learning is based on memory traces within the nervous system, and these memory traces become stronger with repeated practice.

Sprenger (1999) suggests that all factual information is stored in the brain section termed the hippocampus. Semantic memories tend to be organised effectively into schemata that allow new information to be added at any time to what we already know and remember. Schemata may also provide the necessary links between episodic, semantic and procedural memories. Existing schemata can have powerful effects on a learner's comprehension of new situations (Pressley and Schneider, 1997).

Meta-memory

The term 'meta-memory' refers to an individual's awareness of his or her own memory processes and the ways in which storage and retrieval of information can be enhanced. Efficient learners appear to know a great deal about how best to internalise important information, how to offset the effects of forgetting, and what strategies to use to maximise recall (Byrnes, 2001; Pressley and Schneider, 1997).

Meta-memory increases with age, but for some students with learning difficulties, time and effort may need to be spent in intervention programmes to raise children's awareness of their own memory processes and how these can be monitored and made more effective. In particular, as students get older, it becomes possible and desirable to teach the effective use of mnemonic strategies as part of study skill development (Forness *et al.*, 1997). According to Terry (2000), students with learning difficulties are poor at attending closely to the task, poor at encoding information into long-term memory, poor at retrieving information quickly, and lacking in memory-enhancing strategies. As a result, they 'fail to remember' – the problem clearly indicated at the beginning of this section.

Forgetting

It is perfectly natural to forget information. We cannot, and do not need to, remember everything. As Haberlandt (1999, p. 304) points out:

> … forgetting fulfills a selective function by uncluttering our memories and thereby increasing the chance of recalling important information.

The most common reasons for failing to remember something important include:

- The information was of no personal significance.
- Failing to give the information sufficient attention when it is first encountered.

- Not rehearsing the information with the intention of remembering it.

- Decay or fading of information over time; sometimes described as 'passive loss of memory trace'.

- New or conflicting information interfering with storage and recall of earlier information. The term 'proactive interference' is used for situations where something you already know prevents you from easily assimilating and recalling something new. 'Retroactive inhibition' refers to new information preventing the easy recall of prior knowledge.

- Lack of relevance or meaningfulness, in the sense that the new information was not linked effectively with other stored information. It could be said that the information had not been effectively accommodated into existing schemata.

- Failure to use imagery to assist storage and retrieval.

- Inability of the learner to ignore distractions during learning.

- Detrimental emotional states, such as stress and anxiety.

Many of the above factors account for problems in recall that students with learning difficulties exhibit. It is widely acknowledged that students with learning disabilities lack good attention to task and do not use effective study and memorisation strategies (Ormrod, 2003). The problems are most evident in students with attention deficit and hyperactivity disorder (ADHD).

The duration and nature of typical lessons in school also influence learning and remembering. It is said that human attention span, and the active use of working memory, begin to weaken significantly after about 10 to 20 minutes (Sousa, 2001a). To hold students' attention and to optimise their processing and assimilation of information the activities used within the lesson should change at frequent intervals. Variety and active involvement both help students to learn and remember. Gage and Berliner (1998) indicate that the more teachers can get physical, auditory, and visual stimuli combined with the meaningful presentation of information, the more likely that the information will be learned and retrieved easily. Physically active, multisensory learning is more likely to result in longer and fuller retention than passive learning. The challenge for the teacher is to find ways of ensuring that students do store and remember important information and skills.

Remembering

Remembering may involve either *retrieval* (free recall) of information from long-term memory; or it may involve *recognition*, by matching stored information with an outside stimulus. To illustrate the point, a teacher might ask a young student to read aloud a word presented on a flashcard. If the student has already stored this word in long-term memory through practice and repetition, he or she will be able to recall and say the word immediately. If, however, the student has only seen the word once or twice before and has not yet firmly stored the image and its connection to the spoken word, he or she will have difficulty in remembering. Unprompted recall is much more difficult than recognition, and in many early learning tasks teachers need to capitalise on recognition-level activities before expecting children to recall information without cues. Instead of testing recall the teacher might show four different words simultaneously and tell the child, 'Point to the word *breakfast*.' The chances are that the child will recognise (discriminate) the word easily and point to it, even though the word *breakfast* could not be freely recalled.

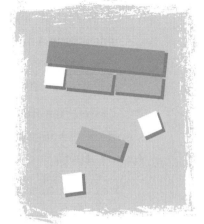

Studies have shown that retention of information is longer and retrieval is easier when material is *overlearned* — that is, practised beyond the point when it first appears to have been mastered. Overlearning is particularly important for topics and concepts that students find difficult (Ausubel, 2000; Sprinthall *et al.*, 1998). Other factors that tend to increase attention and recall include:

- The learner staying cognitively alert.
- Using active learning methods that fully engage students' attention.
- Presenting information or concepts in novel, vivid, or surprising ways.
- Deliberately introducing some degree of incongruity between new and prior knowledge.
- Drawing the learner's attention to key features of the stimulus.
- Teaching the use of mnemonic and rehearsal strategies.
- Reviewing previously taught information at regular intervals.

At the neurological level, Sousa (2001a, p. 113) explains the value of practice and recall of information. He says:

> When memories are continually recalled, the neural networks strengthen with each rehearsal; this process is called consolidation ... Every time we recall information from long-term memory into working memory we relearn it.

On the issue of improving memory, Henderson (1999) states that research suggests there is no such thing as a 'good' or 'bad' memory but rather that an individual's memory is either 'trained' or 'untrained' in its ability to store, organise and access information. As indicated under meta-memory above, teaching students more about memory processes and ways of enhancing their efficiency has proved to be useful, particularly with students exhibiting learning difficulties.

In addition to attention and memory processes, learning is also connected with what we generally term 'intelligence' or mental ability.

Intelligence

There is no universally accepted definition of 'intelligence' although the term and the concept itself enjoy a high degree of acceptance and understanding within the general community. According to Armour-Thomas and Gopaul-McNicol (1998, p. 58):

> Intelligence is a culturally derived abstraction that members of any given society coin to make sense of observed differences in performance of individuals within and between social groups.

The exact nature of intelligence is a very controversial topic that has undergone significant changes in recent years (for example, Gould, 1996; Howe, 1997; A. Jensen, 1998).

Most definitions tend to focus on intelligence as being an individual's capacity for learning, reasoning and understanding, together with aptitude for recognising relationships, comprehending facts, dealing with abstract symbols, and attaching meanings (Eggen and Kauchak, 2003). Other definitions stress intelligence as reflected in the *rapidity* with which information is processed and new concepts acquired. Lohman (1996) uses the general term 'cognitive power', and Guilford (1996, p. 428) talks of intelligence as 'a systematic collection of abilities or functions for processing different kinds of information in various ways'. A concise definition is provided by Hardman, Drew and Egan (2002, p. 286) who state that, 'Intelligence is the ability to acquire, remember, and use knowledge.'

Some theorists conceptualise intelligence as a general innate ability individuals possess that enables them to deal with and learn from the environment. Intelligence is often viewed as distinct from what one has learned; but learning itself enhances intelligence, because the more people know, the more 'intelligently' they can behave (McDevitt and Ormrod, 2002). Ceci (1996) states emphatically that knowledge and intelligence are inseparable. Even with a general consensus on what we mean by intelligence, there are still those who seriously question whether the concept is useful (for example, Schlinger, 2003).

Models of intelligence

The traditional view of intelligence, dating back to the early 1900s and owing much to the work of Spearman (1927) considered that basic intelligence could be conceptualised as an underlying general mental ability that enters into all cognitive endeavours (the so-called '*g*' *factor*) plus a number of specific abilities (*s factors*) that are required in different types of activity, such as mathematics, language, or spatial and mechanical problems.

Arthur Jensen (1996), referring to Thurstone's (1938) early model of *primary mental abilities*, supports the notion of there being a general factor ('g') together with complex sub-sets of abilities comprising reasoning, verbal comprehension, verbal fluency, number, spatial visualisation, perceptual speed, associative memory, and so forth. Pellegrino and Varnhagen (1990) state that it is not known how many specific mental abilities there are, or their degrees of independence from one another. Guilford's (1967) theoretical three-dimensional 'structure of intellect' model visualised 120 or more possible mental abilities. Jensen (1998) claims that all mental abilities are positively correlated.

While some theorists have questioned the value of the notion of 'general intelligence' and 'g' (for example, Schlinger, 2003), others consider them still to be useful concepts. Anderson (2001), for example, has attempted to identify the basic 'cognitive architecture' underpinning intelligence and accounting for 'g'. He suggests that *speed of information processing* (he sometimes says *speed of thinking*) together with *executive mental functioning* (mainly control of attention and focus) may represent two key operational features of 'g'. Anderson suggests that an individual's speed of information processing does not change over time and may constitute the innate component of individual differences in mental ability (Anderson, 1999). Westen (2002) reports that positron emission tomography (PET) research has lent support to Spearman's hypothesis concerning a 'g' factor operating across both verbal and visual tasks. He states:

> The results were striking: tasks associated with general intelligence consistently led to activation of areas of the frontal lobes (particularly the dorsolateral prefrontal cortex) previously shown to be involved in working memory and problem solving (p. 289).

He conjectures that differences in general intelligence may reflect functional differences in frontal lobe neural networks. See Duncan *et al.* (2000) for further details.

It is possible that 'speed of information processing' or 'mental quickness' is based on 'neural efficiency' and is the underlying variable determining differences in intelligence (McRorie and Cooper, 2003). Richardson (1999, p. 14) states that, 'Nearly everyone believes that intelligence somehow resides in the brain [and] intelligence is virtually synonymous with "brain power".' According to Grotzer and Perkins (2000) some theorists suggest that neural functioning contributes to the speed, efficiency, access, and capacity of information processing at the level of synapses and networked memory.

Many years ago Hebb (1949) provided a simple but very useful way of conceptualising the development of intelligence, using the notion of 'Intelligence A' and 'Intelligence B'. A and B can be imagined as two concentric circles, with the smaller circle B inside the larger circle A. Intelligence A represents each individual's innate potential to develop mental ability. Intelligence A is almost certainly genetically predetermined to a large extent, but its rate and extent of development are significantly influenced by environmental factors, including schooling. Intelligence B represents how much of that potential the individual has achieved up to a particular point in time as a result of learning and experience. Given optimum learning experiences, circle B might eventually expand to cover most of circle A. Vernon (1960) added the notion of Intelligence C being that small sample of Intelligence B that intelligence tests can measure. It is argued that Intelligence C is not a particularly good indication of Intelligence B and is a very poor measure indeed of Intelligence A, innate potential. It is widely agreed that standardised tests of mental ability do not sample all aspects or forms of intelligence — for example, creativity, wisdom, practical sense, and social sensitivity (Neisser *et al.*, 1996).

It is interesting to consider that while there is no totally acceptable theory and definition of intelligence, there still exists an elaborate testing technology designed to measure individual differences in intellectual ability and to make predictions and decisions based on the results (Pellegrino and Varnhagen, 1990). The use of intelligence tests to classify and place students in classes or programmes has declined very significantly in recent years, but IQ testing still forms a common part of the assessment process for diagnosing specific learning disability (see Chapter 5). A major problem is that IQ tests are not diagnostic in nature and therefore do not provide helpful information for the planning of adaptive education. Also, measured IQ, although correlating significantly with academic progress in school, is not a completely valid and reliable predictor. A below-average IQ does not necessarily preclude adequate achievement in school; nor does a high IQ guarantee success (Sternberg, 1996). Personal, attitudinal, and environmental factors significantly influence learning, regardless of measured intelligence. Many years ago Vernon (1940) observed that intelligence in action in daily life is not a purely cognitive process but is closely bound up with the individual's emotions, motivations and interests.

Contemporary views

There are currently two main theories concerning the nature of intelligence (Schunk, 2000). The *entity* theory views intelligence as a relatively fixed and stable attribute of the individual, not amenable to improvement. The *incremental* theory on the other hand suggests that intelligence is not a stable commodity and is significantly influenced by experience and learning. The incremental viewpoint implies that given highly effective teaching and productive learning experiences, individuals can increase their intellectual capabilities (for example, Adey and Shayer, 2002). However, whether you can 'teach' intelligence remains a contentious issue. Traditionally, intelligence has been viewed as a static, single general mental ability, with an upper limit for development pre-set genetically for each individual. Recent views have challenged these assumptions.

Mayer (2000) now suggests that:

- Intellectual skills are not fixed and innate but are dynamic and learnable.
- Intelligence is not a single ability but rather a complex collection of component skills.

Contemporary views on the nature of intelligence see intelligence as manifesting itself in different forms or capabilities (for example, Gardner, 1983; Sternberg, 1984). Sternberg's (1985) triarchic theory for example, has intelligence represented in three forms — analytic intelligence, creative intelligence, and practical intelligence. *Analytic* (or *componential*) intelligence relates to the individual's capacity to acquire knowledge, think, reason, plan and monitor performance. The components of this aspect of intelligence include executive mental processes and knowledge-acquisition processes. *Creative* (or *experiential*) intelligence reflects the application of strategies, insights and routine behaviours that are acquired through everyday experiences, but can be used to solve new problems or address new situations. *Practical* (or *contextual*) intelligence is represented in the individual's ability to adapt to changing social and other contexts in order to use analytic and creative intelligence flexibly. Looked at another way, intelligence in action, according to Sternberg, depends upon the environmental context of the moment, the prior experience the individual brings to the situation, and the cognitive processes required in dealing with that situation (McDevitt and Ormrod, 2002).

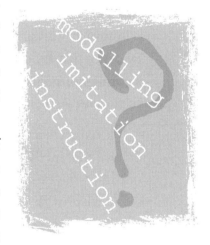

Sternberg (1996) also presents the interesting notion of 'successful intelligence'. He describes successful intelligence as the type that achieves important goals in life for the individual. He suggests that successfully intelligent people motivate themselves, control their impulses, know when to persevere, know how to maintain focus, and make the best of their abilities. Successfully intelligent individuals translate thoughts into actions, complete tasks they set themselves, are not afraid to take risks, do not procrastinate, find ways around difficulties, and have faith in their own capabilities. It is interesting to contrast this list of characteristics with the points made regarding self-efficacy and motivation in the previous chapter. It is also interesting to consider how many of these characteristics are evident (or are lacking) in students who have learning difficulties.

Gardner (1983) has developed the notion of *Multiple intelligences*, suggesting that there are at least eight types of intelligence including verbal-linguistic, logical-mathematical, bodily-kinesthetic, spatial, musical, interpersonal, intrapersonal, and naturalist. He is much more concerned with exploring each type of special ability rather than becoming preoccupied with a search for 'general intelligence' (Anderson, 1999). Although Gardner's model has been influential in stimulating curriculum development and differentiated instruction in schools, it could be argued that he has said little that we did not know already, namely that we are all good at some things and weaker at others. However, on the positive side, the multiple intelligence philosophy supports the belief that we should acknowledge and encourage the development of diverse strengths and talents in all our students.

Can intelligence be taught?

Spitz (1999) provided a useful overview of attempts that have been made to raise intelligence levels of individuals and groups. His conclusion is that intelligence cannot be increased to any significant or lasting degree, even with intensive early childhood intervention. He disputes the claims of researchers that intervention is effective; and he identifies flaws in the studies that appear to have measured gains in IQ. In contrast, Grotzer and Perkins (2000, p. 502) state:

> Efforts to teach for intelligence are promising. There is ample evidence for the malleability of cognitive processes, and earlier interventions have informed later efforts such that they met with greater success in impacting the magnitude, persistence, and transferability of effects.

A similar view is shared by Howe (1997) who considers there to be irrefutable evidence that children's intelligence can be increased substantially. Howe reviews a number of studies in support of this conclusion – interestingly some of the same studies severely criticised by Spitz (1999).

It is natural – and probably highly desirable – that teachers and parents should believe that intellectual functioning can be improved and that a child's IQ does not limit the extent to which he or she can develop and learn. It makes good sense to provide educational environments and teaching methods that will enable all students to develop intellectually to their optimum potential: to think otherwise represents a very pessimistic and possibly self-fulfilling expectation (Pressley and McCormick, 1995).

Neisser *et al.* (1996) have observed that one environmental variable with significant impact on intellectual development is formal schooling. They indicate that schools affect the acquisition of intelligence in many ways, not only by transmitting specific information but also by developing certain intellectual skills and attitudes. However, as Rutter and Maughan (2002) point out, individual differences in response to schooling are striking. They state, 'Schooling can do much to counter family disadvantage, but it cannot be expected to eliminate social or biological inequalities' (p. 459). Major individual differences among learners are inevitable because they are partly biologically determined. Schooling can be helpful in raising ability levels and alleviating individual difficulties, but there will always be marked variations among students.

Beyond intelligence

The ability to participate productively in learning activities requires sufficient intelligence, but also requires motivation, attention, commitment, persistence, and effective use of appropriate learning strategies (Frederickson and Cline, 2002). It may be much easier to improve these components of effective learning than to try to increase intelligence. Evidence from studies involving the teaching of cognitive and self-regulatory strategies appears to show improvements in children's classroom learning and motivation (Swanson, 2000a). While these interventions do not set out specifically to raise IQ, they do seem to help students develop behaviours that enhance learning: to all intents and purposes they make the students more effective learners. For example, Feuerstein's (1980) strategies for 'Mediated Learning Experiences' and 'Structural Cognitive Modifiability' are based on a belief that a student can be guided to become a better thinker and learner, regardless of genetic endowment (Seng *et al.*, 2003). Similarly, endeavours that improve children's receptive and expressive language skills help them to cope much more successfully with the language of the classroom. This in effect makes them 'smarter'. Interest has been shown in recent years in 'accelerated learning' (Silcock, 2003). This approach aims to have students learning at their maximum capacity by:

- making sure students understand and value the learning tasks they are required to engage in, and possess the prerequisite skills and concepts to perform effectively;
- helping students acquire and develop a personal commitment to study;
- giving students enough freedom to develop control over their own learning and motivation (Adey and Shayer, 2002).

A current definition

Finally, perhaps the most useful recent definition of intelligence, compatible with current understanding in the field, is provided by Westen (2002, p. 280):

> Intelligence refers to the application of cognitive skills and knowledge to learn, solve problems, and obtain ends that are valued by an individual or culture. Intelligence is multifaceted and functional, directed at problems of adaptation. It is also to some extent culturally shaped and culturally defined, since cultural practices support and recognize intellectual qualities that are useful in the social and ecological context.

Further reading

Ausubel, D.P. (2000) *The Acquisition and Retention of Knowledge: A Cognitive View*. Dordrecht: Kluwer Academic.

Berninger, V.W. and Richards, T.L. (2002) *Brain Literacy for Educators and Psychologists*. Amsterdam: Academic Press.

Bristow, J., Cowley, P. and Daines, B. (1999) *Memory and Learning: A Practical Guide for Teachers*. London: Fulton.

Heilman, K.M. (2002) *Matter of Mind: A Neurologist's View of Brain-Behavior Relationships*. New York: Oxford University Press.

OECD (2002) *Understanding the Brain: Towards a New Learning Science*. Paris: Organisation for Economic Co-operation and Development.

Purdy, J.E., Markham, M.R., Schwartz, B.L. and Gordon, W.C. (2001) *Learning and Memory* (2nd edn). Belmont, CA: Wadsworth-Thomson.

Ratey, J.J. (2001) *A User's Guide to the Brain: Perception, Attention and the Four Theatres of the Brain*. New York: Pantheon Books.

Smilkstein, R. (2003) *We're Born to Learn*. Thousand Oaks, CA: Corwin Press.

Sousa, D.A. (2001) *How the Brain Learns: A Classroom Teacher's Guide* (2nd edn). Thousand Oaks, CA: Corwin Press.

Squire, L.R. and Schacter, D.L. (2002) *Neuropsychology of Memory* (3rd edn). New York: Guilford Press.

Sternberg, R.J. (ed.) (2000) *Handbook of Intelligence*. Cambridge: Cambridge University Press.

4 Learning difficulties: prevalence and causes

The reasons why children fail are complex. (Daly *et al.*, 1997, p. 554)

In previous chapters passing reference was made in many places to factors that can cause or exacerbate problems in learning. This chapter consolidates much of this information and will present a general overview of learning difficulties in the school context. Later chapters focus in more depth on learning difficulties in particular key areas of the curriculum.

Students with learning difficulties

Over many years students with learning problems have been given a variety of labels, including 'dull', 'educationally subnormal', 'slow learners', 'low achievers', 'at risk', the 'hard-to-teach' and 'learning disabled'. After a period of time each label attracts its own odium and is replaced by another. Most recently the American literature appears to favour the descriptor 'struggling' – as in 'struggling readers' – and the term appears in the title of many books dealing with learning problems. It is to be hoped that 'struggling' goes the way of other inappropriate terms since it implies that the fault lies with the learner.

In most countries the term *learning difficulty* is applied to students who are not making adequate progress within the school curriculum, particularly in basic skill areas covering language, literacy and numeracy. Their problems may be associated with just one particular school subject, or may be evident across all subjects in the academic curriculum. For a variety of reasons these students do not find learning easy in school. The number of students with such learning difficulties varies across schools and across countries. Prevalence rate has been reported as varying anywhere between 12 per cent and 30 per cent of the school population (for example, Gupta, 1999; Silver and Hagin, 2002; Waldron and McLeskey, 2000; Westwood and Graham, 2000). Students with these problems are therefore quite common in schools; and because they are found to flourish almost everywhere the description 'garden variety' learning difficulty has been coined for them (for example, Badian, 1996). Often the intellectual level of these students is somewhat below average and disproportionate numbers come from lower socio-economic and disadvantaged backgrounds.

Within the fairly large group of students with learning difficulties there is a very much smaller sub-group of individuals with normal intelligence and no obvious impairment. These students find the learning of basic literacy and mathematical skills incredibly problematic. The students have been labelled 'learning disabled' (LD) or 'specifically learning disabled' (SpLD) to separate them from 'garden variety' students described above. In the US some 5–6 per cent of the school population has been classified as 'learning disabled' (LD) (Bradley *et al.*, 2002; Silver and Hagin, 2002) but in most other countries the percentage of students diagnosed with genuine learning disability is reportedly lower. This difference may be due to the fact that in US the LD category has become a collecting house for a variety of learning and behaviour problems, not all of which really match the official definition of learning disability. Students with specific learning disabilities are discussed fully in Chapter 5.

Possible causes of learning difficulty

General learning difficulties can occur as a result of any combination of the following influences (collated from Chan, 1998; Cheng, 1998; MacMillan and Siperstein, 2002; Naparstek, 2002; Westwood, 2003):

- inadequate or inappropriate teaching
- irrelevant and unsuitable curriculum
- classroom environment
- socio-economic disadvantage
- poor relationship between student and teacher
- poor school attendance
- health problems
- learning through the medium of a second language
- loss of confidence
- emotional or behavioural problems
- below average intelligence
- sensory impairment
- specific information processing difficulties.

It is important to point out that teachers tend to blame students themselves, or their socio-cultural and family backgrounds for the learning difficulties. Studies by Cheng (1998) and Westwood (1995), for example, indicate that teachers commonly attribute learning problems to weaknesses or impairments *within the student* rather than to deficiencies within the teaching method, curriculum, or teacher–student relationship. They talk about students being 'slow', lacking in intelligence, disorganised and poorly motivated. They also identify them often as coming from 'poor home backgrounds' or 'unsupportive families'. Henderson (2002) refers to this as the 'deficit discourse' surrounding learning difficulty; and

Bearne (1996) suggests that this 'blame the victim' perspective can have a negative impact on teachers' classroom practices and the expectations they hold for students with difficulties. McLaren (2003, p. 236) talks about the trend toward 'psychologizing' failure. He states:

> Psychologizing student failure amounts to blaming it on an individual trait or series of traits (e.g. lack of motivation or low self-concept) … This attitude is particularly frightening because teachers often are unaware of their complicity in its debilitating effects. Psychologizing school failure is part of the hidden curriculum that relieves teachers from the need to engage in pedagogical self-scrutiny or in serious critique of their personal roles within the school, and the school's role within the wider society. In effect, psychologizing school failure indicts the student while simultaneously protecting the social environment from sustained criticism.

While some learning problems are indeed due to specific weaknesses within the learner, it is most unlikely that this is the case with the vast majority of students. Environmental factors, including teaching methods and the curriculum, are much more frequent causes of difficulty. Kershner (2000, p. 280) remarks, 'For most children whose progress causes concern in school, the problems are to do with experience and learning rather than intrinsic intellectual weaknesses or deficits.'

The environmental factor over which teachers have most control is the method of teaching. It seems likely that when methods are not matched to students' interests and capabilities, and when they are not matched well with the type of learning involved in the lesson, learning difficulties will be created.

Teaching methods as a cause of learning difficulty

Insufficient or inappropriate teaching, particularly in the early years, can be a major cause of learning difficulty. Students from backgrounds where there has not been an opportunity to develop what might be termed 'school-learning readiness' are potentially at risk when they enter unstructured early school programmes. The philosophy underpinning early years education is that children should be encouraged to develop at their individual rates; but the outcome can be that without direct teaching some children fail to acquire crucial knowledge, skills and attitudes that would enhance their progress. Instead they experience frustration and failure and develop increasingly negative feelings toward learning in school (Slavin, 1994). To prevent this problem, all effective early intervention programmes tend to place due emphasis on explicit teaching (see Chan and Dally, 2000). The use of explicit teaching methods in the early stages of learning in no way precludes the student from ultimately developing independence in learning; indeed, direct teaching in the early stages facilitates greater confidence and independence in later stages (Heward, 2003b; Pressley and McCormick, 1995).

It takes very little time for lack of success to undermine a child's confidence and interest. There is nothing organically wrong with the student but he or she quickly becomes locked into a failure cycle and attracts the description of slow learner, lazy, or poorly motivated. The 'Matthew Effect' – the poor getting poorer – comes into play and the child falls more and more behind classmates (Stanovich, 1986). There is clear evidence that students who are failing in first year of school generally are still having learning problems in later years (for example, Morris, 2003). For those who get off to a bad start, nothing recedes like success.

It is fairly characteristic of some contemporary classroom approaches based on constructivist philosophy that they rely heavily on students' good independent learning aptitude, high intrinsic motivation, and positive group-working skills. These attributes are singularly lacking in many at-risk students. Their problem  is compounded when direct teaching is frowned upon because it is incompatible with constructivist learning principles. Strategies such as drill and practice, regular revision, and corrective feedback, for example, are not systematically used. For children who get off to a shaky start such programmes do nothing to help them improve (Heward, 2003b).

Direct and explicit forms of instruction appear to achieve most in the early stages of learning basic academic skills (Swanson, 2000a; Wilen *et al.*, 2000). Over many decades, despite the popularity of student-centred, activity-based learning approaches, clear research evidence supports the value of direct and explicit teaching, often delivered through the medium of interactive whole-class teaching (Dickinson, 2003; Galton *et al.*, 1999; OFSTED, 1993). Where explicit teaching is used, students with learning difficulties appear to make much better progress and become more confident and effective learners. Direct teaching not only raises the attainment level of all students but also significantly reduces the prevalence of learning failure.

Effective teaching practices are those that provide students with the maximum opportunity to learn. These practices increase achievement through maintaining students' attention and on-task behaviour (academic engaged time). This active involvement includes listening to instruction from the teacher, asking and answering questions, discussing with teachers and peers, working on assigned tasks independently or with a group, and applying previously acquired knowledge and skills. Studies have shown that students who are receiving explanations, cues and direct instruction from the teacher spend more time attending to the content of the lesson and participating more fully (Jacobsen *et al.*, 2002; Killen, 1998; Rosenshine, 1995). Effective lessons, particularly those covering basic academic skills, tend to be under teacher control and have a clear structure.

Based on a meta-analysis of outcomes from many different types of teaching approach Swanson (1999) draws the conclusion that the most effective method for teaching basic academic skills to students with learning difficulties combines the following features:

- Carefully controlling and sequencing the curriculum content to be studied.

- Providing abundant opportunities for practice and application of newly acquired knowledge and skills.

- Ensuring high levels of participation and responding by the children (for example, answering the teacher's questions; staying on task).

- Using interactive group teaching.

- Modelling by the teacher of effective ways of completing school tasks.

- Direct strategy training (teaching children how best to attempt new learning tasks).

- Making appropriate use of technology (for example, computer-assisted instruction).

- Providing supplementary assistance (for example, in-class support; homework; parental tutoring).

It is unfortunate that some methods of teaching that are known to reduce educational failure and raise achievement levels are not willingly adopted in schools. There is a general resistance among teachers to any approach that seems too highly structured and likely to reduce their freedom and autonomy to use their own preferred methods and style (Waldron and Leskey, 2000). Heward (2003b) provides an excellent critique of the ways in which contemporary thinking about teaching methods creates a barrier to the implementation of effective special education. Two examples of approaches that are known to be highly successful but are not widely used in schools are direct instruction (Adams and Carnine, 2003) and precision teaching (Lindsley, 1992a).

Curriculum

It is not only teaching methods that can contribute to learning difficulties, the content of the curriculum can also create problems (Robertson *et al.*, 1994). Concepts may be pitched at an inappropriately high level relative to the students' ability, or the rate at which new content is introduced may be too rapid. This problem is often more evident in secondary schools where high academic achievement is stressed. Elliott and Garnett (1994, p. 6) use the term 'curriculum disabled' to describe the situation where certain students cannot cope with the cognitive demands of the subject matter or the rate at which new concepts and skills are introduced. From what we know already about the development of cognitive schemata we can appreciate that when students are given work to do that is beyond their current capabilities, they are unable to link the new learning with prior knowledge. The result is fragmented learning, accompanied by a rapid rate of forgetting. Confronting students day after day with work that is frustratingly difficult also has a very serious detrimental effect upon their self-esteem and motivation (Altenbaugh, 1998; Leiding, 2002). According to Howe (1999), many (perhaps most) learning difficulties are not caused by cognitive deficits in the learner but are due to students not having the necessary prior level of knowledge or skill needed for the task at hand.

Van Kraayenoord (2002, p. 398) states, 'Students will quickly become disengaged if classroom teaching does not connect with their lives, and if it does not engage them as learners with topics and issues that have interest and meaning for them.' Brennan (1985) suggested that curriculum content should be selected for students with learning difficulties on the basis that it is *real, relevant, realistic* and *rational*. In this context 'real' means the curriculum should cover topics that feature in the child's life and can be taught in concrete or experiential ways. 'Relevant' implies that in learning this topic the embedded knowledge, skills, strategies and values will be useful to the child. 'Realistic' means it is feasible that the child can attempt the work successfully given his or her age, ability, prior knowledge and motivation. 'Rational' implies that the student understands that there is value and purpose in engaging in this learning. Unfortunately, the content of many school curricula do not stand up well to evaluation against the Brennan's '4 R test', so contribute to or exacerbate learning problems.

Classroom environment

The physical environment of the classroom can exacerbate learning difficulties. The noise level and multiple sources of distraction can have a detrimental impact on the attention span and on-task behaviour of some children. Factors such as temperature, lighting, presence or absence of stimulating display material, availability of resources, adequate working space on desktops, and so forth, can all make learning easier or more difficult for children. Sources of background noise such as air-conditioners, ceiling fans, or moving furniture can be particularly frustrating for distractible students and for students with impaired hearing – whose hearing aids amplify all such environmental sound. Classroom environment is a particularly important factor to consider in the case of students with attention-deficit hyperactivity disorder (ADHD). The evidence is that such students need a calm, structured and highly predictable learning environment if they are to develop better attention to task and improve self-regulation (Alban-Metcalfe and Alban-Metcalfe, 2001; DuPaul and Stoner, 2003).

How children are seated and grouped during lessons also influences time on task, motivation and participation. For example, studies have revealed that on-task behaviour can be significantly better – and students are often more productive – when they are seated in rows rather than in informal groups (Hastings and Schwieso, 1995); yet the common practice in many classrooms operating under constructivist principles is to have children seated in groups to facilitate cooperative learning and discussion. It is not uncommon in primary schools to find classes physically arranged for group work with four or five students seated together around a table, but the students are actually working on different individual assignments. This potentially very distracting arrangement can result in poorer achievement because students have difficulty maintaining concentration (Lyle, 1996). It is also clear that any form of group work can be problematic for students with behavioural or attentional problems (Jenkins *et al.*, 2003).

Class size is one feature of the learning environment that has been thoroughly researched, with literally hundreds of studies carried out (for example, Blatchford, 2003; Goldberg, 2002). It is commonly believed that the smaller the class, the better it is for students' learning. The commonsense argument suggests that with smaller classes teachers are much more able to identify learning problems, provide individual attention, and adapt instruction to individual differences among students. The reality, as revealed in the studies, indicates a much more complex picture. Simply reducing class size does not automatically result in higher achievement and lower failure rates because of many other factors such as behaviour and quality of teaching are important. When class size is reduced, teachers may still tend to teach small classes in exactly the same way they taught large classes, with no adaptations made and limited individual attention for students. A few studies have even found that large classes actually produce a higher general level of achievement, possibly because the teacher is obliged to use a fairly structured approach and maintain good classroom management. However, a sufficient number of studies have shown clear benefits from smaller classes and three tentative conclusions can be reached (Finn, 2002; Wilson, 2002):

- Class size begins to have a positive effect when classes contain fewer than 20 students.

- The benefits are most apparent in the early years of schooling (age 5 to 8 years).

- Smaller classes seem to be of most benefit to children from disadvantaged backgrounds and for students in other at-risk categories.

Socio-economic disadvantage

Socio-economic disadvantage – particularly extreme poverty (see Davies, 1998) – represents one possible domain over which teachers have little or no direct control but it is important that they understand the impact that a child's background environment can have on his or her ability to learn in school. Evidence has accumulated over many years to indicate that socio-economic status (SES) is correlated with school performance (Cox, 2000; Hilty, 1998; OECD, 2001). Students coming from higher SES backgrounds tend to have higher academic achievement while lower SES students tend to have poorer results, irregular attendance, a somewhat higher prevalence of behaviour problems, and leave school at the earliest opportunity (McLoyd, 1998; Ormrod, 2003). Obviously there are many exceptions to this sweeping generalisation and some resilient students from families with many adverse factors, including extreme poverty and lack of emotional support, still manage to achieve well academically (McLaren, 2003; Masten, 1994). It is vitally important that teachers do not lower their expectations for children from disadvantaged backgrounds but instead understand that such children may need massive support if they are to reach their potential.

Ormrod (2003) points out that even when other material factors are satisfactory, many children from lower SES families have fewer experiences that prepare them adequately for learning in school. Some children lack the experiences that are important for smooth entry into literacy and numeracy. Also, the language codes of the school may be very different from the language used in the home, thus creating a communication barrier that adds to the problem. Once the child is in school there is often less parental involvement in children's schoolwork, and the parents may hold low aspirations for their children's educational progress.

Early intervention to ameliorate negative effects of impoverished backgrounds on children's development date back to at least the 1960s, with the book *Teaching Disadvantaged Children in the Preschool* being fairly typical of the thinking at that time (Bereiter and Engelmann, 1966). As noted in the previous chapter, views differ on the effectiveness of early intervention for increasing learning aptitude and intelligence but the consensus tends to be that high quality early intervention, mainly using structured teaching programmes and intensive parental guidance, can prevent many of the learning and behaviour problems that often occur in children exposed to chronic socio-economic disadvantage (Campbell and Ramey, 1994; Hallahan and Kauffman, 2003).

Poor relationship between student and teacher

In his book *Dimensions of Reading Difficulties*, Ravenette (1968) raised the important issue of the 'personal dimension' to a learning problem. Specifically he recommended, 'Find out if the child likes the teacher' (p. 68). For optimum learning to occur there needs to be good rapport between teacher and students. Students want teachers to have faith in them and to care about them (Batten *et al.*, 1993; Hilty, 1998). In a previous chapter it was noted that one of the ways in which some students with learning problems handicap themselves is by failing to seek help from the teacher even though they need it. If students do not feel at ease with the teacher, they are even less likely to seek assistance (Altenbaugh, 1998). The book *Who Am I in the Lives of Children?* (Feeney *et al.*, 2001) contains valuable advice for teachers on building relationships with students.

Poor school attendance

Poor school attendance can be due to unavoidable factors such as health problems, or to avoidable factors such as truancy. Poor attendance is not confined to children from poor home backgrounds although it is more common in such groups (McDevitt and Ormrod, 2002). Truancy rates are positively correlated with socio-economic disadvantage and with delinquency (Mittler, 2000).

It is obvious that frequent absences from school impair the continuity of learning within the curriculum (Carroll, 2000). Subjects such as mathematics, where the concepts and skills tend to be sequential and hierarchical in nature, suffer most when students miss periods of schooling. Absences can have a negative impact on examination results, and poor academic results can begin a child on a downward spiral in terms of confidence and motivation.

Fraser (2002) recognises the problem of being away from school and offers some practical advice for dealing with the confusion a child has when returning to the curriculum after extended absence. Her advice includes pairing the student with another for peer assistance, providing additional explanations, clarifying objectives, and advising parents on useful follow-up for work at home.

Health and physical status

Chronic health problems (for example, asthma, diabetes) are a common reason for school absence; but health problems can also impair a student's energy level and ability to concentrate while in school. In particular, conditions that cause pain or discomfort (for example, juvenile arthritis) are very problematic from a classroom learning perspective. Students with certain types of physical disability (for example, spina bifida with hydrocephalus) may experience headaches preventing them from completing work or participating in the lesson. Many children with health problems may be on daily medication (for example, to control epilepsy) and this can cause problems with concentration. A mild form of epilepsy (*petit mal* or *absence seizure*) can occur in some children and disrupts their attention to task. Petit mal 'absences' can occur as often as 100 times per day. The child loses focus (sometimes momentarily loses consciousness for a few seconds). This constant loss of attention very seriously disrupts learning. Unfortunately, absence seizures are often difficult to detect and a child with this problem may be accused of daydreaming and not listening (Heward, 2003a).

It is worth noting that learning difficulties in school can sometimes themselves cause pseudo illnesses in children – they may feign sickness in order to miss school. Some psychosomatic complaints (headaches, stomach upsets) may be examples of classical conditioning. A stimulus such as a teacher's anger (real or perceived) acts as a conditioned stimulus for physiological responses. Santrock (2001, p. 242) states, 'A teacher's persistent criticism of a student can cause the student to develop headaches, muscle tension, and so on.' Eventually, anything associated with the teacher or the school may trigger the student's stress and physiological response.

Jensen (1995) makes the interesting suggestion that many cases of learning difficulty may actually reflect inappropriate nutrition. Poor nutrition can affect children's general health and their ability to concentrate in school. It is not unusual

to find children coming to school each day without breakfast (Davies, 1998). Lack of food, eating at irregular intervals, or eating the wrong kinds of food can cause problems with the child's physical status and concentration. Morris and Sarll (2001) have confirmed that low blood sugar levels (for example, as a result of having no breakfast) reduce a learner's listening span and this in turn affects listening comprehension. It has already been noted that nutritional deficiencies in the early years may interfere with normal neurological growth and development (McDevitt and Ormrod, 2002).

Lack of sleep can also contribute to learning difficulties in school, mainly by impairing attention and concentration span. Some children are allowed to stay up until very late at night on a regular basis, and then attend school having had perhaps only five hours sleep.

Learning through the medium of a second language

It is easy to understand how difficulties arise for students attempting to learn a new language, and at the same time trying to learn new curriculum concepts, knowledge and skills through the medium of the new language (Hallahan and Kauffman, 2003; OECD, 2001). The challenge for all new immigrant children in school is enormous, and is most problematic if the student is above primary school age when arriving in a new country; language learning through immersion is somewhat easier for younger students (McDevitt and Ormrod, 2002). Often new immigrant children, after a brief but intensive introductory course at a language centre, are left to sink or swim in an unfamiliar language environment and must pick up what they can through incidental learning. The fact that they have difficulties in coping is reflected in their over-representation in special and remedial groups. Some students with English-as-second-language (ESL) are misidentified as learning disabled or even mildly intellectually disabled (Gersten and Baker, 2003; Turnbull *et al.*, 2002).

Some of the classroom learning problems for students from non-English speaking backgrounds include:

- Listening comprehension difficulties due to limited vocabulary, poor grasp of syntax, and the speed at which others speak.

- Reading difficulties due to differences in basic phonology, limited sight vocabulary, and (when reading fiction) not having had first-hand experience of situations or contexts being described.

- Inability to engage meaningfully with new information, concepts and problems due to lack of understanding of the associated language.
- The communication difficulty can also limit social interaction with other children.

To overcome some of the learning obstacles it is recommended that teaching be carried out using a bilingual approach so that the mother tongue can supplement and support the learning of the new language (Brisk, 1998; McIntyre *et al.*, 2001; Smyth, 2003). However, this ideal practice is not feasible in many cases because the regular class teacher may not be fluent in the child's first language, and bilingual aides or volunteers are not always available. Teachers may lack the skills to teach English as a second language within the context of their own school subjects, and they may have a poor understanding of culturally and linguistically different students. For this reason they may have inappropriate expectations of their ability (Jacobsen *et al.*, 2002).

Loss of confidence

As Howe (1999, p. 122) has remarked, 'A lack of confidence in one's capacity to do well, or a fear of failure, can impede a young learner just as effectively as an absence of knowledge or mental skills.' Students with learning difficulties hate to be identified and labelled because they feel that others look down on them and marginalise them. They spend a lot of emotional energy in trying to hide their 'LD' label from their friends (Peters *et al.*, 1998).

Gorman (2001) observes that even the best of intentions in setting out to help children with learning difficulties can result in stigmatising the child and undermining his or her self-confidence. The way in which schools identify students with learning difficulties and then provide remedial intervention through in-class support or group withdrawal can intensify the problem in the child's eyes; he or she feels different and degraded by being identified as someone with a special problem. Vareene and McDermott (1999) have pointed out that when we say there is 'something wrong' and we provide conspicuous special help, we make matters worse. We have seen already that humiliation and loss of feelings of self-worth can result in students giving up completely and making no real effort in school. In many ways this is a natural adaptive response to what the students perceive to be a hopeless situation. Based on the various messages these students receive from teachers, parents and peers, they have constructed very negative and damaging images of themselves as failures with little hope of change (Ravenette, 1999).

Emotional or behavioural problems

Emotional and behavioural problems can be both a cause and an effect of learning difficulty. In individual cases it is often difficult to determine whether an emotional or behavioural problem is the primary underlying cause of a learning difficulty, or is the result of such difficulty (Bauer and Shea, 1999;

Kauffman, 1999). Teachers often say a student is failing in school because of his or her emotional problems, inappropriate behaviour, or bad attitude, but it is more likely in many instances that these are negative consequences arising from persistent failure (Hunt and Marshall, 2002; van Kraayenoord and Elkins, 1998). It is known that bad school experiences can contribute to or exacerbate any pre-existing emotional problems due to outside causes, such as stress and conflict within the home environment – so the interaction among potential causes is complex.

'Emotional and behavioural disorders' (EBD) is a classification given to conditions such as chronic anxiety, phobias, personality disorders, conduct disorders, oppositional defiant disorder, aggression, mood disorders, depression, and immature behaviour patterns (Gupta, 1999). The behaviours or responses regarded as symptomatic of EBD are usually described as either 'externalised' (for example, aggression, temper tantrums, defiance) or 'internalised' (anxiety, withdrawal, depression, phobias). Genuine cases of emotional and behavioural disorder are identified by main three criteria (Gorman, 2001):

- The problem lasts over a long period of time and is not simply a temporary reaction to a situation.

- The problem is severe and the symptoms associated with it are well outside the acceptable range within that age group and culture.

- The problem has a serious impact on the child's learning and development.

Evidence suggests that students with serious emotional and behavioural difficulties or disorders tend to have significant problems in learning within the school curriculum — often they underachieve relative to their basic ability. Emotional disorders disrupt attention, memory, information processing, reasoning and judgement (Williams *et al.*, 1997). In addition, the social skills of many students with EBD are often poor and they have difficulty being accepted in the peer group (Bauer and Shea, 1999; Heward, 2003a). Absence rate is often high among these students, seriously disrupting continuity in learning and compounding their problem.

One of the top priorities in school is to teach these students better self-management so that they can monitor their own reactions when faced with frustrating or threatening situations (Workman and Katz, 1995). It is also vital to increase the time these students spend on task during lessons, since one of the main obstacles to learning is their non-engagement with the classroom tasks and activities (Heward, 2003a). These goals are not easy to achieve, and interventions focused on class work often need to be accompanied by on-going personal counselling and guidance for the student. Where possible, parents and other family members need to be involved in any intervention to ensure a common understanding of what the underlying problem might be and to maintain consistent management and support for the student.

It is beyond the scope of this book to cover in detail the possible interventions for the population of students identified as 'emotionally and behaviourally disordered'. Information on these students can be found in many texts, including those by Bauer and Shea (1999), Gorman (2001) and Kauffman (2001).

Below-average intelligence

The nature of intelligence and its symbiotic relationship to learning have been considered in a previous chapter. It is necessary here only to reiterate that low intelligence is associated with greater likelihood of learning difficulty, or at least a slower rate of learning. Below-average intelligence may also be connected with some of the difficulties to be discussed in a moment under problems with information processing. It is important to reiterate that teachers and parents should not regard a student's below-average intelligence as an insurmountable barrier to learning. Many students with below-average intelligence make perfectly adequate progress in school when provided with a suitable curriculum, effective teaching, and individual support – and when they themselves are prepared to work hard and persist in the face of challenge.

Sensory impairment

The two main senses used in school learning – hearing and sight – can be the source of some difficulty in learning. Hearing impairment and vision impairment can affect students of any ability level, but the extent to which they create learning problems differs markedly from individual to individual. When students exhibit learning problems there is a need to have routine hearing and vision tests carried out to eliminate sensory impairments as possible contributory factors.

Hearing impairment is a fairly low incidence disability but one that can have serious implications for learning. Prevalence rates for hearing loss vary from country to country, reflecting differences in health care services and the availability of identification and rehabilitation services. It is generally estimated that less than 1 per cent of the school population has a significant hearing loss (Steinberg and Knightly, 1997; Turnbull *et al.*, 2002) but in addition there are many other individuals who experience temporary hearing loss as a result of illnesses and ear infections. Impaired hearing is often discovered as an additional disability in students with physical handicaps or with severe intellectual disability. In most developed countries the majority of students with impaired hearing are currently integrated into mainstream classrooms rather than attending schools for the deaf.

Students with impaired hearing are known to have significant problems in some aspects of learning; for example, difficulties in acquiring vocabulary and grammatical awareness have a serious detrimental effect on learning through predominantly auditory-vocal methods in the classroom (Heward, 2003a). The extent to which general intelligence is depressed in deaf students remains a contentious issue (Marschark *et al.*, 2002). Power (1998) concludes that deafness *per se* does not cause intellectual deficit and the learning processes for deaf and partially hearing students are in general the same as those for hearing students. However, deaf students' attainment levels within the curriculum are clearly affected by difficulty in communication and comprehension. It is reported in many studies that the reading, writing and spelling ability of deaf students is typically delayed by two or more years (Kuntze, 2001; Marschark *et al.*, 2002). Deaf students are reported to have poorly developed metacognitive awareness, and this can impair their acquisition of problem-solving and self-regulation strategies in learning (Elkins, 2002).

It is sometimes believed that deaf students compensate for the lack of auditory information by making much more effective use of visual information (the so-called 'sensory compensation theory'). While this theory is difficult to prove, recent studies suggest that deaf students who inevitably rely mainly on visual modes of communication may structure their mental schemata differently from hearing individuals (Marschark *et al.*, 2002). There is also increasing evidence that deaf and hearing individuals may differ in the way they encode information in working memory (Marschark *et al.*, 2002).

Vision impairment can also be a cause of learning difficulty. It is commonly stated that about 80 per cent of learning is through vision (Pagliano, 1998), so any learner who has problems processing visual and spatial information is disadvantaged in most learning situations. The term 'vision impairment' applies to any eye condition affecting sight that cannot be corrected by the wearing of glasses. The prevalence of impaired vision (blindness and partial sight) is estimated to be approximately 0.2 per cent of the school population (Arter *et al.*, 1999). It is reported that in US approximately 0.03 per cent of schoolchildren are actually blind, with others having varying degrees of vision loss. Impaired vision is also identified often as a secondary handicap in individuals with severe and multiple disabilities (Barraga and Erin, 2001).

Lack of sight makes the learning of many concepts extremely difficult for blind students. One big area of difference between sighted children and those with impaired vision is the extent to which they learn through observation and imitation; students with severely impaired vision cannot easily learn by these methods. Even for those students with partial sight (low vision) learning is a great challenge because they must expend much more effort and time to process visual information via magnification aids, enlarged print, tactile diagrams, and so forth. In addition, blind students and some of those with partial sight have to spend time developing mobility, orientation and self-care skills that other students learn incidentally.

It is extremely difficult for vision-impaired learners to organise multiple forms of information in the brain and to develop schemata in the same way as sighted learners. As Barraga and Erin (2001, p. 136) remark:

If the visual system is not used by looking, storing visual images, and coordinating vision with movement, there is no activity in the occipital area of the brain and no visual perceptions are formed. Although most children with low vision gather their major information through vision, their perceptions may not be organized or consistently accurate.

Particular areas of difficulty that are frequently associated with impaired vision include:

- Difficulties in perception and concept formation.
- Delay in physical and motor skill development.
- Difficulties in visual functioning (that is, the effective use of remaining sight).
- Problems with social skill development.
- Emotional problems and low self-esteem.

The exact nature of the learning difficulties encountered by any one individual with impaired vision will depend on many factors, including nature of the vision defect, age of onset, range of experiences the student has had (prior learning), access to assistive technology (for example, magnification aids, braillers), and the student's motivation, persistence and resilience. Many students with severely impaired vision still manage to achieve well within the school curriculum if adequately supported.

More information on hearing impairment and vision impairment can be found in the titles under Further reading.

Specific information processing difficulties

The literature on learning difficulties makes frequent mention of visual processing deficits, perceptual-motor problems, auditory processing deficits, attentional deficits, and memory disorders as correlates of learning problems (for example, Hallahan *et al.*, 1999; Kirk *et al.*, 2000). Most of these difficulties will be discussed in following chapters in relation to the learning of basic skills, but here some general background information is provided.

Visual perceptual difficulties

There was a time in the 1960s and early 1970s when special educators tended to be obsessed with the idea that learning difficulties were all caused by visual perceptual problems or deficits in visual-motor development. Assessment batteries and training programmes were designed to help identify and remediate specific weaknesses – for example, *The Developmental Test of Visual Perception* (Frostig *et al.*, 1966), *The Frostig Program for the Development of Visual Perception* (Frostig and Horne, 1964), and *The Purdue Perceptual-Motor Survey* (Roach and Kephart, 1966). These resources enjoyed popularity for a while only to fall out of favour eventually when research studies generally failed to support any significant benefits from these remedial approaches (for example, Hammill and Larsen, 1974). Deficits in visual perception and in perceptual-motor control are no longer considered major causes in most cases of general learning difficulty, and very few teachers use such approaches today (Hallahan and Kauffman, 2003). However, visual perceptual and perceptual-motor difficulties can be significant in individuals with traumatic brain injury and in those with disabilities such as cerebral palsy, where there is impairment to localised areas of the brain (Tyler and Mira, 1999; Vaughn *et al.*, 2003).

Auditory perception

While interest in visual perceptual difficulties has waned somewhat, interest in *auditory perceptual weakness* (specifically, phonological awareness) has become a major focus of attention. It is now believed, based on reputable research studies, that phonological awareness has a definite causal association with reading and spelling difficulties. The ability to hear speech sounds accurately and identify sounds within words is basic to acquiring an understanding of the alphabetic code on which written English language is based (Torgesen, 1999). Students with literacy problems usually require remedial intervention that is designed to improve their phonemic awareness (Reid, 2003). This issue will be explored fully in Chapter 6.

Attentional difficulties

Another serious potential cause of learning problems is poor attention to task. The first step in learning anything is, in layman's terms, 'paying attention'. Without adequate cognitive focus on the task at hand it is impossible for information to register in working memory and to be actively processed. Eric Jensen (1998) suggests that the average person makes the decision of where to focus attention about 100,000 times a day. Attention is either attracted by some external stimulus or is guided by personal goals. Factors influencing a learner's attention include the novelty, intensity, interest and importance of the stimulus or task, the perceived value and difficulty level of the task, the learner's physical and emotional state, and the learner's ability to ignore distractions. Swanson and Saez (2003) refer to the capacity to maintain attention in the face of interference or distraction as 'controlled attention'. Controlled attention is governed by executive cognitive processes and requires some degree of metacognition and self-regulation. Students with learning difficulties are found frequently to be weak in controlled attention. Even in normal learners the brain is poorly equipped for maintaining continuous high-intensity attention to a single task for more than ten minutes (E. Jensen, 1998).

Some students with poor attending behaviour have a specific 'attention deficit disorder', with or without hyperactivity (ADD and ADHD). In recent years great interest has been shown in this extreme form of attentional deficit and the number of children diagnosed with the syndrome has greatly increased. Typically, a child with ADHD exhibits symptoms of impulsivity, distractibility and hyperactivity in addition to the attentional problems (Gupta, 1999). Estimates of prevalence for ADHD vary widely, but a commonly accepted rate is about 4 per cent of school-age students – with three times more boys than girls. Barkley (2003) reports that ADHD students commonly have serious problems with schoolwork, difficulties in social interaction with peers, and may have language disorders and depressed intelligence level. Children with ADD and ADHD tend to exhibit severe difficulties in the following areas:

- Getting started on tasks.

- Staying on task.

- Completing a task.

- Changing easily from one activity to another.

- Following directions.

- Self-management.

Definitive causes of ADD and ADHD have not been found, but many possible causal factors have been suggested, ranging from inner ear problems, prenatal and postnatal abnormalities, inappropriate diet, environmental toxins, genetic predisposition, and low levels of certain neurotransmitters in the brain. Neuroimaging studies have suggested subtle differences in brain structure and function between non-ADHD and ADHD children. Nielsen (1997), for example, reports that the rate at which the brain utilises glucose is slower in individuals with ADHD. Earlier beliefs that ADD was created by inappropriate child-rearing practices in the home have been largely dismissed, although behaviours similar to those of ADHD can certainly be traced to such causes. Clearly, the labels ADD and ADHD should not be applied to children who are merely bored and restless or are placed in a class 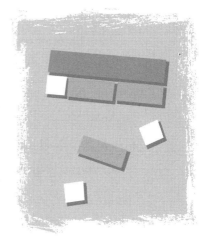 where the teacher lacks good management skills. In cases of genuine attention deficit Barkley (2003, p. 121) has concluded that, 'It should be evident from the research that ADHD arises from multiple factors, and that neurological and genetic factors are substantial contributors.'

In a review of interventions for ADHD, Purdie, Hattie and Carroll (2002) report that pharmacological interventions (for example, the taking of stimulant medication) have the most effect on behaviour, particularly in reducing hyperactivity and impulsivity and by improving attention. However, these interventions alone do not result in improved academic achievement unless the student is also provided with intensive remedial teaching support. Nielsen (1997) states that ADHD treatment generally requires a combination of medication, behaviour modification, and individualised educational programming.

Memory

Finally, learning problems have been associated with difficulties in effective use of memory processes. This topic has been discussed in Chapter 3, where it was indicated that some students with learning difficulties are reported to have problems with working memory and with recall of information from long-term memory (Swanson and Saez, 2003). While these problems could be due to minimal dysfunction or deficits at the neurological level, it is much more likely that failure to give the information full attention when it was presented, together with inefficient (or non-existent) use of rehearsal and retrieval strategies, can account for many of the apparent memory difficulties. Failure to retrieve information from long-term memory can be due to the fact that the information was never effectively linked with prior knowledge to become part of a well-automated cognitive schema. Stress and anxiety can also impair the ability to recall information (Kaufeldt, 1999). More about memory difficulties will be covered in following chapters.

Further reading

Ashman, A. and Elkins, J. (eds) (2002) *Educating Children with Diverse Abilities*. Sydney: Prentice Hall.

Barkley, R.A. (2003) Attention-deficit hyperactivity disorder. In E.J. Mash and R.A. Barkley (eds) *Child Psychopathology* (2nd edn) (pp. 75–143). New York: Guilford Press.

Barraga, N.C. and Erin, J.N. (2001) *Visual Impairments and Learning* (4th edn). Austin, TX: ProEd.

DuPaul, G.J. and Stoner, G. (2003) *ADHD in the Schools: Assessment and Intervention Strategies*. New York: Guilford Press.

Franklin, B.M. (1998) *When Children Don't Learn: Student Failure and the Culture of Teaching*. New York: Teachers College Press.

Marschark, M., Lang, H.G. and Albertini, J.A. (2002) *Educating Deaf Students: From Research to Practice*. Oxford: Oxford University Press.

Minke, K.M. and Bear, G.C. (eds) (2000) *Preventing School Problems: Promoting School Success*. Bethesda, MD: National Association of School Psychologists.

Visser, J., Daniels, H. and Cole, T. (eds) (2001) *Emotional and Behavioral Difficulties in Mainstream Schools*. New York: JAI Press.

5 Specific learning disabilities

> Despite the large numbers of students identified as having specific learning disabilities, there are many challenges to the reality of the condition. Can learning disabilities be reliably differentiated from other problem conditions? (Hallahan and Keogh, 2001, p. 6)

No exploration of learning difficulties would be complete without careful attention to the topic of learning disability and the controversial issues surrounding this concept. This chapter provides a brief overview of a complex field. Chapters that follow will explore some of the implications of learning disability in the domains of literacy and numeracy.

For many years educators have believed that some students have a *specific learning disability* (SpLD) that is not due to a general lack of ability and is quite unlike the problem experienced by other low-achieving students. Students with a specific learning disability are typically of at least average intelligence, are free from sensory impairments, have no significant health problems, emotional disturbance or socio-cultural disadvantage, and have been exposed to appropriate teaching. Even given these positive conditions they still fail to gain normal proficiency in the basic skills of reading, writing and mathematics. Difficulties may also manifest themselves in expressive and receptive oral language, problem solving, physical skills, self-management and social skills development (Block, 2003; Nielsen, 2002; Tur-Kaspa, 2002).

Discrepancy between ability and achievement

Students with learning disability are a puzzle to educators because of the severe discrepancy between their achievement level and their measured intellectual ability or 'potential' (Hallahan and Kauffman, 2003). Fletcher *et al.* (2002, p. 189) indicate that SpLD shows itself most clearly as '… unexpected underachievement in children who seem bright and capable'.

The *Diagnostic and Statistical Manual of Mental Disorders-TR (DSM-4)* (American Psychiatric Association, 2000) refers to learning disabilities as 'disorders' – for example, *reading disorder*, *mathematics disorder*, *disorder of written language*. The *DSM-4* indicates that such disorders may be present when the student's attainment standard falls 'substantially below that expected' given the individual's age, measured intelligence, and appropriate education. In other words, the difficulty in learning is not due to inadequate instruction, environmental factors, or handicapping conditions.

Defining and describing learning disability

Categorising students under the SpLD heading is supposed to differentiate them clearly from the much larger population of students whose learning difficulties are wide-ranging and due perhaps to lack of ability and to environmental factors (OECD, 1999; Silver and Hagin, 2002). As indicated already, students in the larger group have been described as 'low achievers', 'slow learners', 'garden variety learning problems', or simply 'academically weak students' (Naparstek, 2002; Swanson, 2000b). Elksnin (2002, p. 252) even describes the larger group of students with difficulties as 'casualties of the general education curriculum'. Students with specific learning disability are believed to be qualitatively and etiologically different from this group.

Debates concerning definition have continued for more than forty years since Samuel Kirk first coined the term 'learning disability' in the early 1960s (Kirk, 1962; Shaywitz *et al.*, 1992). Definitions maintain currency for a brief time but fall out of favour and are then revised or replaced in the light of new information or changing perspectives. At the time of writing, the following definition of SpLD is used in the US, under the reauthorised and amended version of the *Individuals with Disabilities Education Act* of 1997:

> *Specific learning disability* means a disorder in one or more basic psychological processes involved in understanding or in using language, spoken or written, that may manifest itself in an imperfect ability to listen, speak, read, write, spell, or to do mathematical calculations. The term includes such conditions as perceptual disabilities, brain injury, minimal brain dysfunction, dyslexia and developmental aphasia. The term does not apply to children who have learning problems that are primarily the result of visual, hearing, or motor disabilities, of mental retardation, of emotional disturbance, or environmental, cultural or economic disadvantage. (cited in Lyon, 2002, p. 47)

An alternative current definition favoured by many professionals is:

> Learning disability is a generic term that refers to a heterogeneous group of disorders manifested by significant difficulties in the acquisition and use of listening, speaking, reading, writing, reasoning, or mathematical abilities. These disorders are intrinsic to the individual and presumed to be due to central nervous system dysfunction. Even though a learning disability may occur concomitantly with other handicapping conditions (i.e. sensory impairment, mental retardation), social and economic disturbances or environmental influences (i.e. cultural differences, insufficient/inappropriate instruction, psychogenic factors) it is not the direct result of those conditions or influences. (Hammill *et al.*, 1981, p. 689)

Mather and Goldstein (2001) report that in 1987 the Interagency Committee on Learning Disabilities added 'problems with social skills' to the above list of significant difficulties, reflecting recognition of the fact that learning disability can impact negatively on a student's interpersonal skills and behaviour. Wiener (2002) confirms that many studies have shown that students with SpLD frequently have difficulties with social relationships, have low academic self-concept, and exhibit a variety of emotional problems.

Even having defined specific learning disability, it is still difficult to operationalise the definition to produce criteria for identification purposes. Lloyd (2002, p. 427) advises that:

> … learning disability is not a unitary condition; it is a heterogeneous complex of multiple attributes. Many students with learning disabilities have difficulties with the decoding aspect of reading, but not all do. Some students with learning disabilities have difficulty with attention, but not all do. Some students with learning disabilities have difficulties with planning algorithms for solving mathematical problems, but not all do. There is no student so typical of all students with learning disabilities that we can safely refer to 'the learning-disabled child'.

Given the problems associated with definition and identification it is not surprising that the very existence of such a category of learning difficulty, different from general problems in learning, is frequently challenged (for example, Elkins, 2001; Finlan, 1994; Prior, 1996). Indeed, some educators consider that nothing of value is achieved when two separate groups of students with fairly similar special educational needs are created in this way. It is argued instead that all students with low achievement in basic skills should receive any necessary support to help them improve. The right to effective teaching to overcome learning difficulty is not something that should be decided on the basis of IQ. This point will be discussed in more detail in a moment.

Types of learning disability

Much research effort has been directed toward identifying different types of learning disability. The most obvious broad categories are those that identify the specific skill area in which the individual is having problems:

- severe reading disability (dyslexia);
- severe problems with arithmetic and mathematics (dyscalculia);
- severe problems with written expression and handwriting (dysgraphia);
- severe spelling difficulties (dysorthographia);
- severe problems in recalling names, symbols and vocabulary (dysnomia).

These various types of SpLD are not mutually exclusive and any individual may have difficulties in more than one of the above areas. Dyslexia, for example, usually impairs all aspects of literacy development including reading, writing and spelling – and many dyslexic students also have difficulties with mathematics. Detailed discussion of each type of difficulty will be found in the following chapters covering reading problems, written language problems, and difficulties mathematics.

Prevalence

Estimates of the prevalence of SpLD vary widely (and wildly) from 1 per cent to 30 per cent of the school population (Fuchs *et al.*, 2002; Lyon, 2002). In terms of specific difficulties with literacy, Bradley, Danielson and Hallahan (2002) suggest that some 6 per cent of students have a specific reading disability (dyslexia), although other estimates put the figure for severe reading difficulties lower, at 1.5 per cent to 3 per cent (for example, Vellutino and Scanlon, 2002). This compares with an estimated 16 per cent to 20 per cent of the general school population having 'garden-variety' short term or longer-term problems in acquiring literacy skills. Although severe reading difficulties are reported to occur in all languages, the highest frequency of reading disability is observed in English-speaking countries (Grigorenko, 2001).

Estimates for prevalence of disabilities in written language and mathematics are more difficult to obtain, perhaps because these problem areas have not attracted as much attention from researchers. Some 8 per cent to 15 per cent of students are reported to have significant problems with written expression (dysgraphia) (Lyon, 2002). In addition, it is suggested that approximately 6 per cent of students have a specific disability in mathematics. Their difficulties, and the nature of their errors, are said to be qualitatively different from those found in the very much larger population of students who find mathematics a tough subject to master (see Chapter 8).

The marked variations in reported prevalence rate of SpLD in its various forms are due to a continuing lack of agreement on precise criteria for identification (Silver and Hagin, 2002). There is concern in the USA, for example, that existing criteria are not being applied when students with difficulties are assessed – as a result, too many students are labelled as SpLD. Over-identification may also be occurring in the US because such identification leads to the provision of additional remedial support, whereas low achievers without the SpLD label are not entitled to the same level of service.

Brooks (2002) remarks that in our society today it is 'OK' to be identified as having a learning disability; it is a label that parents, teachers, and society at large do not object to and it opens doors to extra services. However, it seems that some students with mild intellectual disability or emotional disturbance and behaviour problems are being categorised as SpLD, particularly by the schools, because the diagnostic criteria are not being applied rigorously. Hallahan and Keogh (2001) confirm that significant numbers of individuals are misdiagnosed under the SpLD category and are receiving services although they are poor learners for other reasons. MacMillan and Siperstein (2002, p. 319) state, 'As long as the LD category absorbs children with IQ scores in the 70–85 range, as well as those with scores below 70, we will never clean up the LD category.'

A major problem in reporting prevalence rates also hinges on the interpretation of what we mean by 'normal' or 'average' intelligence (Kavale, 2002). When we say, 'A student with specific learning difficulty is of at least average intelligence', do we mean an IQ of 100 and above? Or do we mean IQ above 90? Or above 85? (IQ 85 is one standard deviation below the population average of 100.) Some researchers appear to regard 'normal intelligence' as everything above IQ 70 – that is, anything above mild mental handicap category (Fletcher *et al.*, 2002). Each of these cut-off points would produce very different populations of students in terms of mental ability and number of individuals identified. Further major ambiguity enters when some writers state that *all* low achievers are 'learning disabled' (Fuchs *et al.*, 2002).

Causes

There are many theories concerning the factors that may lead to specific learning disability. In some cases a learning disability may be due to multiple contributory factors.

Genetic factors

It has been known for many years that in some cases of genuine SpLD other members of the child's family may have similar problems, suggesting a genetic influence (Cavey, 2000; Grigorenko, 2001; Stanovich and Siegel, 1998). In the case of reading disability Lyon, Fletcher and Barnes (2003, p. 558) state:

> Genetic studies do provide strong evidence for the heritability of reading difficulties and help explain why reading problems have always been known to run in families … [and] … the quality of reading instruction may be more critical when there is a family history of poor reading.

Prior (1996) reports that the estimated concordance rate for reading disability in identical twins is 71 per cent compared with 49 per cent in non-identical twins. She also reports that at least 33 per cent of reading disabled children have a parent or sibling with reading disability, compared with approximately 9 per cent for non-reading disabled children.

Neurological factors

It is known that in some cases a student with SpLD may exhibit what are termed 'soft' neurological signs, suggesting either immaturity of the child's central nervous system or some slight variation from normal brain function (Silver and Hagin, 2002). These 'soft' signs include a tendency toward clumsiness, confusion of left and right, and a failure to establish a firm lateral preference. But not all SpLD students show these signs.

It has long been assumed that neurobiological factors are the basis of SpLD. Indeed, Vaughn, Gersten and Chard (2000) remark that in the early days of research into SpLD parents and psychologists were hopeful that inherent neurological or neuropsychological underpinnings of children's learning difficulties could be identified and then treated. As discussed in Chapter 3, procedures such as functional magnetic resonance imaging (fMRI) and positron emission tomography (PET) have been used in recent years to study brain structure and function (Berninger and Richards, 2002; Rumsey, 1996). Data from such neuro-imaging studies with adults and children have shown that some individuals with learning disability have slightly different brain structures from those of normal learners. This has been confirmed to some extent by small-scale postmortem studies performed on a few dyslexic adults (Lyon *et al.*, 2003; Rumsey, 1996). It is also apparent that the network of brain activity is slightly different between skilled and unskilled readers when, for example, undertaking word recognition or phonological decoding activities (Fletcher *et al.*, 2002; Zeffiro and Eden, 2000). Stanovich and Siegel (1998) remark that the phonological processing difficulties evident in most reading disability cases may be due in part to atypical brain

symmetry or function. It is hypothesised that in some dyslexic students' poor phonological skills may not be due to lack of teaching or experience but to subtle differences in brain structure and functioning (Miles and Westcombe, 2001).

It is interesting to note that more than a century ago Hinshelwood (1900), one of the first pioneers in the study of what was then called 'congenital wordblindness', was hypothesising that severe reading difficulties were possibly due to impairment or dysfunction in key areas of the brain. In the twenty-first century we are able now to deduce from the findings of fMRI research that the brains of some children with reading disability may indeed be morphologically different from those of children with no problems in reading (Kibby and Hynd, 2001; Miles and Westcombe, 2001).

Comprehensive reviews of the research data on neurological factors in learning disability are provided by Grigorenko (2001) and Lyon, Fletcher and Barnes (2003). It must be noted, however, that while these studies are at the cutting edge of research in neuropsychology, they do not lead immediately to any specific guidance or directions for remedial teaching or therapy. They have served the purpose of establishing that students with SpLD are indeed different from those with garden-variety learning problems. The pedagogical implications for special education are far from clear at this time, although writers such as Berninger and Richards (2002), Given (2002) and Sousa (2001a) do provide some useful general advice to teachers on teaching methods that are compatible with what we now know about brain development and function.

Phonological awareness and rapid automatic naming

In the field of psychology, attention in recent years has focused on significant weaknesses in phonological awareness and rapid automatic naming as the underlying language-based causes of reading and spelling disability. It has been suggested that deficiency in phonological processing may represent the single most important causal factor in specific and general reading problems (Lyon *et al.*, 2003). Inability to understand how words can be decomposed into sounds, or great difficulty in carrying out the process and retrieving sounds from memory, may account for the reading and spelling difficulties typical of SpLD students. Inability to retrieve words or letter-sound correspondences quickly from memory impairs decoding skills, restricts development of a sight vocabulary, and severely disrupts comprehension. More will be said about phonological awareness and rapid naming (*automatised lexical retrieval*) in Chapter 6. A vast literature on the topic of phonological awareness has developed in recent years and it is currently the most widely researched topic in the learning disability field.

Visual perception

It is almost redundant to point out that most school-based learning relies very heavily on vision. This is certainly the case with the learning of basic academic skills such as reading, writing, spelling and arithmetic. Reading, for example, requires accurate visual perception of letters and words, supplemented by phonological information and the meaning of the text (Reid, 2003). In mathematics, numerals and symbols must be identified swiftly and accurately, and calculations must be recorded with correct vertical and horizontal positioning of figures. In reading, writing, spelling and mathematics learners need to have good visuo-spatial skills involving directionality, form constancy, orientation, and sequential order (Cullingford, 2001). It is therefore natural to assume that difficulties in acquiring basic academic skills could be due to problems with visual perception.

In the early years of research into learning disability much attention was given to assessing student's visual perceptual skills (see review by Venezky, 1993). Stein (1993), for example, suggested that some dyslexic students have unstable binocular fixation, giving rise to visual confusion when attempting to process printed text. These are the students who report that the letters 'swim on the page' or 'go blurry' (Stein, 1993, p. 331). Watson and Willows (1993) also confirmed that some students with learning difficulties do have deficits in visual perception, visual memory, visuo-spatial ability, and visual-motor skills. It was soon discovered, however, that while visual perceptual problems were implicated in some cases of SpLD they were certainly not evident in all cases. In reading disability, for example, visual perceptual deficits are the primary causal factor in perhaps only 10 per cent to 16 per cent of the students. Deficiencies in phonological awareness and other language-based difficulties are far more frequent contributory factors (Silver and Hagin, 2002).

Further discussion of visual aspects of reading disability is provided in Chapter 6. See also Reid (2003) for a concise and useful summary.

Learning style

Maladaptive learning style has also been implicated as a causal factor in some cases of SpLD (Chan & Dally, 2001; Culatta *et al.*, 2003; Graham and Harris, 2000a). A maladaptive learning style might be loosely defined as an approach to learning that is self-defeating and likely to lead to failure and frustration. It is almost impossible to determine whether the inefficient approach to learning displayed by many students with learning disabilities is the cause of the difficulty or simply a natural outcome from persistent failure. For example, poor attention to task, distractibility, impulsive guessing, limited self-monitoring, and lack of self-correction are all features of poor learning style – but they are also likely to be outcomes from engaging in tasks that are frustrating and humiliating to the student. But, regardless of whether they are the cause or the outcome from learning failure, inefficient approaches to learning need to be rectified through cognitive intervention or metacognitive training (Conway, 2001; Hallahan and Kauffman, 2003). Improvement in a student's approach to learning must be given high priority in all types of intervention.

Dyspedagogia (inefficient teaching)

It must be stated again that inefficient or insufficient teaching can create learning difficulties but by definition a *learning disability* is not due to poor teaching or restricted opportunity to learn. It is obvious, however, that poor teaching will certainly exacerbate any underlying disability and make a bad situation even worse.

Identification

Early identification of SpLD has long been a priority in schools and Nielsen (2002, p. 106) repeats the commonly agreed principle that:

> It is essential to diagnose learning disabilities and related problems as early as possible. Without recognition and help, students become increasingly frustrated and distressed by persistent failure. By the time they reach high school they may quit trying.

Central to the concept of learning disability has been the notion of an unexpected discrepancy between the student's potential as measured by tests of intelligence and the level of achievement he or she attains in basic academic subjects. Formal testing procedures using IQ tests and norm-referenced attainment tests have been the main method for assessing students with learning problems and detecting these discrepancies. Quite complicated formulae have been used sometimes to calculate a student's expected attainment level and to determine the gap between measured ability and attainment. In recent years the use of discrepancy or expectancy formulae has been widely criticised (for example, Sternberg and Grigorenko, 2001). Most formulae depend upon the student having been in school long enough for his or her measured achievement to reach the required distance between expected level and performance level. Lyon, Fletcher and Barnes (2003, p. 574) refer to this as the 'wait-to-fail model', which is incompatible with any policy of early intervention or prevention.

There has been increasing pressure from some experts to abolish IQ-achievement discrepancy as the main criterion for identification of SpLD (Kavale, 2002; Lloyd, 2002; Shaywitz *et al.*, 1992; Siegel, 1998; Stage *et al.*, 2003; Swanson, 2000b). The faith placed in measures of intelligence assumes that IQ is a very accurate predictor of learning potential but this is not necessarily the case. Some students with below average innate ability succeed in school because of above average effort and commitment (Naparstek, 2002) while others of higher ability may not make particularly impressive academic progress due to lack of effort, poor motivation, or emotional and personal problems. In the literacy domain, measures of IQ have no inherent ability to predict a child's future progress in reading (Vellutino, Scanlon & Lyon, 2000, p. 236) and IQ-achievement discrepancy procedures do not reliably distinguish between readers who will do well within remedial programmes and those who will not (Moats, 2002; Shaywitz *et al.*, 1992; Vellutino *et al.*, 2000).

It has been suggested that SpLD students can be identified more precisely — and ultimately helped more effectively — if their *response to intervention* is used as the criterion (Speece *et al.*, 2003). Under this model, *all* students should be given first level remedial support if they are having difficulty; those who do not respond are likely to be the SpLD students with the more severe learning problems. These students must then receive remedial tuition with greater intensity, frequency and duration (Gross, 2003; Otaiba and Fuchs, 2002). Gresham (2002, p. 477) states, 'What appears to be needed is an approach to defining LD based on how students respond to instructional interventions rather than some arbitrarily defined discrepancy between ability and achievement.'

Differential diagnosis

Intelligence testing has been used in the past not only for initial identification purposes but also for diagnostic purposes. Some psychologists and diagnosticians believe that intelligence test profiles can reveal cognitive and perceptual strengths and weaknesses in the student and can thus lead to the design of a tailor-made intervention programme (for example, Greaves, 1997). Recent research studies have failed to support the use of particular profiles of cognitive skills (for example, scatter analysis of WISC subtest scores) to identify SpLD students or as a basis for designing individualised interventions (D'Angiulli and Siegel,

2003; Kavale, 2002; McKinney and Feagans, 1991). At best this process amounts to what Torgesen (2002, p. 591) refers to as 'psychometric phrenology' ('reading the bumps').

There is also a popular notion that profiles based on the subtests of WISC-R or WISC-III can be used to identify particular *subtypes* of learning disability. For example, poor short-term memory and sequencing difficulties may identify a form of dyslexia that is different from one that reflects weaknesses in language skills. It is often reported that five or six different subtypes can be identified by profile analysis (for example, Blakely *et al.*, 1994), but Ward *et al.* (1999) found that at least 70 per cent of SpLD students show no significant profile deviations from the normal range.

Are students with SpLD really different from other low achievers?

A fundamental question, hinted at earlier in the opening quotation, is whether or not there is really a group of SpLD learners who are quite different from others with learning problems. Differentiation among students with mild difficulties (that is, mild intellectual disability, learning disability, and low achievement) has always been problematic (Gresham, 2002). Are the learning difficulties exhibited by students in these various categories very similar in nature, and simply located at different points on the same continuum? Shaywitz *et al.* (1992) for example, conclude from their studies of poor readers in Grade 2 and Grade 5 that there are many more similarities than differences between SpLD poor readers and other low achievers. Students assessed and labelled as 'SpLD' share very many characteristics in common with low achievers (Shaywitz *et al.*, 1992; Swanson, 2000b). It is argued that there is a 96 per cent overlap between the two groups on measures of intelligence, achievement, perceptual motor skills, classroom behaviour and self-concept (Ysseldyke *et al.*, 2000). Moats (2002) cites the meta-analyses of Hoskyns and Swanson (2000) to suggest there are no significant differences between the two groups, particularly in phonological awareness and rapid naming. In contrast, a meta-analysis by Fuchs *et al.* (2002), comparing low achieving students with SpLD groups, discovered that they differ in several dimensions, particularly the degree of reading retardation and the lack of automaticity in word identification. It is also said that the severity of the weakness in phonological awareness is a marker that sets SpLD students apart from other poor readers (Bailet, 2001).

Some would argue – and have argued over the years – that a separate type of learning problem, qualitatively and etiologically separate from general low achievement, does not exist. But in the domain of reading disability Grigorenko (2001) does not agree, stating that:

> Dyslexia (specific reading disability) is a common, cognitively and behaviorally
> heterogeneous developmental condition, characterized primarily by severe

difficulty in the mastery of reading despite average intelligence and adequate education. *The existence of developmental dyslexia as a complex cognitive and behavioral syndrome is at this point beyond doubt.* (2001, p. 91) [emphasis added]

Having reviewed an enormous volume of research data and expert opinion, the *Learning Disabilities Initiative* (Bradley *et al.*, 2002) reached the following main conclusions:

- SpLD is indeed a valid concept and involves disorders in learning and cognition that are intrinsic to the individual and affect a narrow range of academic and performance skills.

- Schools need to have three levels of prevention and remediation:

    (a) primary prevention, which involves high-quality first teaching for all students;

    (b) secondary intervention, with targeted scientifically-based early intervention for any children not making normal progress; and

    (c) tertiary intervention, with extremely intensive individualised intervention and additional services for those still failing.

Intervention methods

Jenkins and O'Connor (2002, p. 130) concluded that '… it is unlikely that even high-quality general education, no matter how well organized, will be sufficient to meet the needs of students with learning disabilities'. We therefore need to ask, what are the main characteristics of the second and third waves of intervention that students with learning difficulties require?

Some years ago Ogden Lindsley (1992a, p. 21) remarked:

Effective educational methods are available. They have been available for a long time. They are mostly behavioural, structured, fast paced, and require a high proportion of regular daily practice.

He then went on to question why effective teaching methods are not often adopted by teachers, and why educational practice tends, instead, to follow the latest trends and enthusiasms. The latest trends almost always argue for less teacher-direction, less structure and more 'student-centredness'. In general these are the very approaches that may increase the likelihood that some students will experience learning difficulties (see Chapter 4).

Lindsley (1992a) was certainly correct in saying that we do know which methods work best for improving students' attainment levels and reducing failure rates. His views are fully supported by writers who have analysed results from many research studies using different teaching approaches for students with learning problems (for example, Kavale and Forness, 2000b; Lloyd and Forness, 1998; Swanson, 1999; 2000a; Vaughn *et al.*, 2000). These researchers used the statistical procedure known as *meta-analysis* and combined the results from studies carried out with many different students in many different settings. Meta-analysis allows the researcher to compute a statistic called *effect size* (ES) which provides an overall impression of whether a method is generally effective or not – and if it is effective, how well it works. For example:

- effect size of .80 and above is regarded as a 'large effect' (suggesting the method has produced very good results);

- .60 – .70 moderately effective method;

- .40 – .50 some positive effects;

- below .30 suggests only a weak or possibly insignificant effect from the method.

Let us look briefly at some of the outcomes from the meta-analyses of Swanson (1999; 2000a) and of Kavale and Forness (2000b). It is usual to take an effect size greater than .40 as indicating a useful teaching approach (Cohen, 1988; Forness *et al.*, 1997).

Table 1.

Meta-analysis: Effect size from various interventions for learning disabilities

Data selected from Kavale and Forness (2000b) and Swanson (1999; 2000a)

Method or procedure	Effect Size
Training to improve recall (mnemonics)	1.62*
Teaching reading comprehension strategies	1.13*
Direct instruction	0.84*
Formative evaluation/precision teaching	0.70#
Peer tutoring	0.48 – 0.56#
Computer-aided instruction	0.52#
Modality-based instruction	0.14
Visual-perceptual training (e.g. Frostig)	0.10
Perceptual-motor training (e.g. Kephart)	0.06
Social skills training	0.21
Diet modification (for ADD/ADHD)	0.12

* = very successful
\# = moderately successful

It is clear from Table 1 that teaching students how to learn – strategy training in its various forms – combined with high quality direct teaching of curriculum content, is much more effective than trying, for example, to match teaching to students' individual learning styles or modalities, or trying to train particular processes such as visual perception. It is also clear from Table 1 that some popular interventions for students with learning difficulties, such as social skills training, do not produce very convincing results. We always say students with learning difficulties need social skills training, but does it really work? The answer is, in general, probably 'no', although it has possibly helped some individuals. It is also important to point out that certain approaches such as perceptual-motor training and modality-specific teaching, which do not appear to be very effective as interventions for students with general or specific learning difficulties, may still be highly relevant within special school curricula for students with confirmed neurological or sensory impairments.

From a meta-analysis of intervention methods Swanson (1999) draws a general conclusion that the most effective teaching for students with learning disabilities combines direct strategy training with a carefully structured and sequenced curriculum. Methods that provide abundant opportunity for practice with feedback, high participation rates, and supplementary assistance produce the best improvement (see also Chapter 4). All these features of effective intervention are confirmed in the reviews by Vaughn, Gersten and Chard (2000), Elliott, Busse and Shapiro (1999) and Heward (2003b). Many of the same features are identified by Sideridis and Greenwood (1998) who add the following ingredients to create the most effective approach for students with learning difficulties and developmental disabilities:

- Reinforcement, with students being rewarded through descriptive praise and encouragement.

- Fast pacing of lessons.

- Positive student-to-student interactions through peer assistance, group work and discussions.

- Positive student-to-teacher interactions with frequent asking and answering of questions.

Chan (1996) summarised some of the pertinent research on teaching methods related to improving literacy and numeracy skills and concluded that the following factors are positively related to the best progress of students with learning problems:

- Teaching methods that are based on behavioural theories of learning; for example, breaking the learning down into teachable steps, setting clear objectives, using reinforcement.

- Formative assessment, stressing the frequent checking and recording of information on each child's progress and identifying quickly the need to re-teach or revise material with certain individuals or groups.

- Direct and explicit teaching.

In virtually every review of teaching approaches the value of direct and explicit teaching is confirmed (for example, Martens *et al.*, 1999). Carpenter and King-Sears (1997, p. 291) have said, '… explicit instruction is necessary, especially for students with learning disabilities, because they are poor discoverers of new skills and may continue ineffective applications of skills if direct teaching is not used'.

In general, research into the most effective methods for assisting students with learning difficulties has discovered almost the same set of features revealed in earlier studies of what constitutes effective teaching *for all students* (for example, Brophy and Good, 1986; Killen, 1998; Rosenshine, 1986; 1995; Yates, 1988). This finding is very important because the battle to reduce educational failure must focus first on general classroom methods that are most successful with the widest range of students. Prevention of difficulties at the first stage of teaching is so much more effective than applying remedial methods after the student has failed and after he or she has developed secondary affective reactions to failure. It is lamentable that given what we already know about the characteristics of effective first and second wave teaching to reduce learning difficulties, such methods are not widely used in schools (Denton *et al.*, 2003).

Further reading

Bender, W. (2001) *Learning Disabilities: Characteristics, Identification and Teaching Strategies* (4th edn). Boston: Allyn & Bacon.

Bradley, R., Danielson, L. and Hallahan, D.P. (eds) (2002) *Identification of Learning Disabilities: Research to Practice*. Mahwah, NJ: Erlbaum.

Lyon, G.R., Fletcher, J.M. and Barnes, M.C. (2003) Learning disabilities. In E.J. Mash and R.A. Barkley (eds) *Child Psychopathology* (2nd edn) (pp. 520–586). New York: Guilford.

Silver, A.A. and Hagin, R.A. (2002) *Disorders of Learning in Childhood* (2nd edn). New York: Wiley.

Swanson, H.L., Harris, K.R. and Graham, S. (2003) *Handbook of Learning Disabilities*. New York: Guilford Press.

Turkington, C. and Harris, J. (2002) *The Encyclopedia of Learning Disabilities*. New York: Facts on File.

Wong, B.Y.L. and Donahue, M.L. (2002) *The Social Dimensions of Learning Disabilities*. Mahwah, NJ: Erlbaum.

6 Difficulties in reading

All things being equal, everyone should learn to read early and easily and with great pleasure. All things are not equal, and there are many for whom learning to read becomes a barrier, both to their intellectual development and their self-esteem. (Cullingford, 2001, p. 29)

The ability to read is universally recognised as the most important basic academic skill. Reading opens up the pathways to learning across the curriculum, and any child who cannot read is most seriously disadvantaged.

Cullingford (2001, p. 15) says, 'Children learn to read from the moment that they make sense of language, for reading brings together the abilities of visual and auditory discrimination that children explore from birth, and the sense of meaning that language engenders.' However, reading is acknowledged to be a complex skill, and it is not surprising that some students encounter learning difficulties in this area.

Defining and describing reading

There are many differing definitions of reading, some stressing the role of phonic word-analysis skills as components within the process, others playing down the importance of these decoding skills and instead giving emphasis to using language awareness to predict words and build meaning from context (Braunger and Lewis, 1998). For the purposes of this book, Marie Clay's (1991, p. 6) definition of reading is accepted. She states:

> I define reading as a message-getting, problem-solving activity which increases in power and flexibility the more it is practised. My definition states that within the directional constraints of the printer's code, language and visual perception responses are purposefully directed by the reader in some integrated way to the problem of extracting meaning from cues in a text, in sequence, so that the reader brings a maximum of understanding to the author's message.

Understanding is stressed as the core purpose of reading and Clay's definition neatly summarises the key elements involved in becoming a proficient reader able to comprehend text. These elements include the coordinated use of visual perception, language competencies, concepts about print, knowledge of the alphabetic code, contextual cues, and metacognitive strategies to support the search for meaning. Clay's definition also highlights the vital role of practice in becoming a fluent and confident reader. In many ways, Clay's definition brings together several of the skills and competencies discussed in previous chapters.

The ability to read is such an essential skill in the world today that reading difficulties have attracted an enormous amount of research and pedagogical interest. Difficulty in reading is a common criterion used in many local and national surveys to determine prevalence rates for learning difficulty in the community (for example, Louden *et al.*, 2000; van Kraayenoord *et al.*, 2000). Failure to learn to read during the first year in school quickly catches the attention of parents and teachers, and it is probably true to say that difficulties in reading are often the first indication that a student has a learning problem (Clay, 1997). Unfortunately, such problems are not always easily remedied and may stay with the student throughout the school years and beyond (Jordan *et al.*, 2003).

Before summarising some of the current perspectives on possible causes of reading failure, and exploring strategies for intervention, it is necessary to consider normal acquisition of reading skill.

Learning to read

Reading is essentially a language-based skill; anything that impairs or restricts normal language development will impact adversely on the acquisition of reading and writing skills. For children with normal language competence, learning to read may present no problems and some preschool children, given a favourable environment and opportunities, even manage to take the first steps toward reading without direct instruction. Because key elements of emergent reading are present in the preschool years, some educators regard learning to read as a natural process not requiring explicit teaching – like learning to talk. They advocate an informal but supportive exposure to literature in order that children can acquire reading ability by observing the way that others go about the task and by being themselves motivated to try. This is clearly a faulty model because learning to read is *not* a natural process, and most students need explicit instruction in order to acquire and master the various types of knowledge, skills and strategies involved in reading (Lyon, 1998; Spear-Swerling and Sternberg, 2001).

Experts differ in opinion concerning the exact way in which proficient readers process print to obtain meaning (Wolf and Kennedy, 2003). Some regard it as predominantly a 'top-down' process, with the reader's effort to make sense of the message driving his or her recognition or prediction of words in print – the so-called 'psycholinguistic guessing game' referred to by Goodman (1967). Instructional methods based on this principle are usually termed 'meaning emphasis approach', typified by the method called 'Whole Language'. Meaning emphasis approaches tend to stress strategies such as intelligent use of context and syntax rather than phonic decoding to identify unfamiliar words.

In contrast, others experts regard reading as a 'bottom-up' process, with close attention given to individual words on the page to build meaning, aided where necessary by systematic use of phonic cues. It is argued that comprehension depends upon accurate identification of words, not on guesswork or prediction from context; and research evidence strongly supports this view (Heward, 2003b; Lyytinen *et al.*, 1994; Vellutino *et al.*, 1994). Most researchers in the field of literacy acquisition now regard accurate word recognition, not contextual cueing, as the central component of the reading process. Teaching methods based on this principle are termed 'skills-based approaches', with due attention being given to explicit instruction in letter-to-sound correspondences, decoding, and the development of a sight vocabulary.

But increasingly educators have come to recognise that 'meaning emphasis' and 'skills-based' approaches are not mutually exclusive. Skilled reading necessarily involves both top-down and bottom-up strategies, used as required in an interactive way (Stanovich, 1980). Current teaching methodology therefore favours a balanced approach to the teaching of reading, combining explicit instruction in phonic skills, word recognition, use of context cues and comprehension strategies, while at the same time reading widely for information and pleasure (Block, 2003; Graham and Harris, 2000a; Lennon and Slesinski, 1999; Pressley, 1998; Taylor *et al.*, 2002).

Word identification and phonics

Learning to read does not begin at the level of decoding, it begins when children come to understand that the print on the page is language. Children who have stories read to them when they are very young quickly reach this understanding. They also develop concepts about books and print – they know where stories begin on the page; they know that a reader moves along the lines from left to right, and from top to bottom of the page. Quite early in life they will begin to recognise certain words that are repeated on the page, often (but not always) words with an unusual appearance (for example, zoo; toboggan; Rumplestiltskin; moon; Piggy). The beginning of 'real' reading is when children develop a 'word' concept and can begin to identify familiar words in print. Smooth progress into reading occurs as more and more words used in a meaningful context are recognised and added to the child's growing sight vocabulary (Strickland, 1998).

Simultaneously, children are discovering that letters and groups of letters on the page represent the 'sounds' of the language. For example, children who can detect when words rhyme begin to notice that the same string of letters occurs in each of the rhyming words when they are in print; children who can mentally isolate the first sound in a spoken word begin to notice that this sound is usually represented by a certain letter on the page. Children who can play listening games and tell you that the sounds (phonemes) /st/ /o/ /p/ can be put together (blended) make the word 'stop', or can pronounce a word slowly in separate phonemes

(/bl/ /a/ /ck), are demonstrating a very effective and important phonological and metalinguistic skills. This 'phonic' concept is prerequisite for understanding the alphabetic code and applying it logically in reading and spelling. As children acquire strong phonic skills they are able to tackle unfamiliar words successfully, using their awareness of sound-symbol relationships.

Eventually, as children become proficient readers, they reach the mature stage where words are recognised instantly by visual processing of 'orthographic units' (partial spelling patterns) that make up a word. An orthographic unit is a group of letters that represents a pronounceable part of a word – such as *-een*, *pre-*, *-mem-*, *-ic*, *stra-*. The group of letters provides sufficient information to trigger instant recognition of the word and its meaning, without the need to process each letter separately or to process the word as a whole. 'Whole word recognition' is a misnomer as almost all words are not stored or recognised 'wholes' (Harrison, 1996). A combination of sight recognition of familiar words from orthographic units, decoding of unfamiliar words, and an on-going use of contextual clues, heralds a child's growing competence and independence in reading (Braunger and Lewis, 1998; Spear-Swerling and Sternberg, 2001).

Children differ in the amount of direct teaching they require to achieve these component skills in reading. Some children will require specific training in phonological awareness to pave the way for learning the alphabetic code (Scanlon and Vellutino, 1997). Some children require much more time and more practice to build adequate sight vocabularies. The majority will need direct and explicit teaching of phonic skills and word-analysis strategies in order to gain confidence in decoding and spelling (Jenkins and O'Connor, 2002). Perhaps all children need guidance in developing effective strategies to enhance comprehension (Pressley, 1999).

Reading difficulties

The most obvious difficulties exhibited by students with reading problems are poor word recognition and weak decoding skills (Chan and Dally, 2001; Bowers *et al.*, 1999). Their weakness in identifying words prevents them from reading fluently and from focusing on the meaning of what is being read. Slow processing of print overloads working memory capacity that is required for effective comprehension and reflective thought (Jenkins and O'Connor, 2002). Poor fluency gives rise to loss of confidence and motivation, and the student may begin to avoid reading.

There are many and varied factors that can contribute to a child's reading problem, ranging from lack of positive literacy experiences in the pre-school years, inadequate home support, inappropriate or insufficient teaching in the beginning school stages, and cognitive, linguistic, perceptual and motivational problems within the student. The previous chapters touched upon some of these issues in relation to specific and general learning difficulty.

When seeking explanations for a student's problem in learning to read, Richek *et al.* (2002) suggest that we should consider factors in three domains:

(i) the school environment (including the teaching methods and materials);

(ii) factors within the home environment and social or cultural context; and

(iii) factors within the student.

Factors in the school environment that may create learning problems include:

- *Allocating insufficient time to the teaching and practice of reading.* It has been known for many years that the amount of time a child spends engaged in successful study of a particular area of the curriculum is closely correlated with the level of achievement in that subject (Allington, 2001; Wang *et al.*, 1993). This factor is closely related to other variables, such as the teacher's classroom management skills and classroom climate. Recognition of the vital importance of allocated time for reading is reflected in the moves toward introduction of the daily 'literacy hour' in schools in several countries (Berger and Morris, 2001; Fisher, 2002).

- *Providing poor quality or inappropriate instruction.* There is no doubt that some teachers are far more effective than others in promoting good learning (McCoy, 2002). Teachers need to employ teaching methods that actively engage students in their learning and, at the same time, ensure that explicit instruction and ample practice are provided for all basic skills (Allington, 2002; Braunger and Lewis, 1998; Gresham, 2002; Lennon and Slesinski, 1999). Examples of effective teaching with specific reference to reading will be provided in a moment. The basic principles have been identified already in previous chapters.

- *Using inappropriate instructional resources.* While it is possible to teach children to read using minimal or outdated materials, students are much more likely to enjoy learning to read and to be motivated to try if books, computer software, games and other resources are age-appropriate, stimulating, well-designed and personally meaningful (Snow *et al.*, 1998; Strickland *et al.*, 2002). It is also important that reading materials match students' current ability levels so that they can experience success when engaging in independent reading (Allington, 2002; Crawley and Merritt, 2000; Graham and Harris, 2000a).

- *Providing too little individual support for learning.* Some students learn easily when merely provided with opportunities, resources and some basic teaching. Others require opportunities, resources and basic teaching, plus individual support to help them overcome any problems when they arise (Block, 2003). Support for learning within the regular classroom and, if necessary, through additional tuition in a withdrawal group remains an important strategy for reducing or preventing learning difficulties (Robertson *et al.*, 1994; Marston, 1996). But help must be provided in an unobtrusive manner, to avoid the stigmatising and labelling effect described earlier. An important aspect of support is ensuring that the student engages in regular reading practice, rather than avoiding reading throughout the school day (Graham and Harris, 2000a). Students who are poor at reading obviously read less than other students, so they fail to develop necessary automaticity and fluency. They also fail to expand their existing vocabulary and general knowledge, compared with good readers (Ortiz and Yates, 2002). Richek *et al.* (2002, p. 9) state categorically, '… students with reading problems are not practising enough to improve their reading abilities'.

Factors within the home environment and the social and cultural context also cause or exacerbate problems in learning. In recent years more and more importance has been placed on the role that a supportive family environment can play in fostering children's development in literacy skills (Crawley and Merritt, 2000; Cullingford, 2001). Negative influences in the home environment include:

- *Lack of support for or interest in the child's literacy development*: Children who become very good readers tend to have much encouragement and help from home, including the opportunity to practise reading with feedback from an adult (Braunger and Lewis, 1998; Graham and Harris, 2000a). In contrast, some parents may have a low standard of schooling themselves and may not be aware of the importance of encouraging their own children and showing interest in their work. Working parents may not have the time or energy to devote to their children's literacy development at home. However, it is essential not to create a stereotypical 'disadvantaged family syndrome' to explain children's learning failure in school. Many parents whose own educational experiences were limited, or who are socially and economically disadvantaged, still do a magnificent job in supporting their own children's development (Compton-Lilly, 2003). The message here is probably that parents may need encouragement and advice from teachers on how best to help their children at home.

- *Absence of materials and experiences to promote reading out of school.* This factor is really an extension of the one above. Some parents, for whatever reason – poverty, lack of interest – do not themselves read or buy reading material to have in the home.

- *Noise and distractions that prevent study.* Homes where there are many young children, or where the television is playing loudly most of the day, are not conducive to reading.

- *Stress, illness, and family break-ups.* These out-of-school factors can preoccupy children's minds and emotions, and drain them of necessary energy and motivation to read.

- *Peer group pressure*: At secondary school level in particular, a student may avoid reading because his or her peers discredit such an activity.

The final category of factors causing or exacerbating difficulties in learning to read are those considered to reside within the learner (Taylor *et al.*, 1995). As we saw in Chapter 4, teachers, psychologists and parents tend to turn to explanations in this category rather than considering factors in the school environment when a child has problems. This is often referred to as 'blaming the victim' for his or her difficulties. Factors within the learner include:

- *Lack of intelligence (general cognitive ability)*. It is generally accepted that slower-learning children and those with mild intellectual disability will encounter some difficulty in learning to read. Reading involves, in part, the building of a sight vocabulary and the learning and application of a fairly complex system of symbols (26 letters used in specific combinations to represent the 44 sounds in spoken language). This type of learning requires adequate cognitive ability. Nevertheless, Vellutino, Scanlon and Lyon (2000, p. 236) suggest that, '... all things considered, one needs little more than average or even low-average intelligence in order to learn to read'. It must also be noted that many students with intellectual disability, if sufficiently motivated, do learn to read at least to a beginning standard (Sheehy, 2002).

- *Poor language skills*. It is noted that expressive and receptive language competence is often weaker in students with reading difficulties (Graham and Harris, 2000a). Vellutino, Scanlon and Lyon (2000) acknowledge that reading relies heavily on adequately developed aural and oral language skills. They state, '... given adequate pre-literacy experience and adequate reading instruction, the ability to learn to decode print will depend primarily on language and language-based abilities' (p. 236). For this reason, remedial intervention programmes must focus as much on building general language skills as on teaching reading skills and strategies.

- *Specific weaknesses in areas such as attention, memory, auditory perception, visual perception*. These are the factors studied most by educational psychologists (O'Shea *et al.*, 1998). The problems have been touched upon already in previous chapters and will be discussed in more detail in the section below covering dyslexia. In particular, weaknesses in understanding and applying phonological features of language are implicated in most cases of reading difficulty. But deficits in short-term working memory are also implicated in some cases of comprehension difficulty.

- *The presence of psycho-emotional states such as anxiety, depression, learned helplessness, low self-efficacy, and inefficient learning style*. While these factors can be the primary cause of difficulty in learning in some cases, in most cases they are the direct outcome of such difficulty (Block, 2003) (see Chapter 2).

Reading disability: dyslexia

Dyslexia is the best-known form of learning disability. The term is often used to cover severe difficulties with all aspects of literacy, including reading, writing, spelling and comprehension.

Dyslexia is described as:

> … one of several distinct learning disabilities. It is regarded as a specific language-based disorder characterized by difficulties in the development of accurate and fluent word decoding skills, usually associated with insufficient phonological processing and rapid naming abilities. These difficulties in word decoding are unexpected in relation to the learner's age and other cognitive and academic abilities; they are not the result of generalized developmental disability or sensory impairment. Dyslexia is manifest by variable difficulty with different forms of language, often including, in addition to problems reading, a conspicuous problem with acquiring proficiency in writing and spelling. Reading comprehension problems are common, reflecting word decoding and fluency problems. (adapted from the 1994 definition of the International Dyslexia Society: Fletcher *et al.*, 2002, p. 207)

Within the domain of dyslexia, researchers have attempted to identify additional 'subtypes' reflecting the particular areas of difficulty the learner may have. The underlying belief is that if the characteristic pattern of strengths and weaknesses can be identified in each subtype of dyslexia, it should be possible to design effective teaching programmes to meet the students' individual needs (Catts *et al.*, 2003; Cirino *et al.*, 2002; Lyon *et al.*, 2003; Lyytinen *et al.*, 1994; Rourke and Del Dotto, 1994). But sub-typing of students with dyslexia has created much more confusion than clarity in the field. For example, the following subtypes are described in the literature:

- *Visual dyslexia* and *auditory dyslexia* (Johnson and Myklebust, 1967). Children with visual dyslexia are reported to have significant difficulties in discriminating among letter shapes and retaining sequences of letters in long-term memory. They are slow at processing print and often reverse letters and words in their writing. Auditory dyslexics are said to have problems with auditory discrimination, sound blending and phonics. More recently these auditory processing problems would be described as deficits in phonological skills.

- *Dyseidetic* and *dysphonetic dyslexia* (Boder, 1973). Readers with dyseidetic dyslexia have problems in storing and retrieving the visual images of words or significant parts of words (orthographic units). The difficulty is most apparent in their limited sight vocabulary and poor word recognition skills. The dysphonetic form of dyslexia impairs the easy learning of letter-sound correspondences and is reflected in a reader's poor ability at decoding and blending letters and syllables. Silver and Hagin (2002) suggest that the dysphonetic group is by far the largest, outnumbering the dyseidetic group by almost 7 to 1. Students with the most severe reading problems have a combination of dysphonetic and dyseidetic weaknesses.

- *Logographic dyslexia* and *alphabetic dyslexia* (Seymour and Evans, 1999). Logographic subtype is characterised by severe problems in learning and remembering words by sight recognition method. The learner does not easily build a sight vocabulary. Alphabetic dyslexia is diagnosed in learners who have severe difficulty in understanding and applying phonic knowledge.

- *L-type* (fast and inaccurate reading) and *P-type dyslexia* (slow and fragmented reading) (Bakker *et al.*, 1991).

- *Orthographic dyslexia* (Mather and Goldstein, 2001). The reader has difficulty in remembering commonly occurring letter groups (orthographic units) such as *–tion, pre-, -een*.

- *Phonological dyslexia* and *surface dyslexia* (Genard *et al.*, 1998; Manis *et al.*, 1996). Phonological dyslexics have difficulty in applying phonic principles to unfamiliar words or pseudo-words. Surface dyslexics are weak at word identification and building a sight vocabulary. Gernard *et al.* (1998) also report that many dyslexic students have problems with both decoding and sight recognition.

- *Dyslexia associated with scotopic sensitivity syndrome* (Irlen, 1991). The learner reports a blurring, distortion or movement of letters and print on the page, making it impossible to process text without extreme stress and frustration. It has been suggested that perhaps up to 50 per cent of disabled readers experience this problem to some degree (Tan *et al.*, 2003) – but as diagnosis is dependent almost entirely on self-reporting by the learner, it is impossible to place confidence in any exact figure. Students identified as having scotopic sensitivity (also termed *Irlen Syndrome*) often use tinted eyeglasses or coloured overlays to filter out certain wavelengths of light when reading and writing. For some problem readers there seems to be a definite benefit from using these aids (Whiting *et al.*, 1994).

There are very many other categories and subtypes reported in the literature (see reviews by Lyon, 1996, and McKinney and Feagans, 1991).

It is fairly obvious that many of the subtypes or syndromes listed above overlap to a very significant degree; and in some cases researchers appear simply to have coined a new descriptor for an already existing category. For example, dyseidetic subtype seems to be identical to logographic dyslexia. Another problem is that absolutely discrete subtypes do not exist regardless of the criteria used to create the category (Speece, 1993); there is always some overlap in specific areas of difficulty experienced across the categories.

Grimes (2002) regards differential diagnosis of sub-types as an unproductive approach that has failed to deliver in practice what it in theory promises. Similarly, Stanovich and Siegel (1998, p. 105) remarked:

In the history of the reading field, the quest to identify subtypes of reading disability has been as enticing as it has been futile. There is enormous face validity to the idea that poor readers differ among themselves in the way they have become poor readers and in the cognitive underpinnings of their disability. Yet the field has failed to progress beyond step one in defining separable groups of disabled readers – that is, subgroups who are behaviourally, genetically, and physiologically different from other poor readers.

Aptitude-Treatment Interactions

The notion of matching instruction and materials to learners' characteristics is related to *diagnostic-prescriptive teaching* (Collins and Cheek, 1984) and to theories of *aptitude-treatment interaction* (ATI), best represented in the work of Cronbach and Snow (1977). Both ATI and diagnostic-prescriptive teaching are based on the belief that if methods of instruction can be tailored to the learner's strengths and preferences, much better progress will be made. An obvious example would be the use of a predominantly phonic method for teaching reading to students strong on the auditory side, and an alternative visual 'whole-word recognition' method used for those stronger on the visual memory side (Rourke and Del Dotto, 1994). There is little empirical support for such differential prescription of treatments based on different abilities or aptitudes, and the results have been disappointing (Spear-Swerling and Sternberg, 2001). Gresham (2002) concludes that even though such a model is very appealing to practitioners, ATIs may be a myth. It must also be remembered that reading and spelling both require the integrated use of auditory and visual skills; all teaching methods must therefore incorporate both visual and phonological abilities – perhaps even to the point where totally differentiated interventions become counterproductive.

At a more general level too, there has been a significant failure to identify instructional methods that are specifically effective for students with dyslexia but are inappropriate for other poor readers (Christensen 1999). On the issue of differentiating instruction, Rutter and Maughan (2002, p. 469) conclude, 'Despite hopes (and claims) extending over many years that methods of teaching should be adapted to cater for individual patterns of strengths and limitations ... we do not know how this should be done or, indeed, even whether it matters.'

At the present time the ATI field is all but dead, although some individual diagnosticians and remedial tutors still believe that one must teach to students' strengths and avoid their areas of weakness. The movement also lives on in those who believe it is important and feasible to teach according to students' preferred learning styles and differences (for example, Dunn, 1996; Mamchur, 1996; Sprenger, 2002; Tomlinson and Kalbfleisch, 1998).

Phonological awareness

Most recently, attention has focused on dyslexic students' difficulty in phonological awareness and rapid automatic naming. Studies have shown clearly that phonological skills are essential for learning to read and spell (for example, Lundberg *et al.*, 1980; Torgesen, 1999) and that most forms of dyslexia and other reading problems are closely associated with severe difficulties in the phonological aspects of decoding (see Wagner and Garon, 1999, for a summary). The learner seems to have difficulty in all aspects of phonemic awareness (identifying sounds within spoken words) and in understanding the alphabetic principle (that letters and letter groups represent the sounds of language).

It has also been observed that some dyslexic students have problems in rapid naming of pictures, objects, numerals, and letters. This slowness in recall and retrieval of information is a major obstacle in building up and applying a functional sight vocabulary and in the swift recall of letter-sound correspondences required to decode unfamiliar words. Some students with reading disability have a combination of both rapid naming and phonological problems (the so-called 'double deficit'). This smaller group of students exhibits the most impaired reading performance (Sunseth and Bowers, 2002; Wiig, 2001; Wolf and Bowers, 1999). Wise and Snyder (2002) suggest that children with weak rapid naming skill, poor phoneme awareness, deficits in memory and poor decoding appear to be those who turn out to be most resistant to remedial help.

Is dyslexia different from other types of reading difficulty?

'Does dyslexia really exist?' is really the same question as asked in the previous chapter regarding specific learning disabilities. There are some writers and educators who believe that nothing of value is achieved by classifying some students as 'dyslexic' and some as 'low achievers' or 'garden variety' (Finlan, 1994; McGuinness, 1998). Indeed, McGuinness (1998, p. 220) reviews the extant literature and concludes '... these studies provide overwhelming evidence that there is no such thing as dyslexia ... [and] ... children fail to learn to read in school because they aren't being taught correctly'. According to McGuinness, the way to prevent reading difficulties of any type is to teach children to use alphabetic decoding skills early. While contemporary evidence totally supports an emphasis on explicit teaching of phonic skills in the beginning stages of reading (for example, National Reading Panel, 2000; Spear-Swerling and Sternberg, 2001), there is less evidence to suggest that such teaching alone will be the panacea that cures or prevents all reading ills. Teaching phonics is a necessary but not a sufficient condition to ensure successful learning. Children with the most severe problems in reading usually have multiple causes that need to be addressed (Clay, 1997).

The generally accepted position now is that dyslexia does indeed exist as a specific form of reading disability. It shares many features in common with cases of general low achievement in reading, but has a unique etiology and is characterised by a very slow response to remedial intervention (Bradley *et al.*, 2002; Grigorenko, 2001). There has been relatively little success in identifying unique teaching methods required to meet the needs of dyslexic children. The general belief at this time is that intervention methods that have proved to be effective with other problem readers are equally applicable for children with dyslexia. Some of the general principles underpinning such methods will be described now.

General principles of intervention

Early intervention has one main purpose – to *prevent* learning difficulties from arising or becoming more serious. Graham and Harris (2000a) have summarised the evidence of what constitutes effective intervention for reading. They state:

> These same elements are also features of exemplary general reading instruction, but their application is intensified in effective supplementary programs because students are seen individually or in small groups. (p. 57)

Their suggestions include:

- High quality explicit teaching, involving clear explanations, modelling, and scaffolded practice.
- A focus on decoding skills, word recognition and comprehension strategies.
- Promoting writing activities to support reading.
- Using texts that children can read successfully.
- Using regular assessment to monitor the progress of individual students.
- Adjusting instruction according to individual needs.

Having reviewed the extant literature on intervention, Chan and Dally (2000) reached the conclusion that effective programmes for students with reading difficulties require:

- Highly trained professionals, capable of diagnosing difficulties and planning appropriate instruction.
- A programme which links closely with the regular class literacy curriculum and teaches the specific skills the children need.
- The implementation of a very effective teaching approach that accelerates students' acquisition and mastery of skills and strategies.

A review of effective early intervention strategies (Westwood, 1998) revealed that the best outcomes occur when:

- Clear and direct instruction is provided in strategies for decoding, word-analysis, and context cueing.
- Students spend much time practising important skills and strategies at high levels of success.
- The student receives a great deal of encouragement and corrective feedback.
- Texts and resources are selected at an appropriate level of difficulty.
- In reading and spelling instruction, due attention is given to teaching both phonological awareness and phonic decoding.

- Writing is included as an integral part of the literacy programme.
- Any negative behaviour the student may be exhibiting is reduced or eliminated (for example, task avoidance; hyperactivity; distractibility).
- Use is made of other adults and peers to facilitate additional practice.
- Close liaison is established with the parents or caregivers to ensure support and continuity of teaching approach at home.

It is difficult to meet all these requirements through an in-class support model alone, so an essential place still remains for remedial tuition in a withdrawal setting for students with learning difficulties. Taking students with reading difficulties in small groups or individually still provides the best opportunity to give individualised, intensive instruction on a daily basis in a distraction-free environment (Mather and Roberts, 1994). Evidence suggests that intensive one-to-one and small group teaching on a regular basis produces the optimum gains for students with reading problems (for example, Pikulski, 1994; Pinnell, 1997). However, both in-class support and withdrawal systems can also have adverse affective outcomes if a student feels embarrassed by the attention given or has feelings of incompetence reinforced (see Chapter 4).

In terms of teaching methods, Phillips *et al.* (1996) recommend:

- A brisk pace of instruction.
- Variety in format of lesson presentation.
- Maximum active participation by students.
- Scaffolded guidance provided by the teacher or tutor.
- Strategies used to motivate students and keep them on task.
- Completion of all work attempted.
- Use of regular formative assessment against the individual objectives.

Intervention programmes such as *Reading Recovery* (Clay, 1994), *Early Intervention in Reading* (EIR) (Taylor *et al.*, 1994) and *Success for All* (Slavin and Madden, 2001) have proved to be very effective in raising young children's reading achievement and confidence (Richek *et al.*, 2002; Smith-Burke, 2001). These programmes embody many of the basic principles listed above. For example, a typical individualised *Reading Recovery* session includes the following activities:

- Re-reading a familiar book.
- Independent reading aloud of a book introduced the previous day. During this reading the teacher often takes running records of the child's strengths and weaknesses in applying specific reading strategies.
- Writing a message or brief story with help from the teacher (who encourages invented spelling and 'listening to sounds within the words').
- Working with letter-tiles or plastic letters to make words.

- Sentence building using word cards from the day's writing activity.
- Reading a new book with the teacher.

For students with dyslexia, every one of the basic principles of design and implementation described in the sections above is applicable. In particular, making maximum use of the available time, using explicit instruction, providing abundant opportunities for practice with feedback, and encouraging independence in reading are high priorities (Allington, 2001). It is known that often the rate of learning of students with dyslexia will be slower and their need for additional practice is even greater (Gross, 2003; Mastropieri and Scruggs, 2002; Otaiba and Fuchs, 2002) but the teaching strategies they require are no different from those required by other problem readers. Braunger and Lewis (1998, p. 5) suggest that, 'Children learn best when teachers employ a variety of strategies to model and demonstrate reading knowledge, strategies and skills, [and] children need the opportunity to read, read, read.'

The above information builds on points already made in previous chapters, and complements intervention suggestions for mathematics in Chapter 8.

Further reading

Allington, R.L. (2001) *What Really Matters for Struggling Readers: Designing Research-Based Programs*. New York: Addison-Wesley Longman.

Block, C.C. (2003) *Literacy Difficulties* (2nd edn). Boston: Allyn & Bacon.

Chapman, C. and King, R. (2003) *Differentiated Instructional Strategies for Reading in the Content Areas*. Thousand Oaks, CA: Corwin Press.

Morris, D. and Slavin, R. (2003) *Every Child Reading*. Boston: Allyn & Bacon.

Richards, R.G. (1999) *The Source for Dyslexia and Dysgraphia*. East Moline, IL: Linguisystems.

Richek, M.A., Caldwell, J.S., Jennings, J.H. and Lerner, J.W. (2002) *Reading Problems: Assessment and Teaching Strategies* (4th edn). Boston: Allyn & Bacon.

Shanker, J.L. and Ekwall, E.E. (2003) *Locating and Correcting Reading Difficulties* (8th edn). Upper Saddle River, NJ: Merrill.

St John, E.P., Loescher, A.A. and Bardzell, J.S. (2003) *Improving Reading and Literacy in Grades 1–5: A Resource Guide to Research-Based Programs*. Thousand Oaks, CA: Corwin Press.

Strickland, D.S., Ganske, K. and Monroe, J.K. (2002) *Supporting Struggling Readers and Writers*. Portland, ME: Stenhouse.

Westwood, P.S. (2001) *Reading and Learning Difficulties*. Melbourne: Australian Council for Educational Research.

7 Difficulties in writing and spelling

> Learning to express oneself through writing is the most complex language task that children must undertake. (Bain *et al.*, 2001, p. vii)

As we have seen, intense research interest has focused for many years on the phenomenon of reading disability. Much less research has been done on problems with writing, yet almost every student with a reading problem has even greater difficulty in writing and spelling. Cavey (2000) suggests that perhaps some 10 per cent of students (most of them boys) have severe difficulties with written language, while Graham and Harris (2003, p. 944) quote figures from the USA suggesting at least 20 per cent of high school students ' … have not even obtained partial mastery of the writing skills and knowledge needed at that grade level'.

It is clear that many students find writing difficult and try to avoid it, or they engage in writing activities with only limited output and success. Just as skills in reading are of vital importance for independence in learning, and for making good progress in all areas of the curriculum, so too the ability to write with adequate proficiency is important for all students.

The need for explicit instruction

Gould (2001) and Vellutino (2003) are adamant that all students require specific instruction in the writing process and in the use of effective strategies for planning, monitoring, evaluating, revising and editing their written work. In order to develop students' motivation, skills and strategies for writing, teachers may need to use both direct instruction (demonstrations, modelling, 'thinking aloud', guided practice) and indirect instruction (constructive feedback and personal example) (Tompkins, 2000). Even students with the most severe writing problems can be helped to improve their skills through direct teaching, opportunities to write each day, and constructive feedback from teacher and peers (Heward, 2003a).

One possible factor associated with low standards in writing is that some classrooms devote too little time to the teaching and practice of writing. Research has shown that time for practice is particularly important for basic skill development, and children need to write every day to see any real progress toward increased competence (Cavey, 2000; Mastropieri and Scruggs, 2002). It is felt that in some classrooms the development of writing skill is left too much to informal methods and to incidental learning (De La Paz and Graham, 2002) but there are so many different challenges involved in becoming a proficient writer that students need explicit guidance and support, as well as opportunities to experiment.

Writing is a complex skill

Kay (2003) observes that writing is a highly complex process involving multiple brain mechanisms and specific abilities. The act of writing requires the writer to formulate ideas, organize and sequence points in logical order, select vocabulary, check for grammatical correctness, spell words correctly, punctuate, and write legibly. It requires the simultaneous and sequential integration of attention, language, long-term memory and working memory, motor skills, higher-order thinking, and metacognition.

The process usually termed 'transcription' involves converting the thoughts the writer wants to express into written language, correctly arranged and sequenced on the page (Graham and Harris, 2000b). To accomplish this process successfully the writer needs an efficient nervous system, adequate intelligence, motivation, language proficiency (for example, adequate vocabulary, knowledge of grammar, and spelling ability) and an awareness of text organisation and style (Gregg and Mather, 2002). In the past 20 years researchers and theorists have attempted to describe and interrelate the mental operations involved in writing – such as executive control, goal setting, planning, generating ideas, translating ideas into written text, reviewing, editing, evaluating, and judging audience (Graham and Harris, 2003).

Some of the most original and productive work in analysing the writing process stemmed from a model devised by Hayes and Flower (1980) and revised by Hayes in 1996. More recently Lyon, Fletcher and Barnes (2003, p. 572) summed up the field by saying:

> … writing is a complex problem-solving process reflecting the writer's declarative knowledge, procedural knowledge and conditional knowledge, all of which are subserved by a network of neuropsychological factors, personality factors, and other conditions (including teacher-student relationships, amount of writing instruction, and the teacher's knowledge of the writing process). Within this context 'declarative knowledge' refers to the specific writing and spelling subskills that the learner has acquired, whereas 'procedural knowledge' refers to the learner's competence in using such knowledge while writing for meaning.

Developmental aspects of writing and spelling

The acquisition of skills in writing and spelling is generally believed to follow a fairly predictable sequence for all children. This sequence is reflected in the many checklists and inventories available for teachers to use when determining a student's current stage of development in writing (for example, Griffin *et al.*, 2001). Several researchers have described the stages through which children pass as they move from 'emergent writing' at approximately 5 years of age to the final skilled writing stage reached in late adolescence or adulthood (for example, Bissex, 1980; Fitzgerald and Shanahan, 2000; Morrow, 2001). Many of these analyses have focused mainly on normal acquisition of spelling skills, but others have looked also at the strategies the writer uses and the sophistication of the product at various ages and stages (Graham and Harris, 2003). A typical developmental sequence would identify the following stages and features in writing:

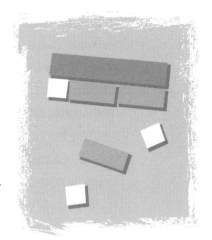

- *Writing as drawing*: Children at this stage use a drawing to record and communicate personally relevant information.

- *Writing as scribbling*: Children imitate the actions of writing and make marks on paper, but with no real awareness of letters and words.

- *Writing with letter-like forms*: Imitation gets closer to real writing, but most of the letters are invented shapes. At this stage children may have grasped the left-to-right directionality of written language through observation of other children or adults writing – but if not, this understanding emerges during the next stage.

- *Writing as reproduced familiar letter strings*: Children write strings of real letters already learned, for example from their own names or from words in the environment. Spelling at this stage is usually referred to as pre-phonetic because there is no connection between what the child writes and the phonemes in the words.

- *Writing with invented spelling*: At this stage children are usually motivated to try to record or communicate information, using simple sentence constructions containing several related words. In terms of spelling, this stage has many levels within it, each one reflecting a growing awareness that letters and groups of letters can represent the speech sounds in words. Phonemic awareness influences competency at this stage; and sensitivity to sounds in words may increase as the child attempts to spell words. The invented words are quite recognizable because at this stage children begin to apply phonic principles as they write (Vellutino, 2003). This is referred to as the *phonetic* stage, with a rapidly emerging knowledge of letter-sound correspondences acquired through incidental learning or direct teaching. It should be noted that the majority of individuals with poor spelling have reached this phonetic stage in their spelling development, but have not progressed beyond it and tend not to employ visual imagery and other strategies for checking words.

- *Increased use of strategies in writing*: As children become more competent in writing they adopt a more strategic and thoughtful approach. Their sentences become more complex and reveal an increasing range of vocabulary and grammatical constructions. They use more efficient and effective strategies for generating ideas, planning, evaluating, revising and correcting mechanical errors (Graham and Harris, 2003). They monitor and modify their own work with greater understanding of audience, style and clarity. In general, they understand the whole process of writing much better and therefore exercise increased control over it. Many writing tasks that at first they would have found challenging they can now accomplish almost automatically, in less time and with much less cognitive effort. For most writers developing normally, motivation and self-efficacy related to writing increase; writing becomes intrinsically rewarding. In terms of spelling, children at this stage can make accurate or reasonable attempts at spelling almost every word they want to use. They apply visual imagery and other strategies more effectively when writing and checking words, and there is clear evidence of a deeper understanding of word structure and word analysis.

- *Independence in writing*. Children now use a wide range of cognitive strategies and self-monitoring skills to manage structure, issues of genre, sense of audience, and text cohesion. Flexible use is made of a wide range of spelling, proofreading, self-help and self-correcting strategies. Spelling at this stage reveals mastery of quite complex grapho-phonic concepts, and children can employ many appropriate strategies (visual, orthographic, phonic, analogic, morphemic, semantic) to spell and check unfamiliar words.

Fitzgerald and Shanahan (2000) identified similar stages of development in writing, closely linked to parallel developmental stages in reading acquisition, and influenced to some degree by reading experience. While reading and writing are separate processes, and in some respects draw upon different areas of knowledge and skill, there is still considerable overlap between reading and writing (Cramer 1998; Graham *et al.*, 2002; Nelson and Calfee, 1998). For example:

- Knowledge of grammar and sentence structure is one of the cueing systems used in fluent reading and is the essential ingredient in writing.

- Awareness of new grammatical constructions grows with increased reading.

- Reading extends vocabulary; and a rich vocabulary is essential for writing.

- Knowledge of phonics helps both reading and spelling.

- Automatic recognition of high frequency words in print is closely linked with automaticity in spelling those words correctly when writing.

It is generally agreed that reading and writing should be taught together from the earliest stages because the teaching of one can positively affect the learning of the other (Cox, 1999). Integrated writing and spelling activities should also form an integral part of any literacy intervention programme, a point to be made again later.

Difficulties in writing

As we have seen, written expression is cognitively demanding and is often considered the most difficult of the language skills for children to acquire. It is not surprising that many students experience problems as they attempt to move upward from the level of novice writer. Williams (2002, p. 73) has observed:

> The demands of writing are particularly problematic for children with learning disabilities. As writers compose, they must juggle not only the ideas that come to mind, but also the many requirements associated with different writing formats. They must also consider the audience to whom the work is directed and the purpose of the writing (descriptive, expository, persuasive, and so forth). Students must know whether they have written 'enough' information, and if their ideas are all connected and relevant. They must ensure that neither these ideas nor the vocabulary they use is unnecessarily repetitive, and that their words and sentences have been constructed correctly. Students with learning disabilities in written expression can have particular difficulties with many of these issues as they write.

In particular, the process of writing requires effective use of metacognition in the form of self-monitoring and self-regulation, as well as adequate proficiency in the lower-level skills involved in handwriting or word-processing. Graham and Harris (2000b) consider that many writing difficulties are due primarily to problems in acquiring and using self-regulatory processes to accompany transcription skills. A priority focus in any intervention approach for writing must be to increase self-regulation through the teaching of effective planning, monitoring and revising strategies.

Another possible contributory factor in some cases of writing difficulty is a limited working memory capacity (Richards, 1999; Swanson and Siegel, 2001). The role of working memory during writing has been the focus of attention in recent years (for example, McCutchen, 2000). It is easy to understand how limitations of working memory or attentional problems can disrupt the processes involved in writing. The heavy demands placed on working memory when an individual is composing and transcribing are reflected in the comment by Richards (1999, p. 69):

> A student must simultaneously maintain the meaning of a sentence while trying to find the right vocabulary and remembering to capitalize, punctuate, and spell correctly.

Anything that disrupts working memory (for example, anxiety, distractions) will also impair the ability to compose and transcribe.

Hess and Wheldall (1999) report that students with learning difficulties often exhibit weaknesses in planning, sequencing ideas, editing and revising. Some students also have problems with mechanical aspects of the task, such as handwriting, spelling and punctuation. Isaacson (1987) reviewed research on the characteristics of unskilled writers and concluded that they tend to spend little or no time planning before starting to write, often do not present ideas in a logical order, use very simple sentence structures (or conversely, write long and rambling sentences with repetitive use of conjunctions), produce very little material in the available time, and are reluctant to review and revise their work. Topping *et al.* (2000) remark that time spent on planning by weak and novice writers is often insufficient. They also report that there are likely to be difficulties with generating ideas for writing, organising the text, and in exercising metacognitive control of the writing process. In their review of the cognitive aspects of writing Graham and Harris (2003) stress that one of the major weaknesses of poor writers is that they lack any effective strategies for approaching the task of writing in a systematic and confident manner. However, these writers go on to conclude (more optimistically), 'Numerous studies have demonstrated that the performance of poor writers can be bolstered by explicitly teaching them the types of planning, revising, and other self-regulatory strategies used by more skilled writers' (Graham and Harris, 2003, p. 944).

Difficulty in writing produces fairly predictable negative affective outcomes. Children who find writing very difficult and frustrating will gain no satisfaction from attempting the task, and will try to avoid writing whenever possible. This avoidance leads to lack of practice and lack of practice in turn results in no improvement. Students who struggle to develop written language quickly construct a negative perception of the writing process and of themselves (Gregg and Mather, 2002). They get locked in the typical 'failure cycle' and lose confidence and self-esteem. A detrimental attitude quickly develops that can be summed up in the words, 'I can't write; I hate writing'. The challenge for the teacher is to motivate such students to write, and to provide them with enough explicit instruction, support and feedback to ensure increased success and satisfaction (Glasswell *et al.*, 2003).

Difficulties with spelling

Cavey (2000, p. 45) reminds us:

> Spelling requires more auditory and visual discrimination, sequence memory, analysis and synthesis, and integration simultaneously than perhaps any other skill. Thus, the majority of children with LD have trouble spelling.

According to Mastropieri and Scruggs (2002), spelling is a more difficult activity than reading because it requires the *production* of a correct sequence of letters. Reading on the other hand requires *recognition* of a set of symbols already displayed on the page. Recognition is usually an easier memory process than recall and production. For most problem spellers, recalling the correct sequence of letters is the major obstacle. The spelling of dyslexic students, for example, is often referred to as 'bizarre' in that the letters they write may not correspond in any way with the sounds within the word, or with the visual appearance of the word in print (Richards, 1999).

For many low-achieving students, spelling continues to present a problem long after reading skills have improved. Most dyslexic adults report having major spelling difficulties and they try to avoid situations where their weakness might be revealed. Many of the difficulties, for both children and adults, appear to stem from three main causes – poor phonological skills, poor visual imagery, and insufficient instruction.

Phonological skills

Children with spelling difficulties quite commonly have poorly developed, or inefficiently applied, phonological skills. They are weak in identifying component sounds within the words they try to spell, and they are poor at linking sounds and syllables to the correct groups of letters. Spelling an unfamiliar word by relating its sound values to another known word (spelling by analogy) requires adequate auditory skills and phonic knowledge. It also requires an efficient mechanism by which to retrieve relevant grapho-phonic information rapidly from long-term memory. Robinson (2001, p. 205) says that, 'For many children, the complex and confusing relationship between letter patterns and sounds in English may not be properly learnt unless specific teaching of these patterns is provided.' There is abundant evidence to indicate that specific training in phonemic awareness, coupled with explicit teaching of phonics, has a positive impact on spelling and reading (for example, Ball and Blachman, 1991; Walton, 1998). This is not to suggest that the key to excellent spelling is phonics alone, because other strategies are also essential for dealing with irregular words often found in the English language.

Visual imagery

Even when children do manage to reach the phonetic stage of spelling development (usually much later than normal spellers), they appear unable to move beyond it because they do not use visual strategies efficiently to help store images of words in visual memory, or to judge whether a word looks correct or incorrect after they have written it. Many years ago Johnson and Myklebust (1967) referred to this as an inability to 'revisualize words', and they devised a teaching procedure that caused the learner to focus more attentively on the sequence of letters to help establish a clear visual image (see Weller and Buchanan, 1988, for details). Peters and Smith (1993) and Richards (1999) also stress the importance in training visual perception of word forms and letter sequences to ensure good development in spelling. The well-known 'Look-Say-Cover-Write-Check' strategy is one effective way of ensuring that visual imagery is applied to spelling.

Insufficient instruction

Learning to spell, like learning to read, is not a natural language process, so children need instruction (Graham *et al.*, 2002). The fact that in recent years the formal teaching of spelling and the use of spelling practice became unpopular has almost certainly increased the number of students who are poor at spelling (Westwood, 1994). Graham (2000) and Richards (1999) indicate that poor spellers are not very adept at acquiring spelling skills merely through reading and other incidental means. They believe that children need to be taught effective word analysis and other strategies to help them become independent spellers. There is evidence that a brief but intensive intervention programme with a focus on strategies for spelling and word analysis can have positive effects on the spelling performance and motivation of children in the primary school years (for example, Lam, 2003).

Some strategies for spelling instruction are described later in the chapter. In general, the approach needs to address spelling improvement within a meaningful reading and writing programme, not as a separate skill to be taught in isolation. However, there may be occasions on which the investigation of 'word families' and 'spelling demons' through the medium of mini lessons will be helpful for all students.

Specific disability in written language: dysgraphia

Dysgraphia is the term used for a specific disability in writing that goes beyond the general difficulties encountered by many students. Sometimes the term is used simply to describe illegible handwriting, but in recent years the meaning has been extended to cover all aspects of poor written language, including expression, clarity, accuracy and spelling. Sometimes the term *dysorthographia* is used to signify a disability specifically related to spelling when other aspects of written language are satisfactory.

There have been attempts to identify subtypes of dysgraphia, each stemming from slightly different underlying causes (Cavey, 2000). One type appears to be due to the phonological coding difficulties underpinning dyslexia. A second subtype seems to result from fine motor coordination deficits. The third type, termed 'spatial dysgraphia', is evident in students who seem unable to set out the work on the page in an organised manner. Subtypes of dysgraphia will not be discussed further here since research in this area appears not to have led to any practical suggestions for differentiated intervention.

According to the *DSM-4* (APA, 2000), to be officially diagnosed as having a 'disorder of written expression' a student must exhibit writing skills that fall substantially below those expected for age, educational opportunity and intelligence. Operationally, it is difficult to interpret the term 'substantially below those expected for age', because there are few reliable standardised tests of written language (Bailet, 2001). Usually the teacher or psychologist has to judge subjectively the student's degree of writing handicap from samples of everyday written work.

DSM-4 describes the main problems associated with this type of learning disability in these terms: poor organisation of ideas; grammatical errors; multiple spelling errors; extremely poor handwriting. These same areas of general difficulty are evident, of course, in all students identified as 'poor writers', so the list does not really help to diagnose or differentiate dysgraphic students from others. Given the very significant overlap in instructional needs of both groups with writing problems, the advice given later for appropriate intervention applies equally to both. There are no specific interventions that are appropriate only for students with a specific learning disability in writing.

Handwriting

The act of handwriting mainly involves the parietal lobe, including the motor cortex, together with the occipital lobe for visual processing (Wing, 2000). Naturally, the language centres of the left hemisphere are also activated during the creative composing aspects of the task.

Sousa (2001b, p. 118) describes the act of handwriting in the following terms:

> When an individual is writing, the visual feedback mechanisms are at work checking the output, adjusting the fine motor skills, and monitoring eye-hand coordination. Meanwhile, kinesthetic monitoring systems are conscious of the position and movement of fingers in space, the grip on the pencil, and the rhythm and pace of writing ... Accomplishing this task [also] requires visual memory for symbols, whole-word memory, and spelling rules.

There is a suggestion that illegible handwriting is sometimes due to difficulty with fine muscle control and poor hand-eye coordination (Cavey, 2000; Sousa, 2001b). These weaknesses are thought to be due to minor neurological dysfunction — with poor coordination being one of the so-called 'soft' neurological signs in cases of SpLD. It is worth noting that very poor handwriting and limited written work output are often seen in students with ADHD (Barkley, 2003), and in their case it is also attributed sometimes to neurological factors (Sousa, 2001b). But most cases of poor handwriting are due to faulty learning and inadequate teaching. Handwriting needs to be taught to children very early in their school life so that it is mastered efficiently and becomes a highly functional tool for communication (Tompkins, 2000). For students with major handwriting difficulties the action of writing has not been automated – largely through lack of practice or lack of clear instruction – and the action of writing each word takes much of the student's attention away from the higher-order processes of planning, generating ideas, self-monitoring, evaluating and revising.

It is not unusual to encounter students with very poor handwriting, and this may constrain a child's development as a creative writer and speller. Baker, Gersten and Graham (2003) stress that effective instruction for students with learning difficulties must include explicit and systematic teaching of handwriting and spelling skills. Writing is not an innate behaviour and the brain is not pre-programmed to develop written language skills in the way it appears to be pre-programmed for oral language acquisition (Sousa, 2001b). For this reason direct instruction in writing is usually required if problems are to be prevented.

If children are not taught an easy and efficient style of writing when they are young, they often develop faulty habits that are extremely difficult to remedy later (Mastropieri and Scruggs, 2002). As with every other basic skill, early intervention can be very effective in preventing later problems in learning (Edwards, 2003). Many handwriting problems stem from improper sitting posture, pencil grip, paper placement, or from insufficient teaching of letter formation (Block, 2003). Difficulties arise if children are not taught correct letter formation and linkages but instead have to 'discover' this knowledge through trial and error. For most students without learning difficulties, once they are instructed appropriately, handwriting rapidly develops to become a highly automatic skill requiring little conscious attention during the composing and transcribing stages of writing (Graham and Harris, 2000b). Handwriting can only become swift and automatic if students engage in it frequently, are motivated to do so, and receive relevant corrective feedback. In the case of students with SpLD, Graham, Harris and Chorzempa (2002) recommend supplementary handwriting instruction be provided with sufficient frequency and intensity to build the required fluency and automaticity.

Difficulties in handwriting are sometimes associated with difficulties in spelling (Cripps, 1990). It is believed that a swift and easy handwriting style facilitates the learning and storage of essential letter sequences within words — learning to spell 'by hand' as well as by eye. In contrast, slow and laborious handwriting style distracts the writer's attention away from aspects of the word that would facilitate spelling. Richards (1999, p. 66) attributes the problems in both handwriting and spelling to an underlying weakness in 'sequential motor memory'.

The book *Source for Dyslexia and Dysgraphia* (Richards, 1999) contains some useful material on handwriting difficulties and their remediation. Additional practical advice can be found in Chapter 6 of *Effective Instruction for Special Education* (Mastropieri and Scruggs, 2002).

Assessment

Assessment is usually the first step in designing effective intervention for individuals or groups of students with difficulties in writing and spelling (Kay, 2003). It is important to determine fairly accurately what the students can do successfully at the moment, and which aspects of the writing process are giving them most difficulty. Assessment strategies might include:

- *Direct observation of the students at work*. What strategies do they use? Attention span and concentration? Motivation and interest? Persistence in the face of difficulty? Self-monitoring and self-correction? Dependence on adult guidance and direction? Effective use of available time?

- *Analysis of work samples*. What do these reveal about the writer's existing knowledge and skills? Quantity written each day? Quality? Neatness? Self-correction?

- *Discussion with the students concerning their approach to writing*. How do they go about planning to write? What strategies do they use? Why do they find writing difficult? What do they perceive to be the problem? What help do they feel they need? What was the best piece of writing they ever produced? Why do they regard it as the best?

- *Testing component skills*. In some cases it will be necessary to assess particular aspects of the writing separately, for example, spelling, phonic knowledge, handwriting, knowledge of conventions, proofreading ability.

Mastropieri and Scruggs (2002) provide some useful suggestions on aspects of written work that should be appraised. These aspects include:

- *Mechanics of writing*: spelling; punctuation; capitalisation; handwriting; format. Error analysis in spelling is often needed to help identify the types of difficulty a student is having.

- *Grammar*: subject-verb agreement; verb tense; pronouns; singular-plural forms.

- *Organisation*: sequence of content; paragraphing.

- *Content*: relevant focus; detail; accuracy; breadth and depth; originality; supporting evidence.

- *Sophistication*: vocabulary; sentence length; sentence complexity; variety; interest.

In the domain of spelling, the current diagnostic approach to spelling combines:

- An evaluation of the overall stage of development the speller has reached.

- An analysis of the types of error the speller makes.

- An assessment of the speller's existing phonic knowledge.

- An appraisal of the strategies the speller uses to generate words and to self-correct.

The following section provides a very brief overview of possible approaches to the improvement of writing and spelling skills. Readers are referred to the sources listed under Further reading for more detailed coverage of practical teaching strategies. Many ideas will be found in Block (2003), Sousa (2001b),

Baker, Gersten and Graham (2003), and Strickland, Ganske and Monroe (2002). Additional strategies for spelling are presented in Westwood (1999a).

Intervention: general principles

Sometimes intervention for writing and spelling must involve individual tuition, but much of value can be gained also by working with small groups (Hodges, 2002). Requiring students to work collaboratively on writing tasks – creating, discussing, reviewing and providing constructive feedback – can motivate them and encourage them to revise and polish their work with an audience in mind (Baker *et al.*, 2002; Furr, 2003).

At the individual level, problems with writing can be addressed in three ways (Sousa, 2001b). These general approaches to writing problems are not mutually exclusive and in most classroom situations they need to be used together to help overcome or bypass the difficulty:

- *By making accommodations for the student*: for example, using a word-processor instead of writing with pen; giving the student an enlarged pencil-holder or grip; allowing more time to complete assignments; allowing manuscript print instead of cursive handwriting; encouraging the student to dictate to a scribe.

- *By modifying the task demands*: for example, reducing the size of the writing task; changing the nature of the task (giving a cloze passage or multiple-choice exercise instead of an essay); giving the student more direct help and guidance during the lesson.

- *By remedying the writing difficulties*: for example, using precision teaching, explicit instruction, modelling, imitation, and guided practice; teaching the use of effective writing strategies (see below); providing corrective feedback. Shapiro and Elliott (1999) recommend using curriculum-based measurement to increase the amount of written work the student produces each day; daily counting and charting can act as an incentive for increased output, accuracy and legibility. While students almost certainly need instruction in the mechanics of writing, if too much of this is work done in the form of isolated drills and routine exercises, it is unlikely that anything useful will generalise to the students' everyday written work (Tompkins, 2000). The teaching of mechanical aspects of writing is best done as an integral part of all meaningful writing activities, and may need to be given high priority with SpLD students.

According to Lyon (2002, p. 57):

> The most successful programs tend to ensure that clear linkages are drawn between oral language, reading, and written language. Successful programs also ensure that basic skills development in spelling and writing (grapho-motor production) are explicitly taught and/or accommodated and that the student is also taught how to employ strategies to guide the formulation of ideas for

writing and the organization of these ideas in writing. These elements are common to many writing programs; however, successful instruction for students with disabilities in written expression depends upon their intensity and explicitness.

Furr (2003) suggests that the two biggest obstacles facing struggling writers are, 'How do I begin?' and, 'What do I write next?' He suggests that much support is needed in the early stages to help children become more confident and independent in their writing. The *Think Sheets* recommended by Englert, Raphael and Anderson (1992) are helpful in this respect. The *Think Sheets* encourage students to think and plan before writing by having them write brief notes in response to key questions before they begin. The personal notes on the *Think Sheet* then provide a framework for beginning to write a more extended version of the topic. The questions on the think sheet typically cover:

- What do I know already about this?
- Who am I writing for?
- What are my main points going to be?
- How will I organise my points?

On similar lines, Richards (1999) suggests improving students' metacognitive approach to writing by providing them with a framework of key questions to guide planning, goal setting and self-monitoring:

- Can I relate this topic to anything I already know?
- Where can I get more information?
- What is the best way to present this information?
- How can I group my ideas?
- Who am I writing this for? (audience?)
- Have I addressed the topic?
- Are my points clear?
- Do my points follow a logical sequence?
- Can I make my writing more interesting?

On the issue of 'how will I organise my points?' several writers have recommended using graphic organisers, or 'idea webs' to present a *visual* plan for writing (Gould, 2001; Richards, 1999; Westwood, 2003). The topic is written at the centre of the 'web' on a blank sheet of paper. Lines (or spokes) radiate from the topic title, and ideas or details related to the topic are then generated and written against separate spokes. Lines connecting ideas in a logical way are inserted, and the spokes are numbered to indicate the order in which each idea will be introduced in the writing. It is thought that having the plan in this visual form, with main points, linkages and sequence readily available for

reference, is particularly helpful for students with difficulties. Graphic organisers can be developed as a group activity.

A different approach is mentioned by Sousa (2001b) who suggests first getting students with writing difficulties to dictate or brainstorm ideas for the story on tape. Then the recorded material can be used later to help with the writing. This method separates the planning stage from the transcription stage and thus frees the student from trying to meet the demands of both processes at the same time (cognitive load). Although written language is not 'talk written down verbatim', talking ideas through first does provide a resource and scaffold for successful writing later (Strickland *et al.*, 2002).

Strategy instruction

A growing body of evidence indicates that the writing of students with learning difficulties can be improved significantly if they are taught effective strategies to use when generating ideas, organising what is to be written, and revising first drafts to improve clarity, interest and cohesion (Baker *et al.*, 2003; Graham and Harris, 2000b; Hallenbeck, 2002; Mayer, 2001; Troia and Graham, 2002). Research has typically found an effect size of 0.8 or above for such interventions, signifying a clear and definite benefit from instructing children in the use of writing strategies (De la Paz and Graham, 2002; Swanson, 2000a). Graham, Harris and Chorzempa (2002) recommend that intervention to improve written expression should focus on the self-regulatory or metacognitive aspects, particularly strategies for planning and revising but other strategies that simply give the student a step-by-step plan of action to follow are also extremely helpful. The effective teaching of such strategies usually requires direct instruction, with demonstrations (thinking aloud), modelling and guided practice (Hartman, 2001).

As an example, Westwood (2003) describes a simple task-approach strategy using the mnemonic LESSER to help students remember the steps. The strategy helps some students to organise their thoughts for writing and then write a longer assignment than they would otherwise produce (*'LESSER helps me write MORE!'*).

L = List your ideas.

E = Examine your list.

S = Select your starting point.

S = Sentence one tells us about this first idea.

E = Expand on this first idea with another sentence.

R = Read what you have written. Revise if necessary. Repeat for the next paragraph.

Hallahan and Kauffman (2003) also describe several composition strategies, including the following adapted from Englert *et al.* (1991):

P = Plan

O = Organise

W = Write

E = Edit

R = Revise

Other advice on plans of action that could be explicitly taught to students (adapted from Mastropieri and Scruggs, 2002; Cavey, 2000) includes:

Prewriting strategies. These might involve:

- Brainstorming topic ideas.

- Generating possible subheadings.

- Organising ideas.

- Writing a first draft.

- Seeking more information.

Editing strategy. This requires the writer to do the following:

- Read each paragraph carefully.

- Examine each sentence for clarity, accuracy, and punctuation.

- Make sure the main idea is clear and that there is necessary supporting detail.

- Where relevant, provide a transition sentence or link to the next paragraph.

- Ask, to make it more interesting, do I need to add or change any words or phrases?

- Read the work aloud. Any improvements needed?

Post-writing strategies. These might include:

- Proofreading for spelling, mechanics and format.

- Proofreading for content, clarity and organisation.

- Revising and polishing.

- Sharing the revised draft with a peer to receive feedback or response.

Additional practical ideas for writing strategies can be found in Wong *et al.* (1997), Harris and Graham (1996) and Gould (2001). Lee (2002) provides some excellent suggestions for strategies and skills that can be taught to learners of English as a second language.

Interventions for spelling

Students with learning difficulties rarely find spelling an enjoyable or self-reinforcing activity, so there may be a need for some form of extrinsic reinforcement to help them maintain attention to task until they begin to recognise their own progress and shift to intrinsic motivation (Mastropieri and Scruggs, 2002). When practice is necessary (*and it usually is necessary*) activities with game-like formats and computer-assisted learning can be effective. Peer tutoring (paired spelling) – learning words together and taking turns to test one another – can also provide opportunities for practice within a social learning context (Watkins and Hunter-Carsch, 1995). In all these cases the words studied should be related closely to the students' genuine writing needs and should derive from the classroom curriculum. Words studied entirely out of context are unlikely to be remembered or used later by the students. Where 'word families' are used to explore orthographic units (phonograms), the basic words selected for the word family should derive from the students' reading or writing materials rather than from vocabulary lists or spelling books. The effective use of word families will always incorporate both the reading and the spelling of the words.

Interventions to improve students' spelling have been reviewed by Gordon, Vaughn and Schumm (1993). Some of the main findings indicated that teachers should:

- Create opportunities for students to engage in frequent writing.
- Instruct students in word analysis strategies.
- Target no more than three words per lesson for students with learning difficulties.
- Aim to develop students' self-monitoring and self-correction strategies.
- Give clear and efficient feedback on errors.
- Use multisensory methods (saying, hearing, seeing, tracing, writing, and checking) to improve retention of difficult words.

Children with spelling difficulties benefit from being taught how to study and check words (Lam, 2003). In particular, children must be taught the following strategies:

- *Look-say-cover-write-check*. This self-help strategy makes use of visual imagery to establish correct spelling patterns in long-term memory. The strategy is particularly valuable for the learning of irregular words, and for helping students progress beyond the phonetic stage of spelling.
- *Phonemic approach*. This strategy is the one that most children discover for themselves at the early stage of inventive spelling. For those who don't discover the 'spell-it-as-it sounds' strategy, they need instruction coupled with phonological awareness training.
- *Spelling by analogy*. Some students will need direct teaching and much practice to realise that knowing the spelling of one word can give clues to the probable spelling of another word that sounds a little like it.
- *Repeated writing*. If a student really wishes to remember a word, writing the word several times is an obvious method of helping with this. The approach brings together motor memory and visual imagery. However, the strategy

is unlikely to be of benefit if the student is not motivated to learn the word, or if the exercise is given as punishment.

Many educators advocate multisensory teaching for improving spelling and for building sight vocabulary (for example, Birsh, 1999; Richards, 1999; Walton, 1998). This approach often involves finger tracing over the sequence of letters in a large flashcard-size version of the target word, while at the same time saying the word in syllables. The word is then written from memory. Multisensory approaches also involve word-building activities with letter tiles or plastic letters. Often different coloured letters are used for this activity, but real words on a page do not normally appear in a mix of red, yellow and blue letters. Rather than using different colours the teacher or tutor should try to have the student practise the word building using black letters on a white background. This aids transfer and generalisation because it creates a 'normal' visual image of the word on a page of print.

Use of computers and spellcheckers

Cavey (2000) strongly recommends the use of any form of technology that will help overcome (or bypass) a student's difficulties in getting ideas on to paper, and Robinson (2001) suggests that using a word-processor may be one way of restoring a student's interest and confidence in composing. Tompkins (2000) reports that when students compose on computers they write more, and both the quality of their writing and their attitude toward writing improve. Van der Kaay, Wilton and Townsend (2000) used a word processor with students aged nine to eleven who were mildly intellectually disabled. They found that the students' written work improved significantly in terms of organisation and control over the writing process.

If teachers have available a large-screen monitor in the classroom, it provides an opportunity for the teacher to demonstrate the whole process of writing, from the initial planning stage, through draft writing, to editing (with cut-and-pastes, deletions, and additions), and final published form (Tompkins, 2000). A word-processor provides excellent opportunities for collaborative writing. Even without the large screen monitor, teachers can still model and discuss the processes of revision with individuals and small groups.

Walton (1998) strongly supports electronic spellcheckers for students with severe spelling difficulties; but she warns that the teacher should make sure the particular device matches the student's needs and capabilities. It is of no great value to buy a spellchecker that is overly comprehensive and provides the learning disabled student with too many alternative words from which to select the one required. She recommends the *Franklin Elementary Spellmaster* for students who have a reading age of about 7 years. When selecting a spellchecker or word-processing program, Cavey (2000) advises choosing a program that lets you add words to the spelling dictionary.

Excellent advice on technological aids for writing, spelling and other purposes can be found in Meyer, Murray and Pisha (2000), Ryba, Curzon and Selby (2002), and Williams (2002).

Further reading

Cavey, D.W. (2000) *Dysgraphia: Why Johnny Can't Write* (3rd edn) Austin, TX: ProEd.

Chapman, C. & King, R. (2003) *Differentiated Instructional Strategies for Writing in the Content Areas*. Thousand, Oaks, CA: Corwin Press.

Edwards, S.A. (2003) *Ways of Writing with Young Kids*. Boston: Allyn & Bacon.

Gould, B.W. (2001) Curricular strategies for written expression. In A.M. Bain, L.L. Bailet and L.C. Moats (eds) *Written Language Disorders* (pp. 185–220). Austin, TX: ProEd.

Lewin, L. (2003) *Paving the Way in Reading and Writing*. San Francisco, CA: Jossey-Bass.

McCarrier, A., Pinnell, G.S. and Fountas, I.C. (2000) *Interactive Writing*. Portsmouth, NH: Heinemann.

Olson, C.B. (2003) *The Reading/Writing Connection: Strategies for Teaching and Learning in the Secondary Classroom*. Boston: Allyn & Bacon.

Richards, R.G. (1999) *The Source Book for Dyslexia and Dysgraphia*. East Moline, IL: Linguisystems.

Strickland, D.S., Gaske, K. and Monroe, J.K. (2002) *Supporting Struggling Readers and Writers*. Portland, ME: Stenhouse.

Tompkins, G.E. (2000) *Teaching Writing: Balancing Process and Product* (3rd edn). Upper Saddle River, NJ: Merrill.

Walton, M. (1998) *Teaching Reading and Spelling to Dyslexic Children*. London: Fulton.

Westwood, P.S. (1999) *Spelling: Approaches to Teaching and Assessment*. Melbourne: Australian Council for Educational Research.

8 Learning difficulties in mathematics

> ... the course of learning formal mathematics is often far from smooth.
> (Ginsberg, 1997, p. 23)

In much the same way that human infants appear to be biologically pre-programmed to acquire language very rapidly and easily in the preschool years, so too it is seems they are pre-programmed with the capacity to deal with quantitative features of their environment (Geary, 2000; Wynn, 1998). A great deal of informal learning of number concepts and skills begins at a very early age, supported in a variety of natural ways by parents and others (Aubrey, 2001). Preschool children appear to have an implicit understanding of numerosity, ordinality, counting, and simple arithmetic (adding, taking away, and sharing) even without direct instruction (Ginsberg, 1997). This informal quantitative experience lays the firm foundation for future skills acquisition and conceptual development when the child begins school.

When children enter school they encounter for the first time a much more formally structured type of mathematics. Children cannot easily discover the properties of school mathematics in an entirely informal way, and they need therefore to be instructed in conventional procedures, terminology, signs and symbols, as well as introduced to new concepts and problems in a sequential manner. They need to encounter age-appropriate mathematical situations and they need to practise and apply new skills in order to maintain interest, build confidence, and develop automaticity.

From the moment children begin school, their success in mathematics depends heavily on the quality of the teaching they receive. In general, research on teacher effectiveness in mathematics has supported the use of a structured approach and carefully sequenced programme, particularly for students with learning difficulties (Heward, 2003a). It is now widely accepted that the most effective teaching approach combines important aspects of direct instruction together with the most meaningful and motivating components of student-centred, learning. High quality teaching in mathematics requires a teacher with excellent subject knowledge who can stimulate students' interest and involvement. The teacher's role is to create a learning environment where there are abundant opportunities for active participation by students, and also to impart relevant information and teach specific skills and strategies.

The changing nature of mathematics education

In many countries, the teaching of mathematics and the content of the mathematics curriculum have undergone drastic reforms in recent years (for example, Australian Education Council, 1990; National Council of Teachers of Mathematics, 2000; Romberg, 1995). The teaching approach most widely advocated now is one based on socio-constructivist learning theory. It is believed that students must be active and critical participants in their own learning experiences. This implies less teacher direction, a more inductive approach, and more collaborative group work and exploratory activity. So-called 'modern methods' call for fewer teacher-directed lessons and less drill and memorisation; the move is toward more investigation, problem solving, discovery, reflection and discussion. Using such an approach, the learning of school mathematics should remain as meaningful to children as were their informal early childhood mathematical experiences.

While the educational reforms have undoubtedly provided a breath of fresh air in many schools – with mathematics lessons becoming more interesting and relevant – it must also be acknowledged that two major problems exist.

First, it is more difficult to use activity-based and enquiry approaches effectively than it is to teach using traditional pedagogy. Most teachers of primary and secondary classes have not learned mathematics themselves in the way they are now expected to teach it (Ginsberg, 1997), so without such prior experience activity-based lessons may sometimes go astray and learning objectives are not always achieved.

Second, the lack of clear explanation and direction in some constructivist classrooms, together with the relative absence of practice exercises using basic skills, can contribute to the learning problems that many low achieving students encounter. Baxter, Woodward and Olson (2001, p. 545) express concern that low achievers are struggling in such classrooms and need '… more time, more attention, and more structured learning experiences'. Students with special educational needs require programmes that emphasise direct teaching of facts, vocabulary, concepts and strategies (Mastrioperi and Scruggs, 2002). Educational reforms have not proved, so far, to be a panacea for learning difficulties.

Learning difficulties in mathematics

It is well recognised that many students find mathematics a difficult subject in school and may experience significant learning problems and frustration (Chinn and Ashcroft, 1998; Larcombe, 1985; Richards, 1982; Wain, 1994). If these problems arise early in the primary school years a student may fail to develop the essential basic skills and concepts necessary for further learning. Frequent failure is also likely to lead to feelings of poor self-efficacy, loss of confidence and motivation, and to a growing aversion to the subject.

It is suggested that approximately 6 per cent of students have severe difficulties in learning mathematical concepts and skills (Fleischner and Manheimer, 1997) but a much higher percentage of students are observed to be 'low achievers' in mathematics, displaying poor results, a negative attitude toward the subject, and having no confidence in their own ability to improve. Some children (and adults too) exhibit learned helplessness in situations where they are expected to demonstrate competence in applying mathematical skills (Battista, 1999). Early experiences of failure, whether through lack of sufficient informal learning in the preschool years, or lack of clear teaching in school, can quickly undermine the development of the firm foundation of concepts and skills needed for further growth. Butterworth (1999, p. 298) has observed:

> There are many reasons for being bad at any school subject. But school maths is like a house of cards: the cards in the bottom layer must be firmly and accurately constructed if they are to support the next layer up. Each stage depends on the last.

Many factors can cause or exacerbate problems in learning basic mathematics. Haskell (2000), for example, suggests that developmental delay, lack of experience, language difficulties, perceptual and motor problems, memory deficits, frequent absences from school, and 'math anxiety' can all contribute to poor learning. Some of these factors will be discussed in more detail in a moment. First, it is important to recognise that the type of instruction the child is receiving may be a significant contributory or causal factor in cases of learning difficulty.

Poor teaching generates poor learning

One of the main causes of learning difficulty in mathematics is poor quality (or insufficient) teaching, or teaching that does not accommodate students' individual needs and differences (Ginsberg, 1997; Reusser, 2000). Before attempting to diagnose the causes of learning difficulty within a student it is more important to diagnose the quality and type of teaching the child receives.

Various studies have revealed the following pedagogical factors to be associated with poor learning in mathematics (Baxter *et al.*, 2001; Harniss *et al.* 2002; Richards, 1982; Westwood, 2003):

- Insufficient total time devoted to teaching and learning.
- Inappropriate instructional methods.
- Demonstrations that are too brief or unclear.
- Insufficient guided practice.
- Too little corrective feedback.

- Unsuitable textbook, in terms of grading, examples, explanations and feedback.
- The teacher's use of language when explaining mathematical relationships or posing questions, does not match the students' levels of comprehension.
- The pace at which the curriculum is covered outstrips the students' ability to assimilate new concepts and skills.
- Abstract symbols introduced too early, in the absence of concrete materials or real-life examples.
- Concrete materials or visual aids removed too soon for some students; or used inappropriately, creating confusion.
- Large numbers involving complications of place-value introduced too soon.
- Students with reading difficulties condemned to a diet of 'pure arithmetic' rather than engaging in interesting problem solving and application.
- Computational tricks are taught, rather than developing number sense and understanding.
- Instead of being planned within a spiral framework, with key concepts and processes revisited at regular intervals, the mathematics programme is presented in a linear sequence, with only a few lessons devoted to each topic before moving on to the next.
- Infrequent reviews and revision.

Unfortunately, many of these weaknesses in teaching occur together in the same classroom and thus have a cumulative effect in exacerbating students' difficulties.

Much more must be done to improve the quality of teaching in order to reduce the prevalence of learning difficulties in mathematics. Traditionally, though, educators, researchers and psychologists have been much more interested in factors within the student, rather than within the teaching approach, to account for failure to learn in mathematics (for example, Fleischner, 1994; Troutman and Lichtenberg, 2003).

Affective components of learning difficulties in mathematics

It is important to consider the affective outcomes from learning failure in mathematics, since these factors exert a very strong influence on the student's future motivation and willingness to persevere in the face of difficulties. Chinn and Ashcroft (1998, p. 14) consider these factors to be 'classroom-acquired difficulties' that add to any inherent problems the learner may already have. Affective factors influence what Mather and Goldstein (2001, p. 7) refer to as the students' 'availability for learning'– are they still willing to make an effort, or have they given up trying? Learned helplessness and avoidance tactics are not uncommon among students who have difficulty in mastering basic mathematics (Houssart, 2002) and they usually attribute their failure to their own lack of ability. Tobias (1993, p. 69) has remarked:

When math-anxious people see that a problem is not going to be easy to solve, they tend to quit right away, believing that no amount of time or rereading or reformulation of the problem will make it any clearer. Freezing and quitting may be as much the result of destructive self-talk as of unfamiliarity with the problem.

The impact of persistent failure has a very damaging effect on a student's self-esteem, self-efficacy, confidence, motivation, and attitude. Much of this has been discussed in a general way already in previous chapters, and it is necessary here only to highlight one area where failure in mathematics appears to have an even more negative affective outcome than failure in other subjects, namely in the level of anxiety it arouses (Buxton, 1981; Henderson, 1998; Quilter and Harper, 1988; Zaslavsky, 1994). The aversion to mathematics created by constant failure and confusion reaches a state of a genuine 'phobia' for some students. They have high levels of anxiety when faced with examinations or assignments, and math anxiety itself can be 'disabling' (Tobias, 1993). Regardless of any other factor that is causing a student's difficulty, anxiety will have a blocking effect on concentration and learning. For example, anxiety can seriously impair a learner's attention to task and can disrupt the operation of working memory (Ashcraft *et al.*, 1998).

Negative affective outcomes from failure in mathematics can be identified in many students, but it is perhaps most apparent in students who have a specific learning disability. They share many of the same difficulties with other low-achievers but they also present a few unique problems (Chinn and Ashcroft, 1998).

Specific learning disability in mathematics: developmental dyscalculia

Dyscalculia is not synonymous with generally low achievement in mathematics. In the same way that the term 'dyslexia' has been applied wrongly by some teachers, parents and the popular press to refer to all types of reading difficulty, so too dyscalculia has been applied too readily to all types of difficulty in learning mathematics. Dyscalculia is a severe learning difficulty presumed to be of neurological origin (Ramaa and Gowramma, 2002; Rourke, 1993; Temple, 2001). Shalev and Gross-Tsur (2001, p. 337) define specific disability in basic mathematics in these terms:

> Developmental dyscalculia is a specific learning disability affecting the acquisition of arithmetic skills in an otherwise normal child. Although poor teaching, environmental deprivation, and low intelligence have been implicated in the etiology of developmental dyscalculia, current data indicate that this learning disability is a brain-based disorder with familial-genetic predisposition.

The *Diagnostic and Statistical Manual of Mental Disorders* (American Psychiatric Association, 2000) uses the term *mathematics disorder* to describe this disability and observes that:

> The essential feature of mathematics disorder is mathematical ability (as measured by individually administered standardized tests of mathematical calculation or reasoning) that falls substantially below that expected for the individual's chronological age, measured intelligence, and age-appropriate education. The disturbance in mathematics significantly interferes with academic achievement or with activities of daily living that require mathematical skills ... A number of different skills may be impaired in mathematics disorder, including *linguistic skills* (e.g. understanding or naming mathematical terms, operations, or concepts, and decoding written problems into mathematical symbols or arithmetic signs, and clustering objects into groups), *attention skills* (e.g. copying numbers or figures correctly, remembering to add in carried numbers, and observing operational signs), and *mathematical skills* (e.g. following sequences of mathematical steps, counting objects, and learning multiplication tables). (*DSM-4-TR, Section 315.1*: American Psychiatric Association, 2000)

The *ICD-10* (World Health Organization, 1992) uses the term 'specific disorder of arithmetic skills' and includes it under the general category of 'specific developmental disorders of scholastic skills' (p. 241). These disorders are considered to stem from 'abnormalities of cognitive processing that derive largely from some type of biological dysfunction' (p. 241). *ICD-10* suggests that the following characteristics are typical of these students:

- poor concept development;
- lack of understanding of mathematical terms and signs;
- confusion over printed symbols;
- poor procedural skills;
- inability to determine which process to use in solving problems;
- poor bookwork with misaligned columns and figures;
- weak multiplication skills.

Many students with severe reading problems also display difficulties in arithmetic and in mathematical problem solving; in fact Miles, Haslum and Wheeler (2001) suggest that all dyslexic students are weak at certain aspects of mathematics. Shalev and Gross-Tsur (2001) anticipate that the prevalence rate for dyscalculia is probably the same as for dyslexia. Some students are found with normal reading and writing skills but who have severe and unusual difficulties in mastering even the most basic of number processes. Grigorenko (2001) reviewed research indicating that perhaps less than 3 per cent of the school population falls in this category, but the *DSM-4* (APA, 2000) suggests 1 per cent – although very many more students find mathematics a difficult subject. Specific disability in mathematics is rarely identified until a child has been in school for more than a year, because he or she may show a delay in mathematical skills initially simply due to lack of pre-school experience. Often students are not referred for assessment until the fifth year of school.

In the same way that research into neuropsychological correlates of reading disability has grown exponentially in recent years, so too researchers have turned to exploration of brain localisation and function to help explain difficulties in learning mathematics (for example, Butterworth, 1999; Lyon, Fletcher and Barnes, 2003). While neuropsychological studies are at the cutting edge of the learning disability field, and have advanced our understanding of the areas of the brain involved in different types of problem solving activities and number operations, the results from such studies are not easy to translate into practices for teaching and intervention.

Specific areas of weakness

Contemporary views on what constitutes proficiency in mathematics suggest that students need to acquire five competencies (Kilpatrick *et al.*, 2001). In the case of students with learning difficulties in mathematics, all the competencies listed below tend to be poorly developed.

- *Conceptual understanding*: The ability to comprehend relations, operations and concepts.

- *Procedural fluency*: Skill, speed and accuracy in carrying out procedures.

- *Strategic competence*: The ability to devise appropriate plans for solving problems or recording experiences.

- *Adaptive reasoning*: Flexibility in thinking, and the capacity to view problems from different perspectives.

- *Productive disposition*: An inclination to enjoy mathematics and appreciate its relevance, together with a personal desire to master mathematical skills.

Students with dyscalculia share many of the same difficulties as other low achievers in mathematics. In particular they exhibit difficulties in recalling basic arithmetic facts from memory and in learning the meaning of specific terms and symbols. They display poor skills in calculation and major weaknesses in reasoning (Culatta, Tompkins and Werts, 2003; Shalev and Gross-Tsur, 2001). Often their bookwork is typified by untidy recording of algorithms, illegible writing of numerals, and evidence in the margins of inefficient strategies (such as tally marks and dot patterns) used for calculation. In addition to these difficulties, Henderson (1998) indicates they have difficulty in reading and understanding word problems; they may read numbers incorrectly and make errors in copying; they are weak in remembering tables, understanding place value, using a calculator correctly, understanding fractions and percentages, estimating, recalling and using formulae, and generalising new learning. While these difficulties are not unique to students with specific learning disability, the extent to which they are difficult to remedy is more apparent in the SpLD groups.

Lyon *et al.* (2003) indicate that the most obvious area of difficulty for students with a specific learning disability is accurate calculation. Various diagnostic error-analysis techniques have been devised to help teachers locate the points of confusion a student may have. For example, Räsänen and Ahonen (1995) developed the following classification system for errors in arithmetic:

- wrong operation; incorrect process selected (for example, + instead of ×);
- digit error; incorrect number written and used; or a number omitted;
- rule error; incorrect borrowing, carrying or exchanging;
- computational error; a slip, or omission when working through a procedure;
- fact error; incorrect recall of a number fact (especially in multiplication);
- algorithm error; incorrect recording of an operation or procedure;
- random errors; not able to be classified.

Of course, all students weak in arithmetic will tend to make errors within this range, but students with arithmetic disability are reported to be significantly worse than control-group in wrong operation, rule, computation and algorithm errors. They are also significantly slower than the controls in all processes (Räsänen and Ahonen, 1995).

Geary (1993) believes that three areas of cognitive skill are involved in calculations:

- The ability to represent, store and retrieve information from long-term memory. Poor skill in this area results in slow and often inaccurate recall of number facts.
- Procedural knowledge and executive functions. This involves correct selection and use of algorithms and strategies, self-monitoring and self-correction.
- Visuo-spatial skills. These are necessary for problems involving spatial relationships, accuracy of recording in bookwork, maintenance of place value, and geometry.

Some of the underlying weaknesses of dyscalculic students have been categorised by Rourke and Del Dotto (1994) under the following headings:

- *Spatial organisation problems*: poor alignment in columns of figures, reversals and transpositions of numbers.
- *Poor grapho-motor skills*: general untidiness in bookwork.
- *Poor visual attention to detail*: misreading numbers; omitting numerals, signs or decimal points.
- *Lack of flexibility in approach*: unable to change easily from one type of operation to another, or to abandon a faulty procedure.

- *Procedural weaknesses*: inaccurate or incorrect steps within algorithms.
- *Memory*: poor recall of number facts and formulae, weak mental arithmetic.

Troutman and Lichtenberg (2003) and Räsänen and Ahonen (1995) suggest that students with learning disabilities may have problems in visual and spatial abilities. Visual perceptual problems may cause difficulties in processing numbers (for example, keeping numerals in correct place-value position; working from right to left in an algorithm; difficulty in recognising number patterns) and in dealing with problems involving spatial relationships. Auditory perceptual difficulties can cause problems in hearing numbers accurately (for example, 16 heard as 60) and in processing oral instructions. Some students with auditory-linguistic problems may need longer to process verbal information. Some have problems dealing with simultaneous processing of visual and auditory input – as when the teacher is explaining while drawing or writing on the blackboard, and thus increasing cognitive load.

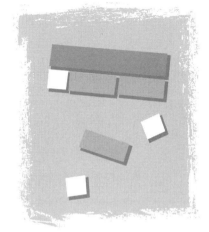

Several researchers have suggested that one of the main underlying weaknesses in students with SpLD is limited capacity in working memory – or an inefficient use of working memory (Cirino *et al.*, 2002; Haskell, 2000; Lyon *et al.*, 2003; McLean and Hitch, 1999). It is clear that working memory and sustained attention to task are very important prerequisites for efficient processing of information needed for mathematical calculation (Macaruso and Sokol, 1998). The learner has to store verbal instructions and information in auditory working memory while at the same time processing various steps within a problem-solving procedure. He or she also has to be able to retrieve relevant information quickly and efficiently when needed from long-term memory. Efficient recall of information and the recognition of numbers and signs have much in common with the 'rapid automatised naming' ability already referred to as a problem area under dyslexia. Räsänen and Ahonen (1995) have hypothesised that poor retrieval of arithmetic facts from memory, slow reading speed, and poor automatised naming may have a common cause, presumably at a neurological level.

An interesting theory has been formulated that links weaknesses in learning and recalling number facts with the same phonological problem that impairs reading and spelling (Robinson *et al.*, 2002). It is suggested that automaticity in recall of number facts is easy for most students because they encode and store the information as an auditory-verbal pattern ('six eights are forty-eight') through repetition and recitation in early school years. Students who have most difficulty in recalling number facts may be those who do not store such clear and powerful auditory-vocal images in long-term memory.

Subtypes within dyscalculia

Attempts have been made to identify subtypes of dyscalculia (Badian, 1983; DeLuca *et al.*, 1991; Geary, 1993; Kosc, 1974; Morrison and Siegel, 1991; Temple, 2001). Although Kosc (1974) identified six subtypes of dyscalculia, Lyon, Fletcher and Barnes (2003) suggest that two main groups exist: those children with significant difficulties in learning and retrieving number facts, and children

who have difficulty in learning and applying the procedures involved in calculating. Geary (1993) concurs on these two groupings, and also adds a third group (a visuo-spatial subtype) with problems in setting out bookwork, misreading or misrepresenting place values, and occasional reversal of numerals.

There is some suggestion that the learning problems of dyscalculic students may be due either to verbal weaknesses or to visuo-perceptual/visuo-spatial difficulties, each requiring quite different forms of intervention (Rourke and Del Dotto, 1994). But there is so much overlap in the patterns of difficulty experienced by learners in the various subgroups identified so far that it is unlikely that such information will be helpful for individualised programme planning. In the same way that searching for subtypes of reading disability has not led to any convincing evidence that teaching methods and materials can then be matched to subtype, so too there is no evidence that subtypes of dyscalculia, however identified, can be matched to particular instructional remedies.

Determining a student's instructional needs

The starting point for remedial intervention in basic mathematics needs to be a careful and sensitive assessment of the student's current knowledge, skills and strategies. It is essential that the teaching programme begin at the appropriate level of difficulty (Baker *et al.*, 2002). Just as interventions to improve reading require a text to match the student's current level of aptitude, so too in mathematics the curriculum content must also match the student's current level. Commencing at too high a level in concepts and skills causes immediate confusion and failure. Too low a level causes boredom and loss of motivation.

Four key questions provide a simple framework for carrying out pre-assessment in mathematics. Answers to these four questions may be obtained by formal or informal testing, by examining the student's exercise books, by direct observation of the student at work, and by discussion with the student (Westwood, 1999b).

1. What can the student already do without assistance?
2. What can the student do if given guidance and support?

3. What gaps exist in the student's previous learning?

4. What does the student need to learn next?

Diagnostic testing in mathematics may span a wide range of concepts and skills. Reference to the school syllabus or curriculum guidelines will provide some indication of the subject content covered so far by the student. The teacher can devise a series of graded problems and arithmetic examples, beginning at the simplest level and progressing to more challenging items. The inventory can then be used to sample and probe the student's existing abilities.

For young students, or those with severe learning problems, it is advisable to assess the student's understanding of everyday mathematics vocabulary, recognition of signs and symbols, ability to count objects, group objects, write numerals, and recall basic number facts. For all students it is valuable to have available concrete materials and aids (such as table squares, number line, calculator) to be used when necessary during the assessment. Silver and Hagin (2002, p. 242) state:

> For students with learning disabilities, verbal concepts usually need to be supported by direct experiences with practical examples, diagrams, manipulatives, models, and field trips. Without concrete, visual, experiential backup, the verbal problem-solving approaches may leave these students lost and confused.

Shapiro and Elliott (1999) recommend that computational skills form an important part of any assessment because these skills are fundamental to success in all problem-solving and application work. Although contemporary approaches to mathematics education are tending to de-emphasise computation, it still represents a major area of weakness for SpLD and other low achieving students. If the student appears to have difficulty with computational skills, it may be helpful to devise a diagnostic number test based on a task-analytic or learning hierarchy approach (see Chapter 1) beginning at the simplest level and moving gradually to more complex items. For example, in the domain of multiplication, the items begin with 'units multiplied by units' (6×4; 7×3) (numbers less than ten). The questions would then move to 'tens and units multiplied by units' with no carrying (23×3), and then with carrying (38×4), etc. The most difficult items would involve multiplication of 'thousands, hundreds, tens and units', and so forth. Such diagnostic number tests are available in published form but it is relatively easy for a teacher to design a suitable substitute.

In an ideal situation the teacher will observe the student completing each item in the test in order to determine the knowledge and skills already firmly established, and to detect the point at which errors begin to occur. A dynamic approach to assessment would enable the teacher to instruct the student on any point of error, and then test again to see if the student has understood and benefited from the feedback.

The most valuable information to help identify a student's specific needs is the *diagnostic interview*. The student is asked to bring to the session any mathematics exercise or any test paper he or she has found troublesome. By working through some of the items together it is usually possible to observe not only the points at which the student encounters difficulty, but also the general pace and style the student uses when working in this area of mathematics. By direct questioning and asking the student to explain or demonstrate (think aloud) how he or she obtained a particular answer or performed a particular process, the teacher can identify the exact point of confusion and thus focus the corrective intervention very precisely. Informal assessment of this type also reveals to what extent the student self-monitors and self-corrects while working, and the extent to which he or she is dependent on the instructor. Informal assessment sessions, if conducted in a warm and supportive context, help to establish rapport and a working relationship with the student.

As well as assessing knowledge, skills and strategies, it is equally important to assess the student's feelings about his or her learning problem, and the student's attitude toward mathematics. A large part of effective tutoring for students with chronic difficulties in mathematics is to help them come to terms with the situation, alleviate anxiety, and to try to restore lost confidence and motivation (Henderson, 1998).

Additional advice on assessment will be found in Westwood (2000; 2003).

Intervention: general principles and strategies

If students have a severe problem in learning mathematics, it is necessary to arrange for one-to-one tutoring. This is known to produce better results than group tuition (Chinn and Ashcroft, 1998; Xin and Jitendra, 1999). The sessions need to be conducted on a daily basis if possible, to ensure sufficient intensity and frequency of assistance. Tuition sessions should continue to be provided for as long as is necessary — often throughout the whole school year.

Techniques such as *precision teaching* (Lindsley, 1992b) are particularly helpful in mathematics intervention programmes. In precision teaching, a student's progress is measured and charted each day to give visual evidence of gains and improvements. This regular assessment also enables the teacher to monitor the effectiveness of the programme and to make changes where necessary. Precision teaching usually ensures that the available tuition time is used to optimum effect, and that students practise basic computational skills to a high degree of automaticity. Practice is believed to result in long-lasting structural changes in the brain because repeated practice at a skill increases the number of neurons the brain assigns to that skill on a more or less permanent basis (Butterworth, 1999).

Early in the chapter some of the weaknesses in poor quality teaching were described. Here a more positive perspective is taken to indicate features of *good teaching* to help students overcome learning difficulties in mathematics and to improve their attitude toward the subject (see also Baker *et al.*, 2002; Fleischner and Manheimer, 1997; Fuchs and Fuchs, 2001; Gucker, 1999; Gersten *et al.*, 2001; Kroesbergen and van Luit, 2003).

Mastriopieri and Scruggs (2002, p. 162) state:

> It is critical for special educators to use teacher effectiveness variables in the delivery of mathematics instruction and, in addition, to examine the type of learned behaviour expected (identification, production, and application), the level of learning (acquisition and fluency), and the type of learning (discriminations, facts, rules, procedures and concepts) to design an optimal set of instructional strategies.

Effective intervention may involve:

- Using a task-analytic approach in teaching, with all new areas of learning broken down into teachable steps.

- Simplifying and restating instructions.

- Asking many questions at the right level of complexity to ensure a high success rate and to build confidence.

- Checking for understanding at every step in the lesson.

- Providing more frequent reviews and revisions of work.

- Setting students more 'practice' type assignments for homework.

- Strongly encouraging students to help one another. Peer assistance is a readily available and powerful resource.

- Making much greater use of concrete materials and visual representation (objects, pictures, sketches, diagrams) to support verbal explanations.

- Selecting or making alternative curriculum resource materials, including the use of different textbooks.

- Utilising appropriate computer programs for drill and practice, and for problem solving.

- Making greater use of the students themselves to work examples on the blackboard or to create new problems for the class to attempt.

- Encouraging the use of a calculator if a student's problem is mainly lack of speed and automaticity in calculations.

- Ensuring that the vocabulary associated with each new topic and within particular word problems is thoroughly taught and understood.

- Close monitoring of the work being done by each student during the lesson.

- Providing more (or less) direct assistance to individual students.

- Looking for students who are working too slowly. Are they confused? Are they unwilling to ask for help? Do they need to be actively encouraged or directly engaged with you to get back on task?

- For in-class support, making regular and appropriate use of group work, enabling students of different abilities and aptitudes to collaborate and to discuss the lesson material.

- Whenever possible, the adaptations made in the teaching of mathematics should aim to help the student understand and succeed with the regular programme, rather than replace it with a different programme.

Chinn and Ashcroft (1998) make the important point that with students whose problems stem from a genuine learning disability in mathematics, it is important to decide whether a particular skill or item of information is so important that it must be memorised, or whether there are ways to bypass the problem. An example would be to teach the student effective use of a calculator instead of spending many hours trying unsuccessfully to rote-learn the multiplication facts.

Two other components are necessary for effective intervention. The first is strategy training. As we have seen already, strategy training means teaching a student appropriate mental plans of action to use independently when approaching mathematical problems and calculations (Alexander and Murphy, 1999; Owen and Fuchs, 2002). This usually involves the teacher in demonstrating highly effective step-by-step, self-regulatory procedures for approaching any new task. Often an important aspect of such strategy training is teaching the student to use 'self-talk' to regulate his or her responses. For example, 'First I do this (look for the smallest number). Then I check. Good. Now I do this (multiply the two numbers). Check again ... etc.' Students then practise the application of similar task-approach strategies for themselves until they become proficient in their application. Greene (1999) has recommended teaching students to use mnemonic devices to help them recall facts or formulae. RAVE CCC represents one of many problem-solving strategies that could be used in mathematics (Westwood, 2003):

R = Read the word problem carefully.

A = Attend to any words that may indicate the process required.

V = Visualise what the problem would look like.

E = Estimate the possible answer.

C = Choose the appropriate numbers and processes.

C = Calculate carefully.

C = Check the result against your estimate.

The value of strategy training has been strongly supported by research and represents a fairly powerful way to improve learning and to overcome learning difficulties (for example, Forness *et al.*, 1997; Meltzer and Montague, 2001; Swanson, 1999, 2000a). Xin and Jitendra (1999, p. 218) have remarked, 'Results of meta-analysis indicated that word-problem solving instruction improved the performance of students with learning problems and promoted the maintenance and generalization of the skill.'

The second component of effective intervention is helping students stay on task and use the available lesson time most productively. In many ways this is another form of cognitive strategy training, but this time the strategy focuses on general *self-monitoring* (Culatta *et al.*, 2003; Mather and Goldstein, 2001). Students who have a history of failure often spend much time off task in the regular classroom, either because the work is too difficult and boring or because they have lost any positive work habits they once possessed. In order to help students remain engaged in the mathematics lesson, it is essential first to provide work that is intrinsically interesting and geared to the student's level of success. Once a student is interested and feeling successful, he or she is almost always able to keep on task for more of the time (Vaughn *et al.*, 2000). For some students with problems of attention it may be necessary to use *cognitive behaviour modification* (CBM) (Kaplan, 1998) to teach them to use self-talk to keep on task. For example, 'I must work for five minutes. After five minutes I must put a tick on my chart. If I need help I must put my hand up immediately to get the teacher's attention. Am I working well? Is this looking good?'

Finally, it is important to help students with learning difficulties develop positive attitudes toward the subject. Some years ago Berrill (1982) highlighted the importance of setting improved attitude as one of the priority goals for intervention. Berrill (1982, p. 111) wrote:

> Mathematics should be seen as a subject to be liked and enjoyed, not as one to be hated or tolerated. Since slow learners tend to require immediate gratification, continuous feedback and encouragement is likely to help to create positive attitudes.

Further reading

Baroody, A.J. and Dowker, A. (2003) *The Development of Arithmetic Concepts and Skills*. Mahwah, NJ: Erlbaum. [See particularly Chapter 13, 'Mathematical thinking and learning difficulties'.]

Bley, N. and Thornton, C.A. (2001) *Teaching Mathematics to Students with Learning Disabilities* (4th edn). Austin, TX: ProEd.

Chinn, S.J. and Ashcroft, J.R. (1998) *Mathematics for Dyslexics: A Teaching Handbook* (2nd edn). London: Whurr.

Henderson, A. (1998) *Maths for the Dyslexic: A Practical Guide*. London: Fulton.

Kroesbergen, E.H. and van Luit, J.E.H. (2003) Mathematics interventions for children with special educational needs. *Remedial and Special Education*, *24*, 2, 97–114.

Mastropieri, M.A. and Scruggs, T.E. (2002) *Effective Instruction for Special Education* (3rd edn). Austin, TX: ProEd.

Meltzer, L. and Montague, M. (2001) Strategic learning in students with learning disabilities: What have we learned? In D.P. Hallahan and B.K. Keogh (eds) *Research and Global Perspectives in Learning Disabilities* (pp. 111–130). Mahwah, NJ: Erlbaum.

Miles, T.R. and Miles, E. (1992) *Dyslexia and Mathematics*. London: Routledge.

Minskoff, E. and Allsopp, D. (2003) *Academic Success Strategies for Adolescents with Learning Disabilities and ADHD*. Baltimore, MD: Brookes.

Reys, R.E., Lindquist, M.M., Lambdin, D.V., Smith, N.L. and Suydam, M.N. (2004) *Helping Children Learn Mathematics* (7th edn). Hoboken, NJ: Wiley.

Temple, C. (1997) *Developmental Cognitive Neuropsychology*. Hove: Psychology Press. [See Chapter 7, 'Arithmetic disorders'.]

Troutman, A.P. and Lichtenberg, B.K. (2003) *Mathematics: A Good Beginning* (6th edn). Belmont, CA: Wadsworth-Thomson.

9 Intellectual disability

> Descriptions of the intellectual functioning and adaptive behaviour of individuals with mental retardation focus on limitations and deficits [but] many children and adults with mental retardation display tenacity in learning, get along well with others, and are positive influences on those around them. (Heward, 2003a, p. 209)

In this final chapter, attention is given to those students who have an impaired ability to learn due to intellectual disability. The quotation above from Heward (2003a) reminds us that it is all too easy to discuss intellectual disability in pessimistic terms, creating a false impression that individuals with impaired cognitive ability can learn very little. While attention will be given here to the learning and adjustment problems experienced by persons with intellectual disability, the overriding message is also that their learning and behaviour can be enhanced significantly. In the 1960s research had begun to show that children with moderate to severe forms of intellectual disability were still capable of substantial learning, particularly when behavioural teaching approaches were used intensively and with precision (Detterman *et al.*, 2000; Dever and Knapczyk, 1997; Ramey and Ramey, 2000). Children with mild intellectual disability can achieve much more, and many are fully integrated into inclusive mainstream classes in most developed countries.

Many years ago Segal (1974) stated that 'no child is ineducable' and in the twenty-first century that belief underpins work with even the most severely disabled students. As Sousa (2001b) indicates, we should look for strengths and abilities, not simply focus on potential limitations imposed by a disability.

Description and definition

Beirne-Smith, Ittenbach and Patton (2002, p. 40) describe mental retardation in the following terms:

> Mental retardation is one type of developmental disability and generally refers to substantial limitations in present levels of functioning. These limitations are manifest in delayed intellectual growth, inappropriate or immature reactions to one's environment, and below-average performance in the academic, psychological, physical, linguistic, and social domains. Such limitations create challenges for individuals to cope with the demands they

encounter each day, those that other people of comparable age and social or cultural background would be expected to deal with successfully on an ongoing basis.

One of several recent definitions of mental retardation states in more detail that:

> Mental retardation refers to substantial limitations in present functioning. It is characterized by significantly subaverage intellectual functioning, existing concurrently with related limitations in two or more of the following applicable adaptive skill areas: communication, self-care, home living, social skills, community use, self-direction, health and safety, functional academics, leisure and work. Mental retardation manifests itself before age 18 years. (American Association on Mental Retardation, 1992; cited in Ysseldyke, Algorzzine & Thurlow, 2000, p. 100)

It is estimated that approximately 2 per cent of the population has some degree of intellectual disability, although there is disagreement on the precise figure and there are differences in prevalence rates across countries. The disability varies in severity and in the characteristics each individual displays (Hodapp and Dykens, 2003). The four degrees of severity are described as mild, moderate, severe, and profound (although in some systems the category 'severe' includes individuals with profound and multiple impairments). Each level of impairment is related to specific IQ ranges, with the mild category beginning below IQ 70. However, the current trend is to pay much less attention to measured IQ and much more attention to an individual's existing skills, the amount of support he or she needs to function adequately, and necessary curricular adaptations (Dockrell and McShane, 1992; Nielsen, 1997; Turnbull *et al.*, 2002).

Mild intellectual disability

Most intellectual disability (90 per cent) falls within the mild category (IQ 70–55) (Drew and Hardman, 2000). Children with mild intellectual disability tend to develop motor, language and social skills at a slower rate than children without disabilities, but their difference often goes unnoticed until they enter school. In many ways these children are not very different from those sometimes described as slow learners or low achievers, although they display more significant learning difficulties. Usually their physical appearance is perfectly normal. In most cases the exact cause of mild intellectual disability is unknown. Students with mild intellectual disability are said to come most frequently (but not exclusively) from lower socio-economic backgrounds, suggesting possible cultural-familial and environmental influences contributing to their developmental delay (Taylor *et al.*, 1995). It is unusual in cases of mild disability to find any organic cause, although a few individuals may be diagnosed with possible fetal alcohol syndrome (FAS). FAS can occur when a mother has consumed excessive amounts of alcohol over the period of pregnancy, causing abnormalities in the developing child.

Students with mild disability can usually acquire basic literacy and numeracy skills but remain significantly below average in attainment – for example, by late adolescence mildly intellectually disabled students may still be operating at a grade six level or below (Santrock, 2001). Many mildly disabled students are successfully accommodated in inclusive classrooms, particularly during the primary school years.

Moderate intellectual disability

There is no clear division between mild and moderate intellectual disability in terms of learning characteristics; students in both categories overlap to some extent in their strengths and weaknesses. Non-cognitive factors such as temperament, personality, motivation, and sensory capabilities also influence learning and development and contribute to differences among individuals (Sue *et al.*, 2000). However, students with moderate intellectual disability (IQ between 40 and 55) do have more learning and adjustment problems than those with mild disability. In particular, they tend to have more attentional and memory problems together with language difficulties or disorders. Some may have challenging behaviours and they frequently have problems developing social skills. Moderately retarded individuals also exhibit more significant deficits in adaptive behaviour (that is, the capacity to perform activities required for personal and social self-sufficiency and to exercise self-management). It is more likely that the cause of moderate intellectual disability is primarily organic rather than environmental. Many students with Down's syndrome or Fragile-X syndrome, for example, will function at this level of retardation, as will some students with brain damage.

Often moderate intellectual disability is recognised during the preschool years. A significant amount of support for learning will be required by these children throughout their school life and often beyond (Hodapp and Dykens, 2003). Ongoing behaviour management is also often required. Students with moderate intellectual disability are proving more difficult to maintain in inclusive classrooms.

Severe intellectual disability

Severe retardation (IQ 40–25) and profound retardation (IQ below 25) result in major problems with learning and self-sufficiency. In addition to intellectual impairment these students frequently have additional handicaps in vision, hearing, mobility and communication (Beirne-Smith *et al.*, 2002). Chronic health problems and conditions such as epilepsy are also common. The more severe the disability, the fewer self-care skills the individual is able to develop without direct teaching; and individuals with severe, profound and multiple disabilities have high support needs throughout their lives. Intensive training, using mainly behavioural principles, is required to help them develop self-help skills such as eating, washing, toileting, dressing and mobility (Mash and Wolfe, 1999). In addition, approaches that help stimulate their sensory awareness (for example, *Snoezelen*; Hutchinson and Kewin, 1994) or will build upon their naturally occurring reflexes and responses (for example, *Interactive Process Approach* or *Intensive Interaction Approach*; Nind, 2000; Kellett and Nind, 2003) are showing some definite benefits. A balanced programme for students with severe retardation and multiple handicaps needs to combine behavioural and socio-cognitive teaching methods.

Individuals with moderate to severe intellectual disability lack the capacity to reflect upon and control their own behaviour. As a consequence, they may exhibit challenging behaviours including temper tantrums, aggression, self-injury, self-stimulation, and ritualistic obsessive-compulsive responses. These behaviours can be very difficult to eliminate and usually require behaviour modification and possibly pharmacological intervention (Gupta, 1999). In many cases it is the negative behaviours, or the need for constant care and monitoring, that make full-time inclusion for most of these students an unrealistic goal.

Autism

A few students with intellectual disability may also exhibit symptoms of autism. Autism is one of several pervasive developmental disorders characterised by severe impairment of communication and social interaction (Klinger *et al.*, 2003; Wong and Westwood, 2002). The condition is not easy to diagnose and has a wide variety of symptoms ranging from mild to severe. Current thinking on the nature of autism views individuals as being placed somewhere on a continuum of symptomatic autistic behaviours, implying that there is no clearly defined single syndrome of autism (Wing, 1996). The term *autistic spectrum disorders* has become popular.

Some individuals with milder forms of autism (for example, Asperger's syndrome) function at a normal or above normal cognitive level and can learn successfully in mainstream classrooms. They may have difficulty in making and retaining friendships due to their quirky behaviours, but they can cope reasonably well academically. More severe forms of autism are almost always accompanied by intellectual disability. Sue *et al.* (2000, p. 480) describe typical autistic children with Kanner's syndrome ('classic autism') in these terms:

> Children with autism often sit for hours, engaging mostly in unusual repetitive habits such as spinning objects, flapping arms, or just staring at their hands. Many exhibit self-injurious behaviours.

Children with autism and accompanying intellectual disability are among the most difficult to integrate and maintain in regular classrooms. Intensive behavioural approaches for teaching and management have proved to be the most effective in helping these students learn and develop social behaviours (Green, 1996; Wong and Westwood, 2002).

Causes of intellectual disability

Causes of intellectual disability are many and varied, including *genetic factors* (for example, chromosomal abnormality resulting in Down's syndrome or Fragile X syndrome), *prenatal factors* such as malnutrition, maternal substance abuse during pregnancy, maternal rubella, prematurity, radiation, toxicity, Rh incompatibility; *perinatal* or *postnatal* factors, such as difficult birth, brain injury; and *environmental factors* including lack of stimulation, malnutrition. In the majority of individual cases it is impossible to determine a definite cause of the disability.

Most introductory texts on intellectual disability discuss causal factors in great detail (for example, Batshaw and Shapiro, 1997; Hallahan and Kauffman, 2003; Taylor *et al.*, 1995) and it is not necessary to discuss the issue in detail here. Causes of an intellectual disability rarely have any direct implications for teaching and management decisions. Educational programming is based instead on an analysis of a student's existing skills and deficits.

Cognition

Hardman, Drew and Egan (2002) state that intelligence is the ability to acquire, remember and use knowledge (see also Chapter 3). Individuals with intellectual disability exhibit a much slower rate of acquiring, remembering and applying knowledge. The most obvious characteristic of these students is that they have significant difficulty in learning almost everything that other children can learn with ease. Intellectual disability presents itself as an inability to think as quickly, reason as deeply, remember as easily, or adapt as rapidly to new situations, when compared with so-called normal children. For students with intellectual disability, interpreting information, reasoning, and problem solving are very difficult processes.

Children with intellectual disability usually appear to be much less mature than their age peers, exhibiting general behaviours typical of much younger children. Their behaviour patterns, skills and general knowledge are related more closely to their mental age than to their chronological age. Children who are developmentally delayed are naturally slower at acquiring cognitive skills. In most aspects of concept development and reasoning children with mild to moderate intellectual disability tend to be functioning at what Piaget referred to as the 'concrete operational' level. They understand and remember only those things and situations that they can directly experience; so teaching for them has to be entirely meaningful and reality-based. Students with severe disability may be operating at even lower levels, the early Piagetian stage of 'sensori-motor' or the 'pre-operational' stage of cognitive development.

It is generally accepted that children with intellectual disability pass through the same sequence of stages in cognitive development as other children — from sensori-motor, through pre-operational to concrete operational, and finally (for a few) formal operational reasoning — but at a much slower rate (Dockrell and McShane, 1992). It is also clear that some intellectually disabled individuals reach a developmental ceiling and never progress beyond the concrete level of thinking and reasoning. It is not known why this occurs, but it is possible that organic factors such as brain damage or dysfunction may change the neural and cognitive architecture of the brain, making it more difficult for information to be encoded and for schemata to be developed and accessed easily (Sousa, 2001b). For example, on the issue of formation of schemata, Kirk, Gallagher and Anastasiow (2000) indicate that students with intellectual impairment have much greater difficulty in linking separate ideas and concepts together and recognising common themes and relationships. One of the ongoing debates concerning intellectual disability relates to the issue of whether the learning problems are due to *delay* in development or to the presence of *specific defects* or impairments (Hodapp and Zigler, 1999). Deficits related to defects might include problems with attentional processes, perception, working memory, or longer-term information storage and retrieval. Anderson (2001) hypothesises, for example, that in the case of organic brain damage the biological underpinnings needed for fast and effective information processing have been compromised, resulting in a much slower speed of processing.

It is often said that students with moderate intellectual disability do not have the capacity to engage in higher-order thinking and problem solving, or to access the mainstream curriculum with understanding. However, there have been attempts to improve the problem-solving strategies of these students (for example, Agran and Wehmeyer, 1999) and to introduce them to school subjects normally covered in the regular classroom, albeit at a greatly simplified level (for example, Marvin and Stokoe, 2003; Turner, 2002). This issue has become increasingly important with the growing trend toward integration and inclusion, since the ability of these students to benefit from placement in regular classes depends in large part upon their ability to access a differentiated version the curriculum. When adapting mainstream curriculum for students with intellectual disability, or making special school curricula more like regular school curricula, it is essential to ensure the content is still relevant and meaningful to the students – otherwise the whole process becomes mere tokenism (Westwood, 2001).

Attention

In Chapter 4 the vital role of attention in learning and in failing to learn was discussed. Individuals with intellectual disability appear often to have problems in attending to the relevant aspects of a learning situation (Detterman *et al.*, 2000; Taylor *et al.*, 1995). For example, when a teacher is showing a student how to use scissors to cut paper, the student is attracted perhaps to the ring on the teacher's finger or to a picture on the paper rather than the task itself. Taylor, Sternberg and Richards (1995) reviewed research that suggests this problem may also relate to the tendency of intellectually disabled students to be 'person-oriented' rather than task-oriented.

Without adequate selective attention to task any student will fail to learn or remember what the teacher is trying to teach. The tendency to focus on irrelevant detail, or to be distracted easily from a task, is potentially a major problem for children with intellectual disability when integrated into mainstream programmes without close supervision. Hunt and Marshall (2002) discuss the importance of all teachers using strategies that will catch and maintain students' attention. Similarly, Snell and Brown (2000) emphasise the rigorous use of attentional cues when working with severely disabled students. Metacognitive training and self-monitoring may help improve a student's personal control over selective attention (Mash and Wolfe, 1999) but this improvement in mental 'executive function' is feasible mainly with mildly disabled learners rather than those with moderate and severe disability.

It is suggested that what a learner already knows (prior knowledge and experience) may have an effect on attention to new information (Dockrell and McShane, 1992). If you are already familiar with most aspects of a stimulus or task you may know immediately which salient features to attend to. Students with intellectual disability may have very limited experience and prior understanding relevant to a classroom task and therefore their attention is random rather than selective. Heward (2003a) suggests that a student's selective and sustained attention to task will improve as he or she experiences greater success in performing the task. To this extent, success and failure also influence future attending behaviours.

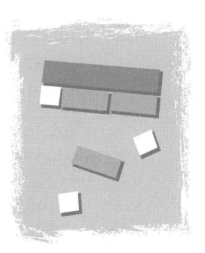

It must be noted that attention deficit hyperactivity disorder (ADHD) is often found as a secondary disability in children with intellectual disability. The problems associated with ADHD were described in Chapter 4.

Memory

Many students with intellectual disability also have difficulty in storing and retrieving information in long-term memory – indeed, poor memory is one of the main deficits identified in individuals with retardation (Nielsen, 1997; Taylor *et al.*, 1995). There is reported evidence of significant weaknesses also in manipulating information in working memory and in processing more than very small amounts of information at one time (Heward, 2003a). These problems with recall and working memory may, in part, be linked with the failure to attend adequately to the learning task or stimulus, as discussed above, but they may also be due to inefficient encoding of information or to anomalies in brain chemistry. Dockrell and McShane (1992, p. 162) state:

> If there are any deficiencies in either the capacity of working memory or in the processes used to manipulate information in working memory, then this is likely to have general effects on cognitive performance. The memory system and memory processes have also been widely studied in relation to general learning difficulties. Of particular importance here is the role that executive processes may play in deploying lower-level memory strategies.

It is also observed that individuals with intellectual disability rarely use any basic strategies to aid memorisation and recall (Ormrod, 2003). Difficulty in storing information in long-term memory suggests that the lower the intellectual ability of the student, the greater the amount of repetition and practice necessary to ensure retention; so the message for the teacher is to provide even more opportunities for guided and independent practice in every area of the curriculum. Very frequent revision and overlearning need to be key features of any teaching programme for students with intellectual disability.

Generalisation

Individuals with intellectual disability have enormous difficulty in generalising learning from one setting to another (Hunt and Marshall, 2002; Meese 2001). For any learner, the most difficult final stage of learning is that of generalisation. In order to master information, skills and strategies to an automatic level a stage must be reached when a student can apply that learning to new situations not directly linked with the context in which it was first taught. Hardman *et al.* (2002) indicate that intelligent behaviour is associated with the ability to apply what is learned to new experiences.

It is generally recommended that teachers consider ways of facilitating generalisation when planning lessons for students with intellectual disability by, for example, re-teaching the same skills or strategies in different contexts, gradually increasing the range of contexts, challenging students to decide whether a skill or strategy could be used to solve a new problem or could be applied to a new situation, and reinforcing any evidence of student's spontaneous generalisation of previous learning. In other words, teachers should anticipate difficulties in transfer and generalisation of learning and should not be surprised when they occur.

Motivation

Many students with intellectual disability are willing to engage in tasks and activities set by the teacher because they enjoy them, or they want to please the teacher, or they simply want to be kept busy (Dever and Knapczyk, 1997). In other cases, because natural intrinsic motivation and confidence may be lacking in relation to school learning, greater use has to be made of positive reinforcement and extrinsic rewarding for effort. As stated previously, behavioural principles appear to have much to offer in the teaching and management of students with intellectual disability (Ashman, 1998).

Students with mild to moderate intellectual disability may have normal motivation to learn in the early years, but once in school their daily experience of difficulty makes them more susceptible to frustration and learned helplessness. Mash and Wolfe (1999, p. 351) report:

> … compared with typically developing children of the same mental age, children with mental retardation expect little success, set low goals for themselves, and settle for minimal success when they could do better. This learned helplessness may be unwittingly condoned by adults [who] are less likely to urge the child to persist following failure than they would for a normal child of the same level of cognitive development.

What Mash and Wolfe are describing really relates to the situation where caregivers and teachers lower their expectations and provide so much help that the learner becomes dependent on such support or on simplification of tasks.

Learned helplessness and a markedly external locus of control can arise from such situations and both states are detrimental to positive motivation for learning. Knight (1992; 1994) has observed such externality in students with intellectual disability but on a positive note reports that, through appropriate teaching and feedback, locus of control is modifiable toward greater internality in this population of students.

There is reported to be an increased potential for emotional problems (for example, depression) and some degree of psychopathology to develop within the population of adolescent and adult persons with intellectual disability. This tendency is due in part to accumulating past failure experiences, negative self-evaluation, peer rejection, ostracism, exploitation and abuse (Mash and Wolfe, 1999; Volkmar and Dykens, 2002). Teachers, particularly in senior special schools, need to monitor students for signs of emotional and behavioural disorders. Specialist advice and services may be needed.

Language delay or disorder

Language is important for cognitive development and learning – without it an individual lacks one efficient encoding system for storing certain types of information that are needed for thinking, reasoning and concept development. Components of mental schemata are more effectively stored and retrieved from memory if they have a representation in words as well as in sensations and perceptions. Language is also the main medium through which school learning is facilitated. Language is also important for social development, and language enables an individual to make his or her needs, opinions and ideas known to others. Positive social interactions with other persons are heavily dependent upon effective communication skills; and language is important for regulating one's own behaviour and responses (self-talk).

One of the main characteristics of children with moderate intellectual disability is the very slow rate at which many of them acquire speech and language. Even the child with mild retardation is likely to be behind the normal milestones for language development. Some individuals with severe and multiple disabilities never develop speech — and for them an alternative or augmented method of communication must be developed (for example, sign language, picture or symbol communication systems) (Dowling, 2002; von Tetzchner and Grove, 2003).

The development of speaking and listening skills in students with intellectual disability is given high priority in special school curricula, and language stimulation will continue to be of vital importance for these students in mainstream settings. While language is best acquired naturally — through using it to express needs, obtain information, and interact socially — for some disabled students a more direct instructional approach may also be necessary (Beirne-Smith *et al.*, 2002). Where possible, naturally occurring opportunities within the school day and at home are used to teach and reinforce new vocabulary and language patterns. This 'milieu approach' is found to be more productive in terms of generalisation and transfer of learning to everyday use than are the more clinical approaches to teaching language in isolation (Kaiser, 2000). Two obvious benefits of placing a child with intellectual disability in a mainstream class are immersion in a naturally enriched language environment, and the increased need for the student to communicate with others.

Some students with intellectual disability require the services of a speech therapist but improvement in speech, voice and articulation can be very slow indeed with the intellectually disabled population. This is because the individuals receiving the therapy may not appreciate the need for it and may therefore have no motivation to practise what is taught. There is also the usual problem of lack of generalisation – what is taught in a clinical 'decontextualised' setting does not transfer to the person's everyday speech.

Social development

The presence or absence of social skills in students with intellectual disability tends to be related to the extent to which they have had an opportunity to socialise in the home and other environments. Within the family, the social interactions between a child with intellectual disability and others are likely to be mainly positive, but the same assumption cannot be made for contacts within the community and at school. Although community attitudes toward people with disabilities are changing, there is still a likelihood that the child with intellectual disability will have experienced difficulty in making friends and gaining acceptance –particularly if he or she has some irritating or challenging behaviours (Snell and Brown 2000). Nielsen (1997, p. 71) observes:

> Most children who are mentally retarded exhibit the social behaviour of a younger child and prefer playing with younger children. Their emotions are usually inappropriate for a particular situation and generally expressed in a childlike manner ... their less-developed social skills may lead to rejection by others and a lowering of self-esteem.

Taylor *et al.* (1995) report studies indicating that some students with intellectual disability are rejected by their peers more on the basis of their irritating behaviour than because they are disabled. For example, the occasional presence of inappropriate responses such as screaming, shouting, aggression, or temper tantrums makes it difficult for a few of these children to be socially accepted. Positive intervention is needed to eliminate the negative behaviours and replace them with pro-social behaviours. If the student with a disability is to make friends and be accepted in the peer group, social skills training must be given a high priority in the programme. Unfortunately, research studies have suggested that, although many social skills training programmes do exist, it is far from easy to teach these social behaviours to students with intellectual disability or to those students with emotional and behavioural disorders (Bullis *et al.*, 2001).

Teaching approaches for students with intellectual disability

Discussion here will focus mainly on teaching principles for students with mild to moderate disability. Some of these same principles apply also for students with severe and multiple impairments, but with lower-functioning students the emphasis is more on the highly structured teaching of self-care, communication, and perceptual-motor skills using direct methods and task analysis. As stated previously, structured teaching is combined with a high degree of personal care and sensory stimulation. Alternative methods of communication may also need to be taught. For additional practical advice on working with severely and profoundly handicapped students, see Snell and Brown (2000), Ryndak and Alper (2003), or Hamill and Everington (2002).

Usually, students with intellectual disability require an individual education plan (IEP) setting out specific goals to meet the student's needs and taking into account his or her current skills and stage of development (Ashman, 1998). The main priority in teaching students with intellectual disability is to make the curriculum reality-based (Hallahan and Kauffman, 2003). It has been mentioned already that for both general cognitive development and for the acquisition of skills these children need to experience things at first hand and to have others help them interpret these experiences (mediated learning). Children with mild to moderate intellectual disability are usually at the concrete operational stage in terms of cognitive development, so the age-old principle of 'learning by doing' certainly applies in their case. For example, if they are to learn important number skills they should learn them not only from books, computer games and other instructional materials but also from real situations such as shopping, stocktaking, measuring, estimating, counting, grouping, recording data and comparing quantities. Reading skills should be developed and practised using real books, real instruction cards, real recipes, real brochures and real comic books, as well as through graded readers, games and flashcards. As far as possible the '4 R Test' should be applied when selecting curriculum content – is the content *real*, *relevant*, *realistic* and *rational*? (Brennan 1985).

In addition to reality-based learning, children with intellectual disability also need some high quality direct teaching of knowledge and skills. Direct instruction is based to a large extent on behavioural views of learning (applied behaviour analysis, see Chapter 2).

• A relevant learning goal is set.

• The teacher models correct responses or skills.

• Students imitate the responses or skills.

• Students' responses are rewarded and shaped.

• Guided and independent practice leads to mastery and automaticity.

The approach is very teacher-directed, with the content to be taught broken down into very simple steps to ensure high success rates. It has been found that direct instruction using these principles is extremely effective for students with disabilities, particularly for teaching basic skills and functional academics (Turnbull *et al.*, 2002).

Lessons that employ direct instructional methods aim to use a fast pace of teaching with as many successful responses from the students as possible in the time available. There is heavy emphasis on practice but lessons are made enjoyable and entertaining. Direct instruction is among the most frequently researched teaching methods and has consistently proved that it is more effective for some types of learning than are the student-centred, independent learning approaches (for example, Forness *et al.*, 1997; Heward, 2003b; Swanson, 2000a).

Other basic principles to consider when working with students with intellectual disability include the following:

• Provide plentiful cues and prompts to enable the learner to manage each step in a task.

• Make all possible use of co-operative group work, and teach the child the necessary group-working skills.

- Frequently assess the learning that has taken place against the child's objectives in the curriculum and IEP.
- Use additional helpers to assist with the teaching (aides, volunteers, parents).
- Involve parents in the educational programme when possible.
- Most importantly, do not sell the students short by expecting too little from them.

In recent years, much emphasis has been placed on trying to increase the self-regulation and self-monitoring strategies of students with intellectual disability using cognitive methods and metacognitive training. While this approach is proving very useful for students with mild disabilities, it is very difficult indeed to employ cognitive training with low-functioning students because it requires a degree of self-reflection and self-monitoring they do not usually possess.

This chapter has provided an overview of the learning difficulties encountered by individuals with intellectual disability. Brief suggestions have been made regarding the types of teaching and management strategies that have proved helpful in fostering the personal, social and cognitive development of these learners. It was stated at the beginning of the chapter, and will be repeated here, that individuals with intellectual disability are capable of learning far more than was once believed possible, and for this reason we should be setting our goals higher. When given appropriate support – and when taught intensively the knowledge and skills required for independent living and self-determination – the quality of life for individuals with intellectual disability is very greatly enhanced.

Further reading

Beirne-Smith, M., Ittenbach, R.F. and Patton, J.R. (2002) *Mental Retardation* (6th edn). Upper Saddle River, NJ: Merrill-Prentice Hall.

Gates, B. (ed.) (2003) *Learning Disabilities: Toward Inclusion* (4th edn). London: Churchill Livingstone.

Hardman, M.L., Drew, C.J. and Egan, M.W. (2002) *Human Exceptionality* (7th edn). Boston: Allyn & Bacon.

Hodapp, R.M. and Dykens, E.M. (2003) Mental retardation. In E.J. Mash and R.A. Barkley (eds) *Child Psychopathology* (2nd edn) (pp. 486–519). New York: Guilford Press.

Hunt, N. and Marshall, K. (2002) *Exceptional Children and Youth* (3rd edn). Boston: Houghton Mifflin.

Klinger, L.G., Dawson, G. and Renner, P. (2003) Autistic disorder. In E.J. Mash and R.A. Barkley (eds) *Child Psychopathology* (2nd edn) (pp. 409–454). New York: Guilford Press.

Snell, M.E. and Brown, F. (2000) *Instruction of Students with Severe Disabilities* (5th edn). Upper Saddle River, NJ: Merrill.

Sue, D., Sue, D.W. and Sue, S. (2003) *Understanding Abnormal Behavior* (7th edn). Boston: Houghton Mifflin.

Wehmeyer, M.L., Sands, D.J., Knowlton, H.E. and Kozleski, E.B. (2002) *Teaching Students with Mental Retardation*. Baltimore, MD: Brookes.

References

Adams, G. and Carnine, D. (2003) Direct instruction. In H.L. Swanson, K.R. Harris and S. Graham (eds) *Handbook of Learning Disabilities* (pp. 403–416). New York: Guilford Press.

Adey, P. and Shayer, M. (2002) Cognitive acceleration comes of age. In M. Shayer and P. Adey (eds) *Learning Intelligence: Cognitive Acceleration across the Curriculum from 5 to 15 Years* (pp. 1–17). Buckingham: Open University Press.

Agran, M. and Wehmeyer, M. (1999) *Teaching Problem Solving to Students with Mental Retardation*. Washington, DC: American Association on Mental Retardation.

Alban-Metcalfe, J. and Alban-Metcalfe, J. (2001) *Managing Attention Deficit-Hyperactivity Disorder in the Inclusive Classroom*. London: Fulton.

Alberto, P.A. and Troutman, A.C. (2003) *Applied Behavior Analysis for Teachers* (6th edn). Upper Saddle River, NJ: Merrill-Prentice Hall.

Alexander, P.A. and Murphy, P.K. (1999) What cognitive psychology has to say to school psychology. In C.R. Reynolds and T.B. Gutkin (eds) *The Handbook of School Psychology* (3rd edn, pp. 167–193). New York: Wiley.

Allington, R.L. (2001) *What Really Matters for Struggling Readers: Designing Research-Based Programs*. New York: Addison-Wesley Longman.

Allington, R.L. (2002) What I've learned about effective reading instruction. *Phi Delta Kappan, 83, 10*, 740–747.

Altenbaugh, R.J. (1998) 'Some teachers are ignorant': Teachers and teaching through urban school leavers' eyes. In B. Franklin (ed.) *When Children Don't Learn* (pp. 52–71). New York: Teachers College Press.

Anderson, J. (2000) *Learning and Memory: An Integrated Approach* (2nd edn). New York: Wiley.

Anderson, M. (1999) Project development: Taking stock. In M. Anderson (ed.) *The Development of Intelligence* (pp. 311–332). Hove: Psychology Press.

Anderson, M. (2001) Conceptions of intelligence. *Journal of Child Psychology and Psychiatry, 42, 3*, 287–298.

APA (American Psychiatric Association) (2000) *Diagnostic and Statistical Manual of Mental Disorders* (DSM-4-TR) (4th edn text revised). Washington, DC: APA.

Armour-Thomas, E. and Gopaul-McNicol, S. (1998) *Assessing Intelligence: Applying a Bio-Cultural Model*. Thousand Oaks, CA: Sage.

Arter, C., Mason, H., McCall, S., McLinden, M. and Stone, J. (1999) *Children with Visual Impairment in Mainstream Settings*. London: Fulton.

Arthur, M., Gordon, C. and Butterfield, N. (2003) *Classroom Management*. Melbourne: Thomson.

Ashcraft, M.H., Kirk, E.P. and Hopko, D. (1998) On the cognitive consequences of mathematics anxiety. In C. Donlan (ed.) *The Development of Mathematical Skills* (pp. 175–196). Hove: Psychology Press.

Ashman, A. (1998) Students with intellectual disabilities. In A. Ashman and J. Elkins (eds) *Educating Children with Special Needs* (3rd edn, pp. 417–461). Sydney: Prentice Hall.

Ashman, A. and Elkins, J. (eds) (2002) *Educating Children with Diverse Abilities*. Sydney: Prentice Hall.

Atkinson, J.W. (1966) Motivational determinants of risk taking behaviour. In J.W. Atkinson and N.T. Feather (eds) *A Theory of Achievement Motivation* (pp. 11–31). New York: Wiley.

Aubrey, C. (2001) Early mathematics. In T. David (ed.) *Promoting Evidence-Based Practice in Early Childhood Education* (pp. 171–210). New York: JAI Press.

Australian Education Council (1990) *A National Statement on Mathematics for Australian Schools.* Melbourne: The Curriculum Corporation.

Ausubel, D.P. (1968) *Educational Psychology: A Cognitive View.* New York: Holt, Rinehart and Winston.

Ausubel, D.P. (2000) *The Acquisition and Retention of Knowledge: A Cognitive View.* Dordrecht: Kluwer Academic.

Ayers, H., Clarke, D. and Murray, A. (2000) *Perspectives on Behaviour* (2nd edn). London: Fulton.

Bachevalies, J. (2001) Neural bases of memory development. In C.A. Nelson and M. Luciana (eds) *Handbook of Developmental Cognitive Neuroscience* (pp. 365–379). Cambridge, MA: MIT Press.

Baddeley, A.D. (1999) *Essentials of Human Memory.* Hove: Psychology Press.

Badian, N.A. (1983) Dyscalculia and nonverbal disorders of learning. In H.R. Myklebust (ed.) *Progress in Learning Disabilities* (pp. 235–264). New York: Grune and Stratton.

Badian, N.A. (1996) Dyslexia: A validation of the concept at two age levels. *Journal of Learning Disabilities, 29, 1,* 102–112.

Bailet, L.L. (2001) Development and disorders of spelling in the beginning school years. In A.M. Bain, L.L. Bailet and L.C. Moats (eds) *Written Language Disorders: Theory into Practice* (2nd edn). Austin, TX: Pro Ed.

Bain, A.M., Bailet, L.L. and Moats, L.C. (2001) *Written Language Disorders.* Austin, TX: ProEd.

Baker, S., Gersten, R. and Graham, S. (2003) Teaching expressive writing to students with learning disabilities: Research-based applications and examples. *Journal of Learning Disabilities, 36, 2,* 109–123.

Baker, S., Gersten, R. and Lee, D.S. (2002) A synthesis of empirical research on teaching mathematics to low-achieving students. *Elementary School Journal, 103, 1,* 51–73.

Bakker, D., Licht, R. and van Strien, J. (1991) Biopsychological validation of L- and P-type dyslexia. In B.P. Rourke (ed.) *Neuropsychological Validation of Learning Disability Subtypes* (pp. 124–139). New York: Guilford Press.

Ball, E.W. and Blachman, B.A. (1991) Does phonemic awareness training in kindergarten make a difference in early word recognition and developmental spelling? *Reading Research Quarterly, 27,* 49–66.

Bandura, A. (1977) *Social Learning Theory.* Morristown, NJ: General Learning.

Bandura, A. (1997) *Self-Efficacy: The Exercise of Control.* New York: Freeman.

Barkley, R.A. (2003) Attention-deficit hyperactivity disorder. In E.J. Mash and R.A. Barkley (eds) *Child Psychopathology* (2nd edn, pp. 75–143). New York: Guilford Press.

Baroody, A.J. and Dowker, A. (2003) *The Development of Arithmetic Concepts and Skills.* Mahwah, NJ: Erlbaum

Barraga, N.C. and Erin, J.N. (2001) *Visual Impairments and Learning* (4th edn). Austin, TX: ProEd.

Batshaw, M.L. and Shapiro, B.K. (1997) Mental retardation. In M.L. Batshaw (ed.) *Children with Disabilities* (4th edn, pp. 335–359). Sydney: Maclennan and Petty.

Batten, M., Marland, P. and Khamis, M. (1993) *Knowing How to Teach Well.* Melbourne: Australian Council for Educational Research.

Battista, M.T. (1999) The mathematical miseducation of America's youth: Ignoring research and scientific study in education. *Phi Delta Kappan, 80, 6,* 425–433.

Bauer, A.M. and Shea, T.M. (1999) *Learners with Emotional and Behavioral Disorders.* Upper Saddle River, NJ: Merrill.

Bauer, P.J., Wenner, J.A., Dropik, P.L. and Wewerka, S.S. (2000) Parameters of remembering and forgetting in the transition from infancy to early childhood. *Monograph of the Society for Research in Child Development, Serial 263, 65,* 4.

Baxter, J.A., Woodward, J. and Olson, D. (2001) Effects of reform-based mathematics instruction on low achievers in five third-grade classrooms. *Elementary School Journal, 101, 5,* 529–547.

Bearne, E. (1996) *Differentiation and Diversity in the Primary School.* London: Routledge.

Begley, S. (1999) How to build a baby's brain. In E.N. Junn and C.J. Boyatzis (eds) *Child Growth and Developments 99/00* (pp. 25–28). Guilford, CT: Dushkin-McGraw-Hill.

Beirne-Smith, M., Ittenbach, R.F. and Patton, J.R. (2002) *Mental Retardation* (6th edn). Upper Saddle River, NJ: Merrill-Prentice Hall.

Bender, W. (2001) *Learning Disabilities: Characteristics, Identification and Teaching Strategies* (4th edn). Boston: Allyn & Bacon.

Bereiter, C. and Engelmann, S. (1966) *Teaching Disadvantaged Children in the Preschool.* Englewood Cliffs, NJ: Prentice Hall.

Berger, A. and Morris, D. (2001) *Implementing the Literacy Hour for Pupils with Learning Difficulties* (2nd edn). London: David Fulton.

Berninger, V.W. and Richards, T.L. (2002) *Brain Literacy for Educators and Psychologists.* Amsterdam: Academic Press.

Berrill, R. (1982) The slow learner and the gifted child. In M. Cornelius (ed.) *Teaching Mathematics* (pp. 106–134). London: Croom Helm.

Biggs, J. (1995) Motivating learning. In J. Biggs and D. Watkins (eds) *Classroom Learning* (pp. 82–102). Singapore: Prentice Hall.

Birsh, J.R. (1999) *Multisensory Teaching of Basic Language Skills.* Baltimore, MD: Brookes.

Bissaker, K. (2001) Students' and teachers' perceptions for perceived learning outcomes. In D. Greaves and D. Barwood (eds) *Creating Positive Futures: Strategies and Methods for Those Who Learn Differently* (pp. 47–58). Melbourne: Australian Resource Educators' Association.

Bissex, G. (1980) *GYNS AT WRK: A Child Learns to Write and Read.* Cambridge, MA: Harvard University Press.

Blakely, T.A., Crinella, F.M., Fisher, T.D., Champaigne, L. and Beck, F.W. (1994) Neuropsychological correlates of learning disabilities: Subtype identification by the Tryon clustering method. *Journal of Developmental and Physical Disabilities, 6, 1,* 1–22.

Blatchford, P. (2003) *The Class Size Debate: Is Small Better?* Maidenhead: Open University Press.

Bley, N. and Thornton, C.A. (2001) *Teaching Mathematics to Students with Learning Disabilities* (4th edn). Austin, TX: ProEd.

Block, C.C. (2003) *Literacy Difficulties* (2nd edn). Boston: Allyn & Bacon.

Block, J.H. (1971) *Mastery Learning: Theory and Practice.* Fort Worth: Holt, Rinehart and Winston.

Boder, E. (1973) Developmental dyslexia: A diagnostic approach based on three atypical reading patterns. *Developmental Medicine and Child Neurology, 15,* 663–687.

Boekaerts, M. (1996) Social, cultural and affective aspects of learning. In E. de Corte and F.E. Weinert (eds) *International Encyclopedia of Developmental and Instructional Psychology* (pp. 585–590). Oxford: Pergamon.

Bourke, S. (1989) Teaching methods. In P. Langford (ed.) *Educational Psychology* (pp. 65–86). Melbourne: Longman-Cheshire.

Bowers, P.G., Sunseth, K. and Golden, J. (1999) The route between rapid naming and reading progress. *Scientific Studies in Reading, 3, 1,* 31–54.

Bradley, R., Danielson, L. and Hallahan, D.P. (eds) (2002) *Identification of Learning Disabilities: Research to Practice.* Mahwah, NJ: Erlbaum.

Bradshaw, K. (1995) Learning disabilities: A cautionary tale. *Australian Journal of Remedial Education, 27, 4,* 15–17.

Braunger, J. and Lewis, J.P. (1998) *Building a Knowledge Base in Reading* (3rd edn). Urbana, IL: National Council of Teachers of English/ International Reading Association.

Brennan, W. (1985) *Curriculum for Special Needs.* Milton Keynes: Open University Press.

Brisk, M. (1998) *Bilingual Education.* Mahwah, NJ: Erlbaum.

Bristow, J., Cowley, P. and Daines, B. (1999) *Memory and Learning: A Practical Guide for Teachers.* London: Fulton.

Brooks, M. (2002) A look at current practice. In R. Bradley, L. Danielson and D.P. Hallahan (eds) *Identification of Learning Disabilities: Research to Practice* (pp. 335–340). Mahwah, NJ: Erlbaum.

Brophy, J.E. (2001) *Motivating Students to Learn.* Boston: McGraw-Hill.

Brophy, J.E. and Good, T.L. (1986) Teacher behaviour and student achievement. In M. Wittrock (ed.) *Handbook of Research on Teaching* (3rd edn, pp. 328–375). New York: Macmillan.

Bruer, J.T. (1999) Neural connections: Some you use, some you lose. *Phi Delta Kappan, 81, 4,* 264–277.

Bruer, J.T. (2001) In search of brain-based education. In K. Cauley, F. Linder and J. McMillan (eds) *Educational Psychology 00–01* (pp. 94–100). Guilford, CT: Dushkin-McGraw-Hill.

Bruner, J.S. (1966) *Toward a Theory of Instruction.* Cambridge, MA: Harvard University Press.

Bullis, M., Walker, H.M. and Sprague, J.R. (2001) A promise unfulfilled: Social skills training with at-risk and antisocial children and youth. *Exceptionality, 9, 1,* 67–90.

Butler, R. (1994) Teacher communications and student interpretations: Effects of teacher responses to failing students on attributional influences in two age groups. *British Journal of Educational Psychology, 64,* 277–294.

Butterworth, B. (1999) *The Mathematical Brain.* London: Macmillan.

Buxton, L. (1981) *Do You Panic about Maths? Coping with Maths Anxiety.* London: Heinemann.

Byrnes, J.P. (2001) *Minds, Brains and Learning.* New York: Guilford Press.

Campbell, F. and Ramey, C.T. (1994) Effects of early intervention on intellectual and academic achievement: A follow-up study of children from low-income families. *Child Development, 65,* 684–698.

Carpenter, S.L. and King-Sears, M. (1997) Strategy instruction. In D. Bradley, M. King-Sears and D. Tessier-Switlick (eds) *Teaching Students in Inclusive Classrooms* (pp. 283–321). Boston: Allyn & Bacon.

Carper, J. (2000) *Your Miracle Brain.* New York: HarperCollins.

Carroll, T. (2000) Pupil absenteeism in the primary school. In T. Cox (ed.) *Combating Educational Disadvantage: Meeting the Needs of Vulnerable Children* (pp. 53–64). London: Falmer.

Catts, H.W., Hogan, T.P. and Fey, M.E. (2003) Subgrouping poor readers on the basis of individual differences in reading-related abilities. *Journal of Learning Disabilities, 36, 2,* 151–164.

Cavey, D.W. (2000) *Dysgraphia: Why Johnny Can't Write* (3rd edn). Austin, TX: ProEd.

Ceci, S.J. (1996) *On Intelligence* (2nd edn). Cambridge, MA: Harvard University Press.

Chan, D. (1996) Special education in Hong Kong: The need for research that informs practice. *Educational Research Journal, 11, 1,* 1–6.

Chan, D. (1998) Perceived competence of students with learning difficulties in Hong Kong. In D.W. Chan (ed.) *Helping Students with Learning Difficulties* (pp. 135–148). Hong Kong: Chinese University Press.

Chan, L.K.S (1991) Metacognition and remedial education. *Australian Journal of Remedial Education, 23, 1*, 4–10.

Chan, L.K.S. (1994) Relationship of motivation, strategic learning and reading achievement in Grades 5, 7 and 9. *Journal of Experimental Education, 62, 4*, 319–339.

Chan, L.K.S. and Dally, K. (2000) Review of literature. In W. Louden, L.K.S. Chan, J. Elkins, D. Greaves, H. House, M. Milton and others (2000) *Mapping the Territory: Primary Students with Learning Difficulties in Literacy and Numeracy* (v.2, pp. 161–331). Canberra: Department of Education, Training and Youth Affairs.

Chan, L.K.S. and Dally, K. (2001) Learning disabilities and literacy and numeracy development. *Australian Journal of Learning Disabilities, 6, 1*, 12–19.

Chapman, C. and King, R. (2003) *Differentiated Instructional Strategies for Reading in the Content Areas*. Thousand Oaks, CA: Corwin Press.

Cheng, P.W. (1998) Primary teachers' perceptions and understanding of learning difficulties. In D.W. Chan (ed.) *Helping Students with Learning Difficulties* (pp. 121–134). Hong Kong: Chinese University Press.

Chinn, S.J. and Ashcroft, J.R. (1998) *Mathematics for Dyslexics: A Teaching Handbook* (2nd edn). London: Whurr.

Christensen, C.A. (1999) Learning disability: Issues of representation, power, and the medicalization of school failure. In R.J. Sternberg and L. Spear-Swerling (eds) *Perspectives on Learning Disabilities* (pp. 227–249). Boulder, CO: Westview Press.

Christison, M.A. (2002) Brain-based research and language teaching. *English Teaching Forum, 40, 2*, 2–7.

Cirino, P.T., Morris, M.K. and Morris, R.D. (2002) Neuropsychological concomitants of calculation skills in college students referred for learning difficulties. *Developmental Neuropsychology, 21, 2*, 201–218.

Clay, M.M. (1991) *Becoming Literate: The Construction of Inner Control*. Portsmouth, NH: Heinemann.

Clay, M.M. (1994) *A Guidebook for Reading Recovery Teachers*. Portsmouth, NH: Heinemann.

Clay, M.M. (1997) The development of literacy difficulties. In V. Edwards and D. Corson (eds) *Encyclopedia of Language and Education* (pp. 37–46). Dordrecht: Kluwer Academic.

Cobb, P. (1994) Constructivism in mathematics and science education. *Educational Researcher, 23, 7*, 4.

Cohen, J. (1988) *Statistical Power Analysis for the Behavioral Sciences* (2nd edn). New York: Academic Press.

Collins, M. and Cheek, E.H. (1984) *Diagnostic-Prescriptive Reading Instruction: A Guide for Classroom Teachers* (2nd edn). Dubuque, IA: Brown.

Compton-Lilly, C. (2003) *Reading Families: The Literate Lives of Urban Children*. New York: Teachers College Press.

Conway, R. (2001) Encouraging positive interactions. In P. Foreman (ed.) *Integration and Inclusion in Action* (2nd edn, pp. 311–359). Melbourne: Nelson-Thomson.

Covington, M.V. (1992) *Making the Grade: A Self-Worth Perspective on Motivation and School Reform*. Cambridge: Cambridge University Press.

Covington, M.V. and Mueller, K.J. (2001) Intrinsic versus extrinsic motivation: An approach/avoidance reformulation. *Educational Psychology Review, 13, 2*, 157–176.

Covington, M.V. and Teel, K.M. (1996) *Overcoming Student Failure: Changing Motives and Incentives for Learning*. Washington, DC: American Psychological Association.

Cox, C. (1999) *Teaching Language Arts* (3rd edn). Boston: Allyn & Bacon.

Cox, T. (2000) Introduction. In T. Cox (ed.) *Combating Educational Disadvantage: Meeting the Needs of Vulnerable Children* (pp. 1–14). London: Falmer.

Cramer, R.L. (1998) *The Spelling Connection: Integrating Reading, Writing and Spelling Instruction*. New York: Guilford Press.

Craske, M. (1988) Learned helplessness, self-worth motivation and attribution retraining for primary school children. *British Journal of Educational Psychology, 58*, 152–164.

Crawley, S.J. and Merritt, K. (2000) *Remediating Reading Difficulties* (3rd edn). Boston: McGraw-Hill.

Creemers, B. (1994) *The Effective Classroom*. London: Cassell.

Cripps, C. (1990) Teaching joined writing to children on school entry as an agent for catching spelling. *Australian Journal of Remedial Education, 22, 3*, 13–15.

Cronbach, L. and Snow, R. (1977) *Aptitudes and Instructional Methods*. New York: Halstead Press.

Culatta, R.A., Tompkins, J.R. and Werts, M.G. (2003) *Fundamentals of Special Education* (2nd edn). Upper Saddle River, NJ: Merrill-Prentice Hall.

Cullingford, C. (2001) *How Children Learn to Read and How to Help Them*. London: Kogan Page.

Daly, E., Witt, J.C., Martens, B.K. and Dool, E. (1997) A model for conducting functional analysis of academic performance problems. *School Psychology Review, 26*, 554–574.

D'Angiulli, A. and Siegel, L.S. (2003) Cognitive functioning as measured by WISC-R. Do children with learning disabilities have distinctive patterns of performance? *Journal of Learning Disabilities, 36, 1*, 48–58.

Daniels, H. (2001) *Vygotsky and Pedagogy*. London: Routledge-Falmer.

Davies, N. (1998) *Dark Heart: The Shocking Truth about Hidden Britain*. London: Vintage.

De La Paz, S. and Graham, S. (2002) Explicitly teaching strategies, skills and knowledge: Writing instruction in middle school classrooms. *Journal of Educational Psychology, 94, 4*, 687–698.

DeLuca, J.W., Rourke, B.P. and Del Dotto, J.E. (1991) Subtypes of arithmetic-disabled children. In B.P. Rourke (ed.) *Neuropsychological Validation of Learning Disability Subtypes* (pp. 180–219). New York: Guilford Press.

Demetriou, A., Christou, C., Spanoudis, G. and Platsidou, M. (2002) The development of mental processing: Efficiency, working memory and thinking. *Monograph of the Society for Research in Child Development, 67, 1, Serial 268*.

Dempster, F.N. (1991) Synthesis of research on reviews and tests. *Educational Leadership, 48, 7*, 71–76.

Denton, C.A., Vaughn, S. and Fletcher, J.M. (2003) Bringing research-based practice in reading intervention to scale. *Learning Disabilities Research and Practice, 18, 3*, 201–211.

Detterman, D.K., Gabriel, L.T. and Ruthsatz, J.M. (2000) Intelligence and mental retardation. In R.J. Sternberg (ed.) *Handbook of Intelligence* (pp. 141–158). Cambridge: Cambridge University Press.

Dever, R.B. and Knapczyk, D.R. (1997) *Teaching Persons with Mental Retardation*. Boston: McGraw-Hill.

De Vries, R. (2002) *Developing Constructivist Early Childhood Curriculum*. New York: Teacher College Press.

Dickinson, P. (2003) Whole class interactive teaching. *SET Research for Teachers, 1*, 18–21. New Zealand Council for Educational Research.

Dixon, R. and Engelmann, S. (1979) *Corrective Spelling through Morphographs*. Chicago, IL: Science Research Associates.

Dockrell, J. and McShane, J. (1992) *Children's Learning Difficulties: A Cognitive Approach*. Oxford: Blackwell.

Dowling, M. (2002) The impact of stress on early development. In J. Fisher (ed.) *The Foundations of Learning* (pp. 41–56). Buckingham: Open University Press.

Drew, C.J. and Hardman, M.L. (2000) *Mental Retardation: A Life Cycle Approach* (7th edn), Upper Saddle River, NJ: Merrill.

Driscoll, M.P. (2000) *Psychology of Learning for Instruction* (2nd edn). Boston: Allyn & Bacon.

Duncan, J., Seitz, R.J., Kolodny, J., Bor, D., Herzog, H., Ahmed, A., Newell, F. and Emslie, H. (2000) A neural basis for general intelligence. *Science, 289, 5478,* 457–460.

Dunn, R. (1996) *How to Implement and Supervise a Learning Style Program*. Alexandria, VA: Association for Supervision and Curriculum Development.

DuPaul, G.J. and Stoner, G. (2003) *ADHD in the Schools: Assessment and Intervention Strategies*. New York: Guilford Press.

Dweck, C.S. and Licht, B.G. (1980) *Learned Helplessness: Theory and Application* (pp. 197–221). New York: Academic Press.

Eccles, J., Wigfield, A. and Schiefele, U. (1998) Motivation to succeed. In W. Damon & N. Eisenberg (eds) *Handbook of Child Psychology* (v.3 pp. 1017–1095). New York: Wiley.

Edwards, L. (2003) Writing instruction in kindergarten: Examining an emerging area of research for children with writing and reading difficulties. *Journal of Learning Disabilities, 36, 2,* 136–148.

Edwards, S.A. (2003) *Ways of Writing with Young Kids*. Boston: Allyn & Bacon.

Eggen, P. and Kauchak, D. (2003) *Educational Psychology: Windows on Classrooms* (6th edn). Upper Saddle River, NJ: Merrill.

Eisner, J.P. and Seligman, M.E.P. (1996) Self-related cognition, learned helplessness, learned optimism and human development. In E. de Corte and F.E. Weinert (eds) *International Encyclopedia of Developmental and Instructional Psychology* (pp. 199–201). Oxford: Pergamon.

Elkins, J. (2001) Learning disabilities in Australia. In D.P. Hallahan and B.K. Keogh (eds) *Research and Global Perspectives in Learning Disabilities* (pp. 181–195). Mahwah, NJ: Erlbaum.

Elkins, J. (2002) Numeracy. In A. Ashman and J. Elkins (eds) *Educating Children with Diverse Abilities* (pp. 436–469). Sydney: Prentice Hall.

Elksnin, L.K. (2002) Redefining LD is not the answer. In R. Bradley, L. Danielson and D.P. Hallahan (eds) *Identification of Learning Disabilities: Research to Practice* (pp. 251–261). Mahwah, NJ: Erlbaum.

Elliott, P. and Garnett, C. (1994) Mathematics power for all. In C.A. Thornton and N. Bley (eds) *Windows of Opportunity: Mathematics for Students with Special Needs*. Reston, VA: National Council of Teachers of Mathematics.

Elliott, S.N., Busse, R.T. and Shapiro, E.S. (1999) Intervention techniques for academic problems. In C.R. Reynolds and T.B. Gutkin (eds) *The Handbook of School Psychology* (3rd edn, pp. 664–685). New York: Wiley.

Engelmann, S. and Bruner, E.C. (1988) *Reading Mastery*. Chicago, IL: Science Research Associates.

Englert, C., Raphael, T. and Anderson, L. (1992) Socially mediated instruction: Improving students' knowledge and talk about writing. *Elementary School Journal, 92,* 411–449.

Englert, C., Raphael, T., Anderson, L., Anthony, H.M. and Stevens, D.D. (1991) Making strategies and self-talk visible. *American Educational Research Journal, 28,* 337–372.

Eysenck, H.J. and Schoenthaler, S. (1997) Raising IQ level by vitamin and mineral supplementation. In R.J. Sternberg and E.L. Grigorenko (eds) *Intelligence, Heredity and Environment* (pp. 363–392). Cambridge: Cambridge University Press.

Eysenck, M.W. and Keane, M.T. (2000) *Cognitive Psychology* (4th edn). Hove: Psychology Press.

Feeney, S., Christensen, D. and Moravcik, E. (2001) *Who Am I in the Lives of Children?* (6th edn). Upper Saddle River, NJ: Merrill-Prentice Hall.

Feuerstein, R. (1980) *Instrumental Enrichment: An Intervention Program for Cognitive Modifiability*. Baltimore, MD: University Park Press.

Finlan, T.G. (1994) *Learning Disability: An Imaginary Disease*. Westport, CT: Bergin and Garvey.

Finn, J.D. (2002) Making the most of small classes: The next steps. In J.D. Finn and M.C. Wang (eds) *Taking Small Classes One Step Further* (pp. 215–221). Greenwich, CT: Information Age Publishing.

Fisher, R. (2002) *Inside the Literacy Hour: Learning from Classroom Experience*. London: Routledge-Falmer.

Fitzgerald, J. and Shanahan, T. (2000) Reading and writing relations and their development. *Educational Psychologist, 35, 1*, 39–50.

Fleischner, J.E. (1994) Diagnosis and assessment of mathematics learning disabilities. In G.R. Lyon (ed.) *Frames of Reference for the Assessment of Learning Disabilities* (pp. 441–472). Baltimore, MD: Brookes.

Fleischner, J.E. and Manheimer, M.A. (1997) Math intervention for students with learning disabilities: Myths and realities. *School Psychology Review, 26, 3*, 397–413.

Fletcher, J.M., Lyon, G.R., Barnes, M., Stuebing, K., Francis, D., Olson, R.K., Shaywitz, S.E. and Shaywitz, B.A. (2002) Classification of learning disabilities: An evidence-based evaluation. In R. Bradley, L. Danielson and D.P. Hallahan (eds) *Identification of Learning Disabilities: Research to Practice* (pp. 185–261). Mahwah, NJ: Erlbaum.

Forness, S., Kavale, K., Blum, I. and Lloyd, J. (1997) A mega-analysis of meta-analyses: What works in special education and related services? *Teaching Exceptional Children, 29, 6*, 4–7.

Franklin, B.M. (1998) *When Children Don't Learn: Student Failure and the Culture of Teaching*. New York: Teachers College Press.

Fraser, J. (2002) *Listen to the Children: From Focused Observation to Strategic Instruction*. Portsmouth, NH: Heinemann.

Frederickson, N. and Cline, T. (2002) *Special Educational Needs, Inclusion and Diversity*. Buckingham: Open University Press.

Frieman, J. (2002) *Learning and Adaptive Behavior*. Belmont, CA: Wadsworth.

Frostig, M. and Horne, D. (1964) *The Frostig Program for the Development of Visual Perception*. Chicago: Follett.

Frostig, M., Lefever, W., and Whittlesey, J. (1966) *The Developmental Test of Visual Perception*. Palo Alto, CA: Consulting Psychologists Press.

Fuchs, D., Fuchs, L., Mathes, P., Lipsey, M. and Roberts, P.H. (2002) Is 'learning disabilities' just a fancy term for low achievement? A meta-analysis of reading differences between low achievers with and without the label. In R. Bradley, L. Danielson and D.P. Hallahan (eds) *Identification of Learning Disabilities: Research to Practice* (pp. 737–762). Mahwah, NJ: Erlbaum.

Fuchs, L. and Fuchs, D. (2001) Principles for the prevention and intervention of mathematics difficulties. *Learning Disabilities Research and Practice, 16, 2*, 85–95.

Furr, D. (2003) Struggling readers get hooked on writing. *The Reading Teacher, 56, 6*, 518–525.

Gabler, I.C. and Schroeder, M. (2003) *Seven Constructivist Methods for Secondary School*. Boston: Allyn & Bacon.

Gage, N.L. and Berliner, D.C. (1998) *Educational Psychology* (6th edn). Boston: Houghton Mifflin.

Gagne, E.D., Yekovich, C.W. and Yekovich, F.R. (1993) *The Cognitive Psychology of School Learning* (2nd edn). New York: HarperCollins.

Gagne, R.M. (1984) *The Conditions of Learning and Theory of Instruction* (4th edn). New York: Holt, Rinehart and Winston.

Gagne, R., Briggs, L. and Wager, W. (1992) *Principles of Instructional Design* (4th edn). Chicago: Holt, Rinehart and Winston.

Gagne, R. and Wager, W. (2002) *Principles of Instructional Design* (5th edn). Belmont, CA: Wadsworth.

Gagnon, G. and Collay, M. (2001) *Designing for Learning*. Thousand Oaks, CA: Corwin Press.

Galloway, D., Leo, E.L., Rogers, C. and Armstrong, D. (1995) Motivational styles in English and mathematics among children identified as having special educational needs. *British Journal of Educational Psychology*, *65*, 477–487.

Galloway, D., Rogers, C., Armstrong, D. and Leo, E. (1998) *Motivating the Difficult to Teach*. London: Longman.

Galton, M., Hargreaves, L., Comber, C., Wall, D. and Pell, A. (1999) *Inside the Primary Classroom: 20 Years On*. London: Routledge.

Gardner, H. (1983) *Frames of Mind: The Theory of Multiple Intelligences*. New York: Basic Books.

Gates, B. (ed.) (2003) *Learning Disabilities: Toward Inclusion* (4th edn). London: Churchill Livingstone.

Gathercole, S.E. and Pickering, S.J. (2000) Working memory deficits in children with low achievements in the National Curriculum at 7 years of age. *British Journal of Educational Psychology*, *70*, 177–194.

Geary, D.C. (1993) Mathematical disabilities: Cognitive, neuropsychological and genetic components. *Psychological Bulletin*, *114*, 2, 345–362.

Geary, D.C. (2000) From infancy to adulthood: The development of numerical abilities. *European Child and Adolescent Psychiatry*, *9*, Supplement 2, 11–16.

Genard, N., Mousty, P., Content, A., Alegria, J., Leybaert, J. and Morais, J. (1998) Methods to establish subtypes of developmental dyslexia. In P. Reitsma and L. Verhoeven (eds) *Problems and Interventions in Literacy Development* (pp. 163–176). Dordrecht: Kluwer Academic.

Gersten, R. and Baker, S. (2003) English-language learners with learning disabilities. In H.L. Swanson, K.R. Harris and S. Graham (eds) *Handbook of Learning Disabilities* (pp. 94–109). New York: Guilford Press.

Gersten, R., Baker, S. and Pugach, M. (2001) Contemporary research on special education teaching. In V. Richardson (ed.) *Handbook of Research on Teaching* (4th edn, pp. 695–722). Washington, DC: American Educational Research Association.

Ginsberg, H.P. (1997) Mathematics learning disabilities: A view from developmental psychology. *Journal of Learning Disabilities*, *30*, 1, 20–33.

Given, B. (2002) *Teaching to the Brain's Natural Learning Systems*. Alexandria, VA: Association for Supervision and Curriculum Development.

Glasswell, K., Parr, J.M. and McNaughton, S. (2003) Working with William: Teaching, learning and the joint construction of a struggling writer. *The Reading Teacher*, *56*, 5, 494–500.

Goldberg, M.F. (2002) *15 School Questions and Discussion*. Lanham, MD: Scarecrow Press.

Good, T.L and Brophy, J.E. (1990) *Educational Psychology: A Realistic Approach* (4th edn). New York: Longman.

Good, T.L. and Brophy, J.E. (2002) *Looking in Classrooms* (9th edn). Boston: Allyn & Bacon.

Goodman, K. (1967) Reading: A psycholinguistic guessing game. *Journal of the Reading Specialist, 6*, 126–135.

Goodman, K. (1986) *What's Whole in Whole Language?* Portsmouth, NH: Heinemann.

Gopnik, A., Meltzoff, A.N. and Kuhl, P.K. (1999) *The Scientist in the Crib: Minds, Brains and How Children Learn*. New York: Morrow.

Gordon, J., Vaughn, S. and Schumm, J.S. (1993) Spelling interventions: A review of the literature and implications for instruction for students with learning disabilities. *Learning Disabilities Research and Practice, 8, 3*, 175–181.

Gorman, J.C. (2001) *Emotional Disorders and Learning Disabilities: Interactions and Interventions*. Thousand Oaks, CA: Corwin Press.

Gould, B.W. (2001) Curricular strategies for written expression. In A.M. Bain, L.L. Bailet and L.C. Moats (eds) *Written Language Disorders* (pp. 185–220). Austin, TX: ProEd.

Gould, S.J. (1996) *The Mismeasurement of Man* (2nd edn). New York: Norton.

Gourgey, A.F. (2001) Metacognition in basic skills instruction. In H.J. Hartman (ed.) *Metacognition in Learning and Instruction* (pp. 17–32). Dordrecht: Kluwer Academic.

Graham, S. (2000) Should the natural learning approach replace spelling instruction? *Journal of Educational Psychology, 92, 2*, 235–47.

Graham, S. and Harris, K.R. (1994) Implications of constructivism for teaching reading and writing to students with special needs. *Journal of Special Education, 28, 3*, 275–289.

Graham, S. and Harris, K. (2000a) Helping children who experience reading difficulties. In L. Baker, M.J. Dreher and J.T. Guthrie (eds) *Engaging Young Readers: Promoting Achievement and Motivation* (pp. 43–67). New York: Guilford Press.

Graham, S. and Harris, K. (2000b) The role of self-regulation and transcription skills in writing and writing development. *Educational Psychologist, 35, 1*, 3–12.

Graham, S. and Harris, K. (2003) Literacy: Writing. In L. Nandel (ed.) *Encyclopedia of Cognitive Science* (v.2, pp. 939–945). London: Nature Publishing Group.

Graham, S., Harris, K. and Chorzempa, B.F. (2002) Contribution of spelling instruction to the spelling, writing and reading of poor spellers. *Journal of Educational Psychology, 94, 4*, 669–686.

Grant, E.R. and Ceci, S.J. (2000) Coding processes. In A.E. Kazdin (ed.) *Encyclopedia of Psychology* (v.5, pp. 162–169). Oxford: Oxford University Press.

Greaves, D. (1997) The educational uses of the WISC-III. *Australian Journal of Learning Disabilities, 2, 2*, 13–20.

Gredler, M.E. (2001) *Learning and Instruction: Theory and Practice* (4th edn). Upper Saddle River, NJ: Merrill-Prentice Hall.

Green, G. (1996) Evaluating claims about treatment for autism. In C. Maurice, G. Green and S.C. Luce (eds) *Behavioural Intervention for Young Children with Autism* (pp. 15–28). Austin, TX: ProEd.

Greene. G. (1999) Mnemonic multiplication fact instruction for students with learning disabilities. *Learning Disabilities Research and Practice, 14, 3*, 141–148.

Greenough, W.T. and Black, J.E. (2000) Molecular and cellular aspects. In A.E. Kazdin (ed.) *Encyclopedia of Psychology* (v.5, pp. 3–5) Oxford: Oxford University Press.

Gregg, N. and Mather, N. (2002) School is fun at recess: Informal analyses of written language for students with learning disabilities. *Journal of Learning Disabilities, 35, 1*, 7–22.

Gregory, G. and Chapman, C. (2002) *Differentiated Instructional Strategies: One Size Does Not Fit All*. Thousand Oaks, CA: Corwin Press.

Gresham, F.M. (2002) Responsiveness to intervention: An alternative approach to the identification of learning disabilities. In R. Bradley, L. Danielson and D.P. Hallahan (eds) *Identification of Learning Disabilities: Research to Practice* (pp. 467–519). Mahwah, NJ: Erlbaum.

Griffin, P., Smith, P.G. and Ridge, N. (2001) *The Literacy Profiles in Practice*. Portsmouth, NH: Heinemann.

Grigorenko, E.L. (2001) Developmental dyslexia: An update on genes, brains and environments. *Journal of Child Psychology and Psychiatry, 42*, 91–125.

Grimes, J. (2002) Responsiveness to interventions: The next step in special education identification, service, and exiting decision-making. In R. Bradley, L. Danielson and D.P. Hallahan (eds) *Identification of Learning Disabilities: Research to Practice* (pp. 531–547). Mahwah, NJ: Erlbaum.

Gross, J. (2003) Waves of intervention. *Special Children, 153*, 16–20.

Grotzer, T.A. and Perkins, D.N. (2000) Teaching intelligence: A performance conception. In R.J. Sternberg (ed.) *Handbook of Intelligence* (pp. 492–515). Cambridge: Cambridge University Press.

Gucker, G. (1999) Teaching mathematics to students with different learning styles. *Mathematics Teachers' Journal, 49, 1*, 39–41.

Guilford, J.P. (1967) *The Nature of Human Intelligence*. New York: McGraw-Hill.

Guilford, J.P. (1996) Human intelligence. In R.J. Corsini and A.J. Auerbach (eds) *Concise Encyclopedia of Psychology* (pp. 425–428). New York: Wiley.

Gunter, M.A., Estes, T.H. and Schwab, J. (2003) *Instruction: A Models Approach* (4th edn). Boston: Allyn & Bacon.

Gupta, V.B. (1999) *Manual of Developmental and Behavioral Problems in Children*. New York: Dekker.

Haberlandt, K. (1999) *Human Memory: Exploration and Application*. Boston: Allyn & Bacon.

Hallahan, D.P. and Kauffman, J.M. (2003) *Exceptional Learners: Introduction to Special Education* (9th edn). Boston, MA: Allyn & Bacon.

Hallahan, D.P., Kauffman, J.M. and Lloyd, J.W. (1999) *Introduction to Learning Disabilities* (2nd edn). Boston: Allyn & Bacon.

Hallahan, D.P. and Keogh, B.K. (2001) Introduction. In D.P. Hallahan and B.K. Keogh (eds) *Research and Global Perspectives in Learning Disabilities* (pp. 1–12). Mahwah, NJ: Erlbaum.

Hallenbeck, M.J. (2002) Taking charge: Adolescents with learning disability assume responsibility for their own writing. *Learning Disability Quarterly, 25, 4*, 227–247.

Hamill, L.B. and Everington, C. (2002) *Teaching Students with Moderate to Severe Disabilities*. Upper Saddle River, NJ: Merrill-Prentice Hall.

Hammill, D.D. and Larsen, S.C. (1974) The effectiveness of psycholinguistic training. *Exceptional Children, 41*, 5–15.

Hammill, D.D., Leigh, E., McNutt, G. and Larsen, S. (1981) A new definition of learning disabilities. *Learning Disability Quarterly, 4*, 689–699.

Hardman, M.L., Drew, C.J. and Egan, M.W. (2002) *Human Exceptionality* (7th edn). Boston: Allyn & Bacon.

Harniss, M.K., Carnine, D.W., Silbert, J. and Dixon, R.C. (2002) Effective strategies for teaching mathematics. In E.J. Kameenui and D.C. Simmons (eds) *Effective Teaching Strategies that Accommodate Diverse Learners* (2nd edn, pp. 121–148). Upper Saddle River, NJ: Merrill-Prentice Hall.

Harris, K. and Graham, S. (1996) *Making the Writing Process Work: Strategies for Composition and Self-Regulation*. Cambridge, MA: Brookline.

Harrison, C. (1996) *Methods of Teaching Reading: Key Issues in Research and Implications for Practice*. Edinburgh: Scottish Office of Education and Industry Department.

Hartman, H.J. (2001) Developing students' metacognitive knowledge and skills. In H.J. Hartman (ed.) *Metacognition in Learning and Instruction* (pp. 33–68). Dordrecht: Kluwer Academic.

Haskell, S.H. (2000) The determinants of arithmetic skills in young children: Some observations. *European Child and Adolescent Psychiatry, 9, Supplement 2,* 77–86.

Hastings, N. and Schwieso, J. (1995) Tasks and tables: The effects of seating arrangements in primary classrooms. *Educational Research, 37, 3,* 279–291.

Hauser-Cram, P. (1998) 'I think I can, I think I can': Understanding and encouraging mastery motivation in young children. *Young Children, 53,* 67–71.

Hayes, J. (1996) A new framework for understanding cognition and affect in writing. In M. Levy and S. Ransdell (eds) *The Science of Writing* (pp. 1–27). Mahwah, NJ: Erlbaum.

Hayes, J. and Flower, L. (1980) Identifying the organization of writing processes. In L. Gregg and E. Steinberg (eds) *Cognitive Processes in Writing* (pp. 3–30). Hillsdale, NJ: Erlbaum.

Healy, J.M. (1994) *Your Child's Growing Mind* (2nd edn). New York: Doubleday.

Hebb, D.O. (1949) *Organization of Behavior.* New York: Wiley.

Heilman, K.M. (2002) *Matter of Mind: A Neurologist's View of Brain-Behavior Relationships.* New York: Oxford University Press.

Henderson, A. (1998) *Maths for the Dyslexic: A Practical Guide.* London: Fulton.

Henderson, J, (1999) *Memory and Forgetting.* London: Routledge.

Henderson, R.W. (2002) Queensland Year 2 Diagnostic Net and teachers' explanations of literacy failure. *Australian Journal of Education, 46, 1,* 50–64.

Henley, M., Ramsey, R.S. and Algozzine, R. (2002) *Characteristics of and Strategies for Teaching Students with Mild Disabilities* (4th edn). Boston: Allyn & Bacon.

Henson, K.T. and Eller, B.F. (1999) *Educational Psychology for Effective Teaching.* Belmont, CA: Wadsworth.

Hess, M. and Wheldall, K. (1999) Strategies for improving the written expression of primary children with poor writing skills. *Australian Journal of Learning Disabilities* 4, 4, 14–20.

Heward, W.L. (2003a) *Exceptional Children* (7th edn). Upper Saddle River, NJ: Merrill-Prentice Hall.

Heward, W.L. (2003b) Ten faulty notions about teaching and learning that hinder the effectiveness of special education. *Journal of Special Education, 36, 4,* 186–205.

Hill, W. (2002) *Learning: A Survey of Psychological Interpretations* (7th edn). New York: Longman.

Hilty, E.B. (1998) The professionally challenged teacher: Teachers talk about school failure. In B. Franklin (ed.) *When Children Don't Learn* (pp. 72–98). New York: Teachers College Press.

Hinshelwood, J. (1900) Congenital wordblindness. *Lancet, 1,* 1506–1508.

Hirsch, E.D. (1996) *The Schools We Need and Why We Don't Have Them.* New York: Doubleday.

Hirsch, E.D. (2000) Reality's revenge: Research and ideology. In L. Abbeduto (ed.) *Taking Sides: Clashing Views on Controversial Issues in Educational Psychology* (pp. 158–175). Guilford, CT: Dushkin-McGraw Hill.

Hodapp, R.M. and Dykens, E.M. (2003) Mental retardation. In E.J. Mash and R.A. Barkley (eds) *Child Psychopathology* (2nd edn, pp. 486–519). New York: Guilford Press.

Hodapp, R.M. and Zigler, E. (1999) Intellectual development and mental retardation: Some continuing controversies. In M. Anderson (ed.) *The Development of Intelligence* (pp. 295–308). Hove: Psychology Press.

Hodges, G.C. (2002) Learning through collaborative writing. *Reading: Literacy and Language, 36, 1,* 4–10.

Hoskyn, M. and Swanson, H.L. (2000) Cognitive processing of low achievers and children with reading disabilities: A selective meta-analytic review of the published literature. *School Psychology Review, 29*, 102–119.

Houssart, J. (2002) Count me out: Task refusal in primary mathematics. *Support for Learning, 17, 2*, 75–79.

Howe, M.J.A. (1997) *IQ in Question: The Truth about Intelligence.* London: Sage.

Howe, M.J.A. (1998) *Principles of Abilities and Human Learning.* Hove: Psychology Press.

Howe, M.J.A. (1999) *A Teacher's Guide to the Psychology of Learning* (2nd edn). Oxford: Blackwell.

Howse, R.B., Lange, G., Farran, D.C. and Boyles, C.D. (2003) Motivation and self-regulation as predictors of achievement in economically disadvantaged young children. *Journal of Experimental Education, 71, 2*, 151–174.

Hunt, N. and Marshall, K. (2002) *Exceptional Children and Youth* (3rd edn). Boston: Houghton Mifflin.

Hutchinson, R. and Kewin, J. (1994) *Sensations and Disability.* London: ROMPA.

Irlen, H. (1991) *Scotopic Sensitivity Syndrome: Screening Manual.* Long Beach, CA: Perceptual Development Corporation.

Isaacson, S.L. (1987) Effective instruction in written language. *Focus on Exceptional Children 19, 6*, 1–12.

Jacobsen, D.A., Eggen, P. and Kauchak, D. (2002) *Methods for Teaching: Promoting Student Learning* (6th edn). Upper Saddle River, NJ: Merrill.

Jenkins, J.R., Antil, L.R., Wayne, S.K. and Vadasy, P.F. (2003) How cooperative learning works for special education and remedial students. *Exceptional Children, 69, 3*, 279–292.

Jenkins, J.R. and O'Connor, R. (2002) Early identification and intervention for young children with reading/learning disabilities. In R. Bradley, L. Danielson and D.P. Hallahan (eds) *Identification of Learning Disabilities: Research to Practice* (pp. 99–148). Mahwah, NJ: Erlbaum.

Jensen, A. (1996) General intelligence factor. In R.J. Corsini and A.J. Auerbach (eds) *Concise Encyclopedia of Psychology* (pp. 371–372). New York: Wiley.

Jensen, A. (1998) *The g Factor: The Science of Mental Ability.* Westport, CT: Praeger.

Jensen, E. (1995) *The Learning Brain.* San Diego: Turning Point Publishing.

Jensen, E. (1998) *Teaching with the Brain in Mind.* Alexandria, VA: Association for Supervision and Curriculum Development.

Johnson, D.J. and Myklebust, H.R. (1967) *Learning Disabilities: Educational Principles and Practices.* New York: Grune and Stratton.

Jonassen, D.H. (1992) Evaluating constructivistic learning. In T.M. Duffy and D.H. Jonassen (eds) *Constructivism and Technology of Instruction* (pp. 137–148). Hillsdale, NJ: Erlbaum.

Jones, C.B. (2002) *The Source for Brain-Based Learning.* East Moline, IL: Linguisystems.

Jordan, N.C., Hanich, L.B. and Uberti, H.Z. (2003) Mathematical thinking and learning difficulties. In A.J. Baroody and A. Doweker (eds) *The Development of Arithmetic Concepts and Skills* (pp. 359–383). Mahwah, NJ: Erlbaum.

Kaiser, A.P. (2000) Teaching functional communication skills. In M.E. Snell and F. Brown (eds) *Instruction of Students with Severe Disabilities* (5th edn, pp. 453–492). Upper Saddle River, NJ: Merrill.

Kameenui, E.J. and Carnine, D.W. (2002) *Effective Teaching Strategies that Accommodate Diverse Learners* (2nd edn). Upper Saddle River, NJ: Prentice Hall.

Kaplan, J.S. (1998) *Beyond Behavior Modification* (3rd edn). Austin, TX: ProEd.

Kauchak, D.P. and Eggen, P.D. (2003) *Learning and Teaching: Research-Based Methods* (4th edn). Boston: Allyn & Bacon.

Kaufeldt, M. (1999) *Begin with the Brain*. Tucson, AZ: Zephyr Press.

Kauffman, J.M. (1999) How we prevent the prevention of emotional and behavioral disorders. *Exceptional Children, 65, 4*, 448–468.

Kauffman, J.M. (2001) *Characteristics of Emotional and Behavioral Disorders of Children and Youth* (7th edn). Upper Saddle River, NJ: Merrill-Prentice Hall.

Kauffman, J.M. (2002) *Education Deform: Bright People Sometimes Say Stupid Things about Education*. Lanham, MD: Scarecrow Press.

Kavale, K. (2002) Discrepancy models in the identification of learning disability. In R. Bradley, L. Danielson and D.P. Hallahan (eds) *Identification of Learning Disabilities: Research to Practice* (pp. 369–426). Mahwah, NJ: Erlbaum.

Kavale, K. and Forness, S.R. (2000a) What definitions of learning disability say and don't say. *Journal of Learning Disabilities, 33, 3*, 239–256.

Kavale, K. and Forness, S. (2000b) Policy decisions in special education: The role of meta-analysis. In R. Gersten, E. Schiller and S. Vaughn (eds) *Contemporary Special Education Research* (pp. 281–326). Mahwah, NJ: Erlbaum.

Kay, M.J. (2003) *Diagnosis and Intervention Strategies for Disorders of Written Language*. On line: http://www.udel.edu/bkirby/asperger/dysgraphia_mjkay.html

Kellett, M. and Nind, M. (2003) *Implementing Intensive Interaction in Schools*. London: Fulton.

Kershner, R. (2000) Teaching children whose progress in learning is causing concern. In D. Whitebread (ed.) *The Psychology of Teaching and Learning in the Primary School* (pp. 277–299). London: Routledge-Falmer.

Kibby, M.Y. and Hynd, G.W. (2001) Neurobiological basis of learning disabilities. In D.P. Hallahan and B.K. Keogh (eds) *Research and Global Perspectives in Learning Disability* (pp. 25–42). Mahwah, NJ: Elbaum.

Killen, R. (1998) *Effective Teaching Strategies: Lessons from Research and Practice* (2nd edn). Wentworth Falls, NSW: Social Science Press.

Kilpatrick, J., Swafford, J. and Findell, B. (eds) (2001) *Adding It Up: Helping Children Learn Mathematics*. Washington, DC: National Academy Press.

Kirk, S. (1962) *Educating Exceptional Children*. Boston: Houghton Mifflin.

Kirk, S., Gallagher, J. and Anastasiow, N. (2000) *Educating Exceptional Children* (9th edn). Boston: Houghton Mifflin.

Klassen, R. (2002) Writing in early adolescence: A review of the role of self-efficacy. *Educational Psychology Review, 14, 2*, 173–203.

Klinger, L.G., Dawson, G. and Renner, P. (2003) Autistic disorder. In E.J. Mash and R.A. Barkley (eds) *Child Psychopathology* (2nd edn, pp. 409–454). New York: Guilford Press.

Knight, B.A. (1992) The development of a locus of control measure designed to assess intellectually disabled students' beliefs in adaptive behaviour situations. *Australasian Journal of Special Education, 16, 2*, 13–21.

Knight, B.A. (1994) The effects of a teaching perspective of guided internality on intellectually disabled students' locus of control. *Educational Psychology, 14, 2*, 55–166.

Kosc, L. (1974) Developmental dyscalculia. *Journal of Learning Disabilities, 7*, 46–59.

Krasuski, J., Horwitz, B. and Rumsey, J.M. (1996) A survey of functional and anatomical neuroimaging techniques. In G.R. Lyon and J.M. Rumsey (eds) *Neuroimaging: A Window to the Neurological Foundations of Learning and Behaviour in Children* (pp. 25–52). Baltimore, MD: Brookes.

Kroesbergen, E.H. and van Luit, J.E.H. (2003) Mathematics interventions for children with special educational needs. *Remedial and Special Education, 24, 2*, 97–114.

Kuntze, M. (2001) Literacy and deaf children. *Topics in Language Disorders, 18, 4*, 1–15.

Lam, B.F.Y. (2003) The effect of training in word analysis strategies on primary school children's spelling attainment. Unpublished BEd dissertation, Faculty of Education, University of Hong Kong.

Larcombe, A. (1985) *Mathematical Learning Difficulties in Secondary School*. Milton Keynes: Open University Press.

Leahey, T.H. and Harris, R.J. (2001) *Learning and Cognition* (5th edn). Upper Saddle River, NJ: Prentice Hall.

LeDoux, J. (2002) *Synaptic Self: How Our Brains Become Who We Are*. New York: Viking.

Lee, I. (2002) Helping students develop coherence in writing. *English Teaching Forum, 40, 3*, 32–39.

Leiding, D. (2002) *The 'Won't' Learners: An Answer to Their Cry*. Lanham, MD: Scarecrow Press.

Lennon, J.E. and Slesinski, C. (1999) Early intervention in reading: Results of a screening and intervention program for kindergarten students. *School Psychology Review, 28, 3*, 353–364.

Leo, E. and Galloway, D. (1994) A questionnaire for identifying behavioural problems associated with maladaptive motivational style. *Educational and Child Psychology, 11, 2*, 91–99.

Lewin, L. (2003) *Paving the Way in Reading and Writing*. San Francisco, CA: Jossey-Bass.

Lieberman, D.A. (2000) *Learning, Behaviour and Cognition*. Belmont, CA: Wadsworth.

Linden, N. (2002) Special educational needs in mathematics: A problem developed in school? In S. Goodchild and L. English (eds) *Researching Mathematics Classrooms* (pp. 67–89). Westport, CT: Praeger.

Lindsley, O. (1992a) Why aren't effective teaching tools widely adopted? *Journal of Applied Behavior Analysis, 25, 1*, 21–26.

Lindsley, O. (1992b) Precision teaching: Discoveries and effects. *Journal of Applied Behaviour Analysis, 25, 1*, 51–57.

Lloyd, J.W. (2002) There's more to identifying learning disability than discrepancy. In R. Bradley, L. Danielson and D.P. Hallahan (eds) *Identification of Learning Disabilities: Research to Practice* (pp. 427–435). Mahwah, NJ: Erlbaum.

Lloyd, J.W. and Forness, S.R. (1998) Some methods are more effective than others. *Intervention in School and Clinic, 33, 4*, 195–201.

Lohman, D.F. (1996) Intelligence, learning and instruction. In E. de Corte and F.E. Weinert (eds) *International Encyclopedia of Developmental and Instructional Psychology* (pp. 660–665). Oxford: Pergamon.

Long, M. (2000) *The Psychology of Education*. London: Routledge-Falmer.

Louden, W., Chan, L.K.S., Elkins, J., Greaves, D., House, H., Milton, M. and others (2000) *Mapping the Territory: Primary Students with Learning Difficulties in Literacy and Numeracy*. Canberra: Department of Education, Training and Youth Affairs.

Lundberg, I., Olofsson, A. and Wall, S. (1980) Reading and spelling skills in the first school years predicted from phonemic awareness skills in kindergarten. *Scandinavian Journal of Psychology, 21*, 159–173.

Lyle, S. (1996) An analysis of collaborative group work in the primary school and factors relevant to its success. *Language and Education, 10, 1*, 13–31.

Lyon, G.R. (1996) Learning disabilities. In E.J. Mash and R.A. Barkley (eds) *Child Psychopathology* (pp. 390–435). New York: Guilford Press.

Lyon, G.R. (1998) Why reading is not a natural process. *Educational Leadership, 55, 6*, 14–18.

Lyon, G.R. (2002) Learning disabilities. In K.L. Freiberg (ed.) *Educating Exceptional Children – 02/03* (pp. 46–62). Guilford, CT: McGraw-Hill-Dushkin.

Lyon, G.R., Fletcher, J.M. and Barnes, M.C. (2003) Learning disabilities. In E.J. Mash and R.A. Barkley (eds) *Child Psychopathology* (2nd edn, pp. 520–586). New York: Guilford Press.

Lyytinen, H., Ahonen, T. and Räsänen, P. (1994) Dyslexia and dyscalculia in children: Risks, early precursors, bottlenecks and cognitive mechanisms. *Acta Paedpsychiatrica*, *56*, 179–192.

McCarrier, A., Pinnell, G.S. and Fountas, I.C. (2000) *Interactive Writing*. Portsmouth, NH: Heinemann.

McCarty, H. and Siccone, F. (2001) *Motivating your Students*. Boston: Allyn & Bacon.

McCombs, B.L. and Pope, J.E. (1994) *Motivating Hard to Reach Students*. Washington, DC: American Psychological Association.

McCoy, W.C. (2002) *What We Work With: Troubling Times for Educators*. Lanham, MD: Scarecrow Press.

McCutchen, D. (2000) Knowledge, processing, and working memory: Implications for a theory of writing. *Educational Psychologist, 35, 1,* 13–23.

McDevitt, T.M. and Ormrod, J.E. (2002) *Child Development and Education*. Upper Saddle River, NJ: Merrill-Prentice Hall.

McGuinness, D. (1998) *Why Children Can't Read*. Harmondsworth: Penguin Books.

McInerney, D. and McInerney, V. (2002) *Educational Psychology: Constructing Learning* (3rd edn). Sydney: Prentice Hall.

McIntyre, E., Rosebery, A. and Gonzalez, N. (2001) *Classroom Diversity: Connecting Curriculum to Students' Lives*. Portsmouth, NH: Heinemann.

McKinney, J.D. and Feagans, L.V. (1991) Subtypes of learning disability: A review. In L.V. Feagans, E.J. Short and L.J. Meltzer (eds) *Subtypes of Learning Disabilities: Theoretical Perspectives and Research* (pp. 3–31). Hillsdale, NJ: Erlbaum.

McLaren, P. (2003) *Life in Schools: An Introduction to Critical Pedagogy in the Foundations of Education* (4th edn). Boston: Allyn & Bacon

McLean, J.F. and Hitch, G.J. (1999) Working memory impairments in children with specific arithmetic learning difficulties. *Journal of Experimental Child Psychology, 74,* 240–260.

McLoyd, V. (1998) Socioeconomic disadvantage and child development. *American Psychologist, 53,* 185–204.

MacMillan, D.L. and Siperstein, G.N. (2002) Learning disabilities as operationally defined by schools. In R. Bradley, L. Danielson and D.P. Hallahan (eds) *Identification of Learning Disabilities: Research to Practice* (pp. 287–333). Mahwah, NJ: Erlbaum.

McRorie, M. and Cooper, C. (2003) Neural transmission and general mental ability. *Learning and Individual Differences, 13,* 335–338.

Macaruso, P. and Sokol, S.M. (1998) Cognitive neuropsychology and developmental dyscalculia. In C. Donlan (ed.) *The Development of Mathematical Skills* (pp. 201–225). Hove: Psychology Press.

Mamchur, C. (1996) *A Teacher's Guide to Cognitive Type Theory and Learning Style*. Alexandria, VA: Association for Supervision and Curriculum Development.

Manis, F.R., Seidenberg, M.S., Doi, L.S., McBride-Chang, C. and Petersen, A. (1996) On the bases of two sub-types of developmental dyslexia. *Cognition, 58,* 157–195.

Marlowe, B.A. (1998) *Creating and Sustaining the Constructivist Classroom*. Thousand Oaks, CA: Corwin Press.

Marschark, M., Lang, H.G. and Albertini, J.A. (2002) *Educating Deaf Students: From Research to Practice*. Oxford: Oxford University Press.

Marston, D. (1996) A comparison of inclusion only, pull-out only, and combined service models for students with mild disabilities. *Journal of Special Education, 30, 2,* 121–132.

Martens, B.K., Witt, J.C., Daly, E.J. and Vollmer, T.R. (1999) Behavior analysis: Theory and practice in educational settings. In C.R. Reynolds and T.B. Gutkin (eds) *The Handbook of School Psychology* (3rd edn, pp. 638–663). New York: Wiley.

Martin, A.J. and Marsh, H.W. (2003) Fear of failure: Friend or foe? *Australian Psychologist, 38, 1*, 31–38.

Marvin, C. and Stokoe, C. (2003) *Access to Science: Curriculum Planning and Practical Activities for Pupils with Learning Difficulties*. London: Fulton.

Mash, E.J. and Wolfe, D.A. (1999) *Abnormal Child Psychology*. Belmont, CA: Wadsworth.

Masten, A.S. (1994) Resilience in individual development: Successful adaptation despite risk and adversity. In M.C. Wang and E.W. Gordon (eds) *Educational Resilience in Inner-City America: Challenges and Prospects* (pp. 3–26). Hillsdale, N.J: Erlbaum.

Mastropieri, M.A. and Scruggs, T.E. (2002) *Effective Instruction for Special Education* (3rd edn). Austin, TX: ProEd.

Mather, N. and Goldstein, S. (2001) *Learning Disabilities and Challenging Behaviour.* Baltimore, MD: Brookes.

Mather, N. and Roberts, R. (1994) Learning disabilities: A field in danger of extinction. *Learning Disabilities Research and Practice, 9, 1*, 49–58.

Mayer, R.E. (2000) Intelligence and education. In R.J. Sternberg (ed.) *Handbook of Intelligence* (pp. 519–533). Cambridge: Cambridge University Press.

Mayer, R.E. (2001) Cognitive, metacognitive and motivational aspects of problem solving. In H.J. Hartman (ed.) *Metacognition in Learning and Instruction* (pp. 87–101). Dordrecht: Kluwer Academic.

Mazur, J.E. (2001) *Learning and Behavior* (5th edn). Upper Saddle River, NJ: Prentice Hall.

Meade, A. (2001) One hundred billion neurons: How do they become organised? In T. David (ed.) *Promoting Evidence-Based Practices in Early Childhood Education: Research and its Implications* (v.1, pp. 3–26). New York: JAI Press.

Meese, R.L. (2001) *Teaching Learners with Mild Disabilities: Integrating Research and Practice* (2nd edn). Belmont, CA: Wadsworth-Thomson.

Meltzer, L. and Montague, M. (2001) Strategic learning in students with learning disabilities: What have we learned? In D.P. Hallahan and B.K. Keogh (eds) *Research and Global Perspectives in Learning Disabilities.* (pp. 111–130). Mahwah, NJ: Erlbaum.

Meyer, A., Murray, E. and Pisha, B. (2000) More than words: Learning to write in the digital world. In A.M. Bain, L.L. Bailet and L.C. Moats (eds) *Written Language Disorders* (pp. 137–184). Austin, TX: ProEd.

Miles, T. R., Haslum, M. N. and Wheeler, T. (2001) The mathematical abilities of dyslexic 10-year-olds. *Annals of Dyslexia, 51*, 299–322.

Miles, T.R. and Miles, E. (1992) *Dyslexia and Mathematics*. London: Routledge.

Miles, T.R. and Westcombe, J. (eds) (2001) *Music and Dyslexia*. London: Whurr.

Miller, G.A. (1956) The magical number seven, plus or minus two: Some limits on our capacity for processing information. *Psychological Review, 63*, 81–97.

Minke, K.M. and Bear, G.C. (eds) (2000) *Preventing School Problems: Promoting School Success*. Bethesda, MD: National Association of School Psychologists.

Minskoff, E. and Allsopp, D. (2003) *Academic Success Strategies for Adolescents with Learning Disabilities and ADHD*. Baltimore, MD: Brookes.

Mittler, P. (2000) *Working Towards Inclusive Education: Social Contexts*. London: Fulton.

Moats, L.C. (2002) Learning disabilities and low achievement are not meaningfully different categories for classification or treatment of reading disabilities. In R. Bradley, L. Danielson and D.P. Hallahan (eds) *Identification of Learning Disabilities: Research to Practice* (pp. 777–782). Mahwah, NJ: Erlbaum.

Morris, D. (2003) Reading instruction in first grade. In D. Morris and R.E. Slavin (eds) *Every Child Reading* (pp. 33–57). Boston: Allyn & Bacon.

Morris, D. and Slavin, R. (2003) *Every Child Reading*. Boston: Allyn & Bacon.

Morris, N. and Sarll, P. (2001) Drinking glucose improves listening span in students who miss breakfast. *Educational Research, 43*, 2, 201–207.

Morrison, S.R. and Siegel, L.S. (1991) Arithmetic disability: Theoretical considerations and evidence for this subtype. In L.V. Feagans, E.J. Short and L.J. Meltzer (eds) *Subtypes of Learning Disabilities* (pp. 189–208). Hillsdale, NJ: Erlbaum.

Morrow, L.M. (2001) *Literacy Development in the Early Years: Helping Children Read and Write* (4th edn). Boston: Allyn & Bacon.

Naparstek, N. (2002) *Successful Educators: A Practical Guide for Understanding Children's Learning Problems and Mental Health Issues*. Westpoint, CT: Bergin and Garvey.

Nash, J.M. (2001) Fertile minds. In E. Nunn and C. Noyatzis (eds) *Child Growth and Development 01-02* (pp. 24–28). Guilford, CT: McGraw-Hill-Dushkin.

National Council of Teachers of Mathematics (2000) *Principles and Standards for School Mathematics*. Reston, VA: National Council.

National Reading Panel (US) (2000) *Teaching Children to Read: An Evidence-Based Assessment of the Scientific Research Literature on Reading and its Implications for Reading Instruction*. Washington, DC: National Institute of Child Health and Human Development. http://www.nichd.nih.gov/publications/pubslist.cfm#RR

Neal, J. and Kelly, P.R. (2002) Delivering the promise of academic success through late intervention. *Reading and Writing Quarterly, 18*, 101–117.

Neisser, U. and associates (1996) Intelligence: Knowns and unknowns. *American Psychologist, 51*, 2, 77–101.

Nelson, N. and Calfee, R.C. (1998) *The Reading-Writing Connection*. Chicago, IL: National Society for the Study of Education.

Newton, D.P. (2000) *Teaching for Understanding: What It Is and How to Do It*. London: Routledge-Falmer.

Nielsen, L.B. (1997) *The Exceptional Child in the Regular Classroom*. Thousand Oaks, CA: Corwin Press.

Nielsen L.B. (2002) *Brief Reference of Student Disabilities*. Thousand Oaks, CA: Corwin Press.

Nind, M. (2000) Teachers' understanding of interactive approaches in special education. *International Journal of Disability, Development and Education, 47*, 2, 183–199.

Numminen, H., Service, E. and Ruoppila, I. (2002) Working memory, intelligence and knowledge base in adult persons with intellectual disability. *Research in Developmental Disabilities, 23*, 105–118.

Nuthall, G. (1999) Learning how to learn: The evolution of students' minds through the social processes and culture of the classroom. *International Journal of Educational Research, 31*, 141–256.

O'Brien, T. and Guiney, D. (2001) *Differentiation in Teaching and Learning*. London: Continuum.

OECD (Organisation for Economic Cooperation and Development) (1999) *Inclusive Education at Work: Students with Disabilities in Mainstream Schools*. Paris: OECD Centre for Educational Research and Innovation.

OECD (Organisation for Economic Cooperation and Development) (2001) *Knowledge and Skills for Life*. Paris: OECD.

OECD (Organisation for Economic Cooperation and Development) (2002) *Understanding the Brain: Towards a New Learning Science*. Paris: OECD.

OFSTED (Office for Standards in Education) (1993) *The Teaching and Learning of Number in Primary Schools*, London: HMSO.

Olson, C.B. (2003) *The Reading/Writing Connection: Strategies for Teaching and Learning in the Secondary Classroom*. Boston: Allyn & Bacon.

Ormrod, J.E. (2003) *Educational Psychology: Developing Learners* (4th edn). Upper Saddle River, NJ: Merrill-Prentice Hall.

Ortiz, A.A. and Yates, J.R. (2002) Response to 'Is learning disabilities just a fancy term for low achievement?' In R. Bradley, L. Danielson and D.P. Hallahan (eds) *Identification of Learning Disabilities: Research to Practice* (pp. 783–789). Mahwah, NJ: Erlbaum.

O'Shea, L.J., O'Shea, D.J. and Algozzine, B. (1998) *Learning Disabilities from Theory to Practice*. Upper Saddle River, NJ: Merrill.

Otaiba, S.A. and Fuchs, D. (2002) Characteristics of children who are unresponsive to early literacy intervention. *Remedial and Special Education, 23, 5*, 300–316.

Owen, R.L. and Fuchs, L.S. (2002) Mathematical problem-solving strategy instruction for third-grade students with learning disabilities. *Remedial and Special Education, 23, 5*, 268–278.

Paas, F., Renkl, A. and Sweller, J. (2003) Cognitive load theory and instructional design: Recent developments. *Educational Psychologist, 38, 1*, 1–4.

Pagliano, P. (1998) Students with vision impairment. In A. Ashman and J. Elkins (eds) *Educating Children with Special Needs* (3rd edn, pp. 383–416). Sydney: Prentice Hall.

Paris, S.G. and Turner, J.C. (1994) Situated motivation. In P. Pintrich, D. Brown and C.E. Weinstein (eds) *Student Motivation, Cognition, and Learning* (pp. 213–237). Hillsdale, NJ: Erlbaum.

Pellegrino, J.W. and Varnhagen, C.K. (1990) Abilities and aptitudes. In R.M. Thomas (ed.) *The Encyclopedia of Human Development and Education* (pp. 214–221). Oxford: Pergamon.

Penso, S. (2002) Pedagogical content knowledge: How do student teachers identify and describe the causes of their pupils' learning difficulties? *Asia-Pacific Journal of Teacher Education, 30, 1*, 25–37.

Perutz, M. (2001) Review of the book 'It ain't necessarily so: The dream of the human genome and other illusions' by Richard Lewontin. (2000: London: Granta). *The Times Higher Education Supplement, 1475*, 24–25.

Peters, M. and Smith, B. (1993) *Spelling in Context*. Windsor: NFER-Nelson.

Peters, S.J., Klein, A. and Shadwick, C. (1998) From our voices: Special education and the 'alter-eagle' problem. In B. Franklin (ed.) *When Children Don't Learn* (pp. 99–115). New York: Teachers College Press.

Phillips, D.C. (1995) The good, the bad and the ugly: The many faces of constructivism. *Educational Researcher, 24, 7*, 5–12.

Phillips, N.B., Fuchs, L., Fuchs, D. and Hamlett, C. (1996) Instructional variables affecting student achievement: Case studies of two contrasting teachers. *Learning Disabilities Research and Practice, 11, 1*, 24–33.

Piaget, J. (1929) *The Child's Conception of the World*. New York: Harcourt Brace.

Piaget, J. (1952) *The Origins of Intelligence in Children*. New York: International University Press.

Pikulski, J. (1994) Preventing reading failure: A review of five effective programs. *The Reading Teacher, 48, 1*, 30–39.

Pinnell, G.S. (1997) Reading recovery: A summary of research. In J. Flood, S.B. Heath and D. Lapp (eds) *Handbook of Research on Teaching Through Communicative and Visual Arts* (pp. 638–654). New York, Macmillan.

Porter, L. (2000) *Behaviour in Schools: Theory and Practice for Teachers*. Buckingham: Open University Press.

Pound, L. (1999) *Supporting Mathematical Development in the Early Years*. Buckingham: Open University Press.

Pound, L. (2002) Breadth and depth in early foundations. In J. Fisher (ed.) *The Foundations of Learning* (pp. 9–24). Buckingham: Open University Press.

Power, D. (1998) Deaf and hard of hearing students. In A. Ashman and J. Elkins (eds) *Educating Children with Special Needs* (3rd edn., pp. 345–381). Sydney: Prentice Hall.

Premack, D. (1959) Toward empirical behavior laws: Positive reinforcement. *Psychological Review, 66*, 219–233.

Pressley, M. (1998) *Reading Instruction that Works: The Case for Balanced Teaching.* New York: Guilford Press.

Pressley, M. (1999) Self-regulated comprehension processing and its development through instruction. In L. Gambrell, L.M. Morrow, S.B. Neuman and M. Pressley (eds) *Best Practices in Literacy Instruction* (pp. 90–97). New York: Guilford Press.

Pressley, M. and Harris, K. (1997) Constructivism and instruction. *Issues in Education, 3, 2*, 245–256.

Pressley, M. and McCormick, C.B. (1995) *Advanced Educational Psychology for Educators, Researchers and Policymakers.* New York: HarperCollins.

Pressley, M. and Schneider, W. (1997) *Introduction to Memory Development during Childhood and Adolescence.* Mahwah, NJ: Erlbaum.

Prior, M. (1996) *Understanding Specific Learning Difficulties.* Hove: Psychology Press.

Purdie, N., Hattie, J. and Carroll, A. (2002) A review of the research on interventions for attention deficit hyperactivity disorder: What works best? *Review of Educational Research, 72, 1*, 61–99.

Purdy, J.E., Markham, M.R., Schwartz, B.L. and Gordon, W.C. (2001) *Learning and Memory* (2nd edn). Belmont, CA: Wadsworth-Thomson.

Quilter, D. and Harper, E. (1988) 'Why we didn't like mathematics, and why we can't do it'. *Educational Research, 30, 2*, 121–134.

Ramaa, S. and Gowramma, I.P. (2002) A systematic procedure for identifying and classifying children with dyscalculia among primary school children in India. *Dyslexia, 8*, 67–85.

Ramey, C.T. and Ramey, S.L. (2000) Intelligence and public policy. In R.J. Sternberg (ed.) *Handbook of Intelligence* (pp. 534–548). Cambridge: Cambridge University Press.

Räsänen, P. and Ahonen, T. (1995) Arithmetic disabilities with and without reading difficulties: A comparison of arithmetic errors. *Developmental Neuropsychology, 11*, 275–295.

Ratey, J.J. (2001) *A User's Guide to the Brain: Perception, Attention and the Four Theatres of the Brain.* New York: Pantheon Books.

Ravenette, A.T. (1968) *Dimensions of Reading Difficulties.* Oxford: Pergamon.

Ravenette, A.T. (1999) *Personal Construct Theory in Educational Psychology.* London: Whurr.

Reid, G. (2003) *Dyslexia: A Practitioner's Handbook* (3rd edn). Chichester: Wiley

Reusser, K. (2000) Success and failure in school mathematics: Effects of instruction and school environment. *European Child and Adolescent Psychiatry, 9, Supplement 2*, 17–26.

Reys, R.E., Lindquist, M.M., Lambdin, D.V, Smith, N.L., and Suydam, M.N. (2004) *Helping Children Learn Mathematics* (7th edn). Hoboken, NJ: Wiley.

Ricciuti, H.N. (1993) Nutrition and mental development. *Current Directions in Psychological Science, 2*, 43–46.

Richards, P. (1982) Difficulties in learning mathematics. In M. Cornelius (ed.) *Teaching Mathematics* (pp. 59–80). London: Croom Helm.

Richards, R.G. (1999) *The Source Book for Dyslexia and Dysgraphia.* East Moline, IL: Linguisystems.

Richardson, K. (1999) *The Making of Intelligence.* London: Weidenfeld and Nicolson.

Richek, M.A., Caldwell, J.S., Jennings, J.H. and Lerner, J.W. (2002) *Reading Problems: Assessment and Teaching Strategies* (4th edn). Boston: Allyn & Bacon.

Riding, R. (2002) *School Learning and Cognitive Style*. London: Fulton.

Roach, E. and Kephart, N. (1966) *The Purdue Perceptual-Motor Survey*. Columbus, OH: Merrill.

Robertson, P., Hamill, P. and Hewitt, C. (1994) Effective support for learning. *Interchange*, 2, 1–8. Edinburgh: Education Department Scottish Office.

Robinson, C.S., Menchetti, B.M. and Torgesen, J.K. (2002) Toward a two-factor theory of one type of mathematics disability. *Learning Disabilities Research and Practice*, 17, 2, 81–89.

Robinson, G. (2001) Problems in literacy and numeracy. In P. Foreman (ed.) *Integration and Inclusion in Action* (2nd edn, pp. 169–229). Melbourne: Nelson-Thomson.

Roediger, H.L. and Meade, M.L. (2000) Cognitive approaches for humans. In A.E. Kazdin (ed.) *Encyclopedia of Psychology* (v.5, pp. 8–11). Oxford: Oxford University Press.

Romberg, T.A. (1995) *Reform in School Mathematics and Authentic Assessment*. Albany, NY: University of New York Press.

Rooney, K.J. (2002) Clinical judgment in the assessment of learning disabilities. In R. Bradley, L. Danielson and D.P. Hallahan (eds) *Identification of Learning Disabilities: Research to Practice* (pp. 713–723). Mahwah, NJ: Erlbaum.

Rosenshine, B. (1986) Synthesis of research on instruction. *Educational Leadership*, 43, 7, 60–78.

Rosenshine, B. (1995) Advances in research on instruction. *Journal of Educational Research*, 88, 5, 262–268.

Rosner, J. (1993) *Helping Children Overcome Learning Difficulties* (3rd edn). New York: Walker.

Rotter, J.B. (1966) Generalized expectancies for internal versus external control of reinforcement. *Psychological Monographs 80*, 1, 609.

Rourke, B.P. (1993) Arithmetic disabilities specific and otherwise: A neuropsychological perspective. *Journal of Learning Disabilities*, 26, 4, 214–226.

Rourke, B.P. and Del Dotto, J.E. (1994) *Learning Disabilities: A Neuropsychological Perspective*. Thousand Oaks, CA: Sage Publications.

Rumsey, J.M. (1996) Neuro-imaging in developmental dyslexia. In G.R. Lyon and J.M. Rumsey (eds) *Neuroimaging: A Window to the Neurological Foundations of Learning and Behaviour in Children* (pp. 57–77). Baltimore, MD: Brookes.

Rutter, M. and Maughan, B. (2002) School effectiveness findings 1979–2002. *Journal of School Psychology*, 40, 6, 451–475.

Ryan, A.M., Pintrich, P.R. and Midgley, C. (2001) Avoiding seeking help in the classroom: Who and why? *Educational Psychology Review*, 13, 2, 93–114.

Ryan, R.M. and Deci, E.L. (2000) Intrinsic and extrinsic motivations: Classic definitions and new directions. *Contemporary Educational Psychology*, 25, 54–67.

Ryba, K., Curzon, J. and Selby, L. (2002) Learning partnerships through information and communication technology. In A. Ashman and J. Elkins (eds) *Educating Children with Diverse Abilities* (pp. 500–529). Sydney: Prentice Hall.

Ryndak, D. and Alper, S. (2003) *Curriculum and Instruction for Students with Significant Disabilities in Inclusive Settings* (2nd edn). Boston: Allyn & Bacon.

Santrock, J.W. (2001) *Educational Psychology*. New York: McGraw-Hill.

Sasson, G.M. (2001) The retreat from inquiry and knowledge in special education. *Journal of Special Education*, 34, 4, 178–193.

Scanlon, D.M. and Vellutino, F.R. (1997) A comparison of the instructional backgrounds and cognitive profiles of poor, average and good readers who were initially identified as at risk for reading failure. *Scientific Studies of Reading*, 1, 3, 191–215.

Schlinger, H.D. (2003) The myth of intelligence. *The Psychological Record*, 53, 15–32.

Schneider, W. and Bjorkland, D. (2003) Memory and knowledge development. In J. Valsiner and K.J. Connolly (eds) *Handbook of Developmental Psychology* (pp. 370–403). London: Sage.

Schunk, D.H. (2000) *Learning Theories: An Educational Perspective* (3rd edn). Upper Saddle River, NJ: Merrill-Prentice Hall.

Schunk, D.H. (2003) *Learning Theories: An Educational Perspective* (4th edn). Upper Saddle River, NJ: Merrill-Prentice Hall.

Segal, S.S. (1974) *No Child is Ineducable* (2nd edn). Oxford: Pergamon.

Seligman, M.E.P. (1995) *The Optimistic Child*. Boston: Houghton Mifflin.

Selley, N. (1999) *The Art of Constructivist Teaching in Primary School*. London: Fulton.

Seng, A.S.H., Pou, L.K.H. and Tan, O.S. (2003) *Mediated Learning Experience with Children*. Singapore: McGraw-Hill.

Seymour, P. and Evans, H.M. (1999) Foundation-level dyslexia: Assessment and treatment. *Journal of Learning Disabilities, 32*, 394–405.

Shalev, R.S. and Gross-Tsur, V. (2001) Developmental dyscalculia. *Pediatric Neurology, 24*, 337–342.

Shanker, J.L. and Ekwall, E.E. (2003) *Locating and Correcting Reading Difficulties* (8th edn). Upper Saddle River, NJ: Merrill.

Shapiro, E.S. and Elliott, S.N. (1999) Curriculum-based assessment and other performance-based assessment strategies. In C.R. Reynolds and T.B. Gutkin (eds) *The Handbook of School Psychology* (3rd edn, pp. 383–408). New York: Wiley.

Shaywitz, B.A., Fletcher, J.M., Holahan, J.M. and Shaywitz, S.E. (1992) Discrepancy compared to low-achievement definitions of reading disability: Results from the Connecticut longitudinal study. *Journal of Learning Disabilities, 25, 10*, 639–648.

Sheehy, K. (2002) The effective use of symbols in teaching word recognition to children with severe learning difficulties. *International Journal of Disability, Development and Education, 49, 1*, 47–59.

Shulman, L.S. (1987) Knowledge and teaching: Foundations of the new reform. *Harvard Educational Review, 57, 1*, 1–22.

Sideridis, G. and Greenwood, C. (1998) Identification and validation of effective instructional practices for children from impoverished backgrounds and those with learning and developmental disabilities using ecobehavioural analysis. *European Journal of Special Needs Education, 13, 2*, 145–154.

Siegel, L. (1998) The discrepancy formula: Its use and abuse. In B. Shapiro, P.J. Accardo and A.J. Capute (eds) *Specific Reading Disability: A View of the Spectrum* (pp. 123–153). Timonium, MD: York Press.

Silcock, P. (2003) Accelerated learning: A revolution in teaching method? *Education, 3–13, 31, 1*, 48–52.

Silver, A.A. and Hagin, R.A. (2002) *Disorders of Learning in Childhood* (2nd edn). New York: Wiley.

Silverman, S.L. and Casazza, M.E. (2000) *Learning and Development: Making Connections to Enhance Teaching*. San Francisco: Jossey-Bass.

Slavin, R.E. (1994) Preventing early school failure. In R.E. Slavin, N.L. Karweit and B.A. Wasik (eds) *Preventing Early School Failure* (pp. 1–12). Boston: Allyn & Bacon.

Slavin, R. (2003) *Educational Psychology* (7th edn). Boston: Allyn & Bacon.

Slavin, R. and Madden, N.A. (2001) *One Million Children: 'Success for All'*. Thousand Oaks, CA: Corwin Press.

Smilkstein, R. (2003) *We're Born to Learn*. Thousand Oaks, CA: Corwin Press.

Smith, C. (1998) *Learning Disabilities: The Interaction of Learner, Task and Setting* (4th edn). Boston: Allyn & Bacon.

Smith-Burke, M.T. (2001) Reading Recovery: A systematic approach to early intervention. In L.M. Morrow and D.G. Woo (eds) *Tutoring Programs for Struggling Readers* (pp. 216–236). New York: Guilford Press.

Smyth, G. (2003) *Helping Bilingual Pupils Access the Curriculum*. London: Fulton.

Snell, M.E. and Brown, F. (2000) *Instruction of Students with Severe Disabilities* (5th edn). Upper Saddle River, NJ: Merrill.

Snow, C.E., Burns, M.S. and Griffin, P. (1998) *Preventing Reading Difficulties in Young Children*. Washington, DC: National Academy Press.

Snowman, J. and Biehler, R. (2003) *Psychology Applied to Teaching* (10th edn). Boston: Houghton Mifflin.

Sousa, D.A. (2001a) *How the Brain Learns: A Classroom Teacher's Guide* (2nd edn). Thousand Oaks, CA: Corwin Press.

Sousa, D.A. (2001b) *How the Special Needs Brain Learns*. Thousand Oaks, CA: Corwin Press.

Spearman, C. (1927) *The Abilities of Man*. London: Macmillan.

Spear-Swerling, L. & Sternberg, R.J. (2001) What science offers teachers of reading. *Learning Disabilities Research and Practice, 16, 1*, 51–57.

Speece, D.L. (1993) Broadening the scope of classification research. In G.R. Lyon, D.B. Gray, J.F. Kavanagh and N.A. Krasnegor (eds) *Better Understanding Learning Disabilities* (pp. 57–72). Baltimore, MD: Brookes.

Speece, D.L., Case, L.P. and Molloy, D.E. (2003) Responsiveness to general education instruction as the first gate to learning disabilities identification. *Learning Disabilities Research and Practice, 18, 3*, 147–156.

Spitz, H.H. (1999) Attempts to raise intelligence. In M. Anderson (ed.) *The Development of Intelligence* (pp. 275–293). Hove: Psychology Press.

Sprenger, M.B. (1999) *Learning and Memory: The Brain in Action*. Alexandria, VA: Association for Supervision and Curriculum Development.

Sprenger, M.B. (2002) *Becoming a "Wiz" at Brain-Based Teaching*. Thousand Oaks, CA: Corwin Press.

Sprinthall, R., Sprinthall, N. and Oja, S.N. (1998) *Educational Psychology: A Developmental Approach* (7th edn) Boston: McGraw-Hill.

Squire, L.R. and Schacter, D.L. (2002) *Neuropsychology of Memory* (3rd edn). New York: Guilford Press.

Stage, S.A., Abbott, R.D., Jenkins, J.R. and Berninger, V.W. (2003) Predicting response to early reading intervention from verbal IQ, reading-related language abilities, attention ratings, and verbal IQ-word reading discrepancy: Failure to validate discrepancy method. *Journal of Learning Disabilities, 36, 1*, 24–33.

Stanovich, K.E. (1980) Toward an interactive compensatory model of individual differences in the development of reading fluency. *Reading Research Quarterly, 16*, 32–71.

Stanovich, K.E. (1986) Matthew effects in reading: Some consequences of individual differences in the acquisition of literacy. *Reading Research Quarterly, 21*, 360–406.

Stanovich, K.E. (1994) Constructivism in reading education. *Journal of Special Education, 28, 3*, 259–274.

Stanovich, K.E. and Siegel, L.S. (1998) The role of IQ in the diagnosis of reading disorders: The quest for a subtype based on aptitude/achievement discrepancy. In J. Rispens, T.A. van Yperen and W. Yule (eds) *Perspectives on the Classification of Specific Developmental Disorders* (pp. 105–136). Dordrecht: Kluwer Academic Publishing.

Stein, J.F. (1993) Visuospatial perception in disabled readers. In D.M. Willows, R.S. Kruk and E. Corcos (eds) *Visual Processes in Reading and Reading Disabilities* (pp. 331–346). Hillsdale, NJ: Erlbaum.

Steinberg, A.G. and Knightly, C.A. (1997) Hearing. In M. Batshaw (ed.) *Children with Disabilities* (4th edn, pp. 241–274). Sydney: MacLennan and Petty.

Sternberg, R.J. (1984) Toward a triarchic theory of human intelligence. *Behavior and Brain Sciences, 2,* 269–315.

Sternberg, R.J. (1985) *Beyond IQ: A Triarchic Theory of Human Intelligence.* New York: Freeman.

Sternberg, R.J. (1996) *Successful Intelligence.* New York: Simon and Schuster.

Sternberg, R.J. (ed.) (2000) *Handbook of Intelligence.* Cambridge: Cambridge University Press.

Sternberg, R.J. and Grigorenko, E. (2001) Learning disabilities, schooling and society. *Phi Delta Kappan, 83, 4,* 335–338.

Stipek, D.J. and Greene, J.K. (2001) Achievement motivation in early childhood: Cause for concern or celebration? In S.L. Golbeck (ed.) *Psychological Perspectives on Early Childhood Education* (pp. 64–91). Mahwah, NJ: Erlbaum.

St John, E.P., Loescher, A.A. and Bardzell, J.S. (2003) *Improving Reading and Literacy in Grades 1–5: A Resource Guide to Research-Based Programs.* Thousand Oaks, CA: Corwin Press.

Strickland, D.S. (1998) What's basic in beginning reading? *Educational Leadership, 55, 6,* 6–10.

Strickland, D.S., Ganske, K. and Monroe, J.K. (2002) *Supporting Struggling Readers and Writers.* Portland, ME: Stenhouse.

Sue, D., Sue, D.W. and Sue, S. (2003) *Understanding Abnormal Behaviour* (7th edn). Boston: Houghton Mifflin.

Sunseth, K. and Bowers, P. (2002) Rapid naming and phonemic awareness: Contributions to reading, spelling and orthographic knowledge. *Scientific Studies of Reading, 6, 4,* 401–430.

Swanson, H.L. (1999) *Interventions for Students with Learning Disabilities: Meta-Analysis of Treatment Outcomes.* New York: Guilford Press.

Swanson, H.L. (2000a) What instruction works for students with learning disabilities? In R. Gersten, E. Schiller and S. Vaughn (eds) *Contemporary Special Education Research* (pp. 1–30). Mahwah, NJ: Erlbaum.

Swanson, H.L. (2000b) Issues facing the field of learning disabilities. *Learning Disabilities Quarterly, 23,* 37–50.

Swanson, H.L. (2002) Learning disabilities is a specific processing deficit, but it is much more than phonological processing. In R. Bradley, L. Danielson and D.P. Hallahan (eds) *Identification of Learning Disabilities: Research to Practice* (pp. 643–651). Mahwah, NJ: Erlbaum.

Swanson, H.L., Harris, K.R. and Graham, S. (2003) *Handbook of Learning Disabilities.* New York: Guilford Press.

Swanson, H.L. and Siegel, L. (2001) Learning disabilities as a working memory deficit. *Issues in Education, 7, 1,* 1–48.

Swanson, H.L. and Saez, L. (2003) Memory difficulties in children and adults with learning disabilities. In H.L. Swanson, K.R. Harris and S. Graham (eds) *Handbook of Learning Disabilities* (pp. 182–198). New York: Guilford Press.

Sweller, J. (1999) *Instructional Design in Technical Areas.* Melbourne: Australian Council for Educational Research.

Sylwester, R. (2003) *A Biological Brain in a Cultural Classroom* (2nd edn). Thousand Oaks, CA: Corwin Press.

Tan, O.S., Parsons, R.D., Hinson, S.L. and Sardo-Brown, D. (2003) *Educational Psychology: A Practitioner-Researcher Model of Teaching.* Belmont, CA: Wadsworth-Thomson.

Tarpy, R.M. (1997) *Contemporary Learning Theory and Research.* New York: McGraw-Hill.

Tate, M.L. (2003) *Worksheets Don't Grow Dendrites: 20 Instructional Strategies that Engage the Brain*. Thousand Oaks, CA: Corwin Press.

Taylor, B., Harris, L.A., Pearson, P.D. and Garcia, G. (1995) *Reading Difficulties: Instruction and Assessment* (2nd edn). New York: McGraw-Hill.

Taylor, B., Peterson, D., Pearson, P.D. and Rodriguez, M.C. (2002) Looking inside classrooms: Reflecting on the 'how' as well as the 'what' in effective reading instruction. *The Reading Teacher, 56*, 3, 270–279.

Taylor, B., Strait, J. and Medo, M.A. (1994) Early intervention in reading. In E.H. Hiebert and B. Taylor (eds) *Getting Reading Right from the Start* (pp. 107–121). New York: Allyn & Bacon.

Taylor, G.R. (2002) *Using Human Learning Strategies in the Classroom*. Lanham, MD: Scarecrow Press.

Taylor, R.L., Sternberg, L. and Richards, S.B. (1995) *Exceptional Children: Integrating Research and Teaching*. San Diego, CA: Singular Publishing.

Temple C. (1997) *Developmental Cognitive Neuropsychology*. Hove: Psychology Press.

Temple, C.M. (2001) Developmental dyscalculia. In S.J. Segalowitz and I. Rapin (eds) *Handbook of Neuropsychology* (v.7, pp. 211–222). Amsterdam: Elsevier.

Terry, W.S. (2000) *Learning and Memory: Basic Principles, Processes and Procedures*. Boston: Allyn & Bacon.

Thorkildsen, T.A. and Nicholls, J.G. (2002) *Motivation and the Struggle to Learn: Responding to Fractured Experience*. Boston: Allyn & Bacon.

Thorndike, E.L. (1927) The law of effect. *American Journal of Psychology, 39*, 212–222.

Thurstone, L.L. (1938) *Primary Mental Abilities*. Chicago: University of Chicago Press.

Tobias, S. (1993) *Overcoming Math Anxiety*. New York: Norton.

Tomlinson, C.A. and Kalbfleisch, M.L. (1998) Teach me, teach my brain: A call for differentiated classrooms. *Educational Leadership, 56*, 3, 52–55.

Tompkins, G.E. (2000) *Teaching Writing: Balancing Process and Product* (3rd edn). Upper Saddle River, NJ: Merrill.

Topping, K., Nixon, J., Sutherland, J. and Yarrow, F. (2000) Paired writing: A framework for effective collaboration. *Reading 34*, 2, 79–89.

Torgesen, J.K. (1999) Phonologically based reading disabilities: A coherent theory of one kind of learning disability. In R.J. Sternberg and L. Spear-Swerling (eds) *Perspectives in Learning Disabilities* (pp. 106–135). Boulder, CO: Westview Press.

Torgesen, J.K. (2002) Empirical and theoretical support for direct diagnosis of learning disabilities by assessment of intrinsic processing weaknesses. In R. Bradley, L. Danielson and D.P. Hallahan (eds) *Identification of Learning Disabilities: Research to Practice* (pp. 565–613). Mahwah, NJ: Erlbaum.

Troia, G.A. and Graham, S. (2002) The effectiveness of a highly explicit, teacher-directed strategy instruction routine: Changing the writing performance of students with learning disabilities. *Journal of Learning Disabilities, 35*, 4, 290–305.

Troutman, A.P. and Lichtenberg, B.K. (2003) *Mathematics: A Good Beginning* (6th edn). Belmont, CA: Wadsworth-Thomson.

Tuovinen, J.E. and Sweller, J. (1999) A comparison of cognitive load associated with discovery learning and worked examples. *Journal of Educational Psychology, 91*, 2, 334–341.

Tur-Kaspa, H. (2002) Social cognition in learning disabilities. In B.Y.L. Wong and M. Donahue (eds) *The Social Dimensions of Learning Disabilities* (pp. 11–31). Mahwah, NJ: Erlbaum.

Turkington, C. & Harris, J. (2002) *The Encyclopedia of Learning Disabilities*. New York: Facts on File.

Turnbull, R., Turnbull, A., Shank, M., Smith, S. and Leal, D. (2002) *Exceptional Lives* (3rd edn). Upper Saddle River, NJ: Merrill-Prentice Hall.

Turner, A. (2002) *Access to History: Curriculum Planning and Practical Activities for Pupils with Learning Difficulties*. London: Fulton.

Tyler, J.S. and Mira, M.P. (1999) *Traumatic Brain Injury in Children and Adolescents: A Sourcebook for Teachers and Other School Personnel* (2nd edn). Austin, TX: ProEd.

Urdan, T. and Midgley, C. (2001) Academic self-handicapping: What we know, what more there is to learn. *Educational Psychology Review, 13*, 2, 115–138.

Valas, H. (2001) Learned helpless and psychological adjustment II: Effects of learning disabilities and low achievement. *Scandinavian Journal of Educational Research, 45*, 2, 101–114.

Van der Kaay, M., Wilton, K. and Townsend, M. (2000) Word processing and written composition: An intervention for children with mild intellectual disability. *Australasian Journal of Special Education, 24*, 2, 53–9.

Van Kraayenoord, C. (2002) Focus on literacy. In A. Ashman and J. Elkins (eds) *Educating Children with Diverse Abilities* (pp. 388–435). Sydney: Prentice Hall.

Van Kraayenoord, C. and Elkins, J. (1998) Learning difficulties in regular classrooms. In A. Ashman and J. Elkins (eds) *Educating Children with Special Needs* (3rd edn, pp. 131–176). Sydney: Prentice Hall.

Van Kraayenoord, C., Elkins, J., Palmer, C., Rickards, F. and Colbert, P. (2000) *Literacy, Numeracy and Students with Disabilities*. Canberra: Commonwealth of Australia.

Vareene, H. and McDermott, R. (1999) *Successful Failure: The School that America Builds*. Boulder, CO: Westview Press.

Vaughn, S., Bos, C.S., and Schumm, J. (2003) *Teaching Exceptional, Diverse, and At-risk Students in the General Education Classroom* (3rd edn). Boston: Allyn & Bacon.

Vaughn, S., Gersten, R. and Chard, D.J. (2000) The underlying message in LD intervention research: Findings from research syntheses. *Exceptional Children, 67*, 1, 99–114.

Vellutino, F.R. (2003) Literacy: reading (early stages). In L. Nandel (ed.) *Encyclopedia of Cognitive Science* (v.2, pp. 922–930). London: Nature Publishing Group.

Vellutino, F.R. and Scanlon, D.M. (2002) The interactive strategies approach to reading intervention. *Contemporary Educational Psychology, 27*, 573–635.

Vellutino, F.R., Scanlon, D.M. and Lyon, G.R. (2000) Differentiating between difficult-to-remediate and readily remediated poor readers. *Journal of Learning Disabilities, 33*, 3, 223–238.

Vellutino, F.R., Scanlon, D.M. and Tanzman, M.S. (1994) Components of reading ability. In G.R. Lyon (ed.) *Frames of Reference for the Assessment of Learning Disabilities* (pp. 279–332). Baltimore, MD: Brookes.

Venezky, R.L. (1993) History of interest in the visual component of reading. In D.M. Willows, R.S. Kruk and E. Corcos (eds). *Visual Processes in Reading and Reading Disabilities* (pp. 3–30). Hillsdale, NJ: Erlbaum.

Vernon, P.E. (1940) *The Measurement of Abilities*. London: University of London Press.

Vernon, P.E. (1960) *Intelligence and Attainment Testing*. London: University of London Press.

Visser, J., Daniels, H. and Cole, T. (eds) (2001) *Emotional and Behavioural Difficulties in Mainstream Schools*. New York: JAI Press.

Volet, S. (2001) Emerging trends in recent research on motivation in learning contexts. In S. Volet and S. Jarvela (eds) *Motivation in Learning Contexts* (pp. 319–334). Amsterdam: Pergamon.

Volkmar, F.R. and Dykens, E. (2002) Mental retardation. In M. Rutter and E. Taylor (eds) *Child and Adolescent Psychiatry* (4th edn, pp. 697–710). Oxford: Blackwell.

von Tetzchner, S. and Grove, N. (2003) *Augmentative and Alternative Communication*. London: Whurr.

Vygotsky, L.S. (1962) *Thought and Language*. Cambridge, MA: MIT Press.

Wagner, R.K. and Garon, T. (1999) Learning disabilities in perspective. In R.J. Sternberg and L. Spear-Swerling (eds) *Perspectives in Learning Disabilities* (pp. 83–105). Boulder, CO: Westview Press.

Wain, G (1994) Mathematics education and society. In A. Orton and G. Wain (eds) *Issues in Teaching Mathematics* (pp. 21–34). London: Cassell.

Waite-Stupiansky, S. (1997) *Building Understanding Together*. Albany, NY: Delmar.

Waldron, N.L. and McLeskey, J. (2000) Preventing academic failure. In K.M. Minke and G.C. Bear (eds) *Preventing School Problems: Promoting School Success* (pp. 171–209). Bethesda, MD: National Association of School Psychologists.

Walker, J.T. (1996) *The Psychology of Learning: Principles and Processes*. Upper Saddle River, NJ: Prentice Hall.

Wall, K. (2003) *Special Needs in Early Years*. London: Paul Chapman Publishing.

Walton, M. (1998) *Teaching Reading and Spelling to Dyslexic Children*. London: Fulton.

Wang, M.C., Haertel, G.D. and Walberg, H.J. (1993) What helps students learn? *Educational Leadership*, *51*, *4*, 74–79.

Ward, T.J., Ward, S.B., Glutting, J.J. and Hatt, C.V. (1999) Exceptional LD profile types for WISC-III and WIAT. *School Psychology Review*, *28*, *4*, 629–643.

Watkins, D. and Biggs, J. (2001) The paradox of the Chinese learner and beyond. In D. Watkins and J. Biggs (eds) *Teaching the Chinese Learner* (pp. 3–23). Melbourne: Australian Council for Educational Research.

Watkins, G. and Hunter-Carsch, M. (1995) Prompt spelling: A practical approach to paired spelling. *Support for Learning*, *10*, *3*, 133–137.

Watson, C. and Willows, D.M. (1993) Evidence for a visual-processing-deficit subtype among disabled readers. In D.M. Willows, R.S. Kruk and E. Corcos (eds) *Visual Processes in Reading and Reading Disabilities* (pp. 287–309). Hillsdale, NJ: Erlbaum.

Wearmouth, J. (2002) The role of the learning support coordinator: Addressing the challenges. In G. Reid and J. Wearmouth (eds) *Dyslexia and Literacy* (pp. 213–228). Chichester: Wiley.

Wehmeyer, M.L., Sands, D.J., Knowlton, H.E. and Kozleski, E.B. (2002) *Teaching Students with Mental Retardation*. Baltimore, MD: Brookes.

Weiner, B. (1972) *Theories of Motivation from Mechanism to Cognition*. Chicago: Markham.

Weiner, B. (1985) An attributional theory of achievement motivation and emotion. *Psychological Review*, *92*, 548–573.

Weiner, B. (1995) *Judgements of Responsibility: A Foundation for a Theory of Social Conduct*. New York: Guilford Press.

Weinstein, R.S. (2002) *Reaching Higher: The Power of Expectations in Schooling*. Cambridge, MA: Harvard University Press.

Weller, C. and Buchanan (1988) *Educators' Desk Reference for Special Learning Problems*. Boston: Allyn & Bacon.

West, J. (2002) Motivation and access to help: The influence of status on one child's motivation for literacy learning. *Reading and Writing Quarterly*, *18*, 205–229.

Westen, D. (2002) *Psychology: Brain, Behavior and Culture* (3rd edn). New York: Wiley.

Westwood, P.S. (1993) Striving for positive outcomes for students with learning difficulties. *Special Education Perspectives*, *2*, *2*, 87–94.

Westwood, P.S. (1994) Issues in spelling instruction. *Special Education Perspectives*, *3*, *1*, 31–44.

Westwood, P.S. (1995) Teachers' beliefs and expectations concerning students with learning difficulties. *Australian Journal of Remedial Education*, *27*, *2*, 19–21.

Westwood, P.S. (1996) Current issues in effective teaching and learning. In NSW Board of Studies: *Nature of the Learner Forum* (pp. 28–43). North Sydney: Board of Studies New South Wales.

Westwood, P.S. (1998) Which intervention? Effective strategies to overcome learning difficulties. In D. Greaves and P. Jeffery (eds) *Strategies for Intervention with Special Needs Students* (pp. 177–199). Melbourne: AREA Press.

Westwood, P.S. (1999a) *Spelling: Approaches to Teaching and Assessment*. Melbourne: Australian Council for Educational Research.

Westwood, P.S. (1999b) Teaching basic mathematics to students with learning difficulties: Priorities and issues. In D. Barwood, D. Greaves and P. Jeffery (eds) *Teaching Numeracy and Literacy: Interventions and Strategies for 'At Risk' Students* (pp. 215–231). Melbourne, AREA Press.

Westwood, P.S. (2000) *Numeracy and Learning Difficulties*. Melbourne: Australian Council for Educational Research.

Westwood, P.S. (2001) Making special schools ordinary: Is this inspirational or confused thinking? *International Journal of Special Education, 16, 1*, 7–20.

Westwood, P.S. (2003) *Commonsense Methods for Children with Special Educational Needs* (4th edn). London: Routledge-Falmer.

Westwood, P.S. and Graham, L. (2000) How many children with special needs in regular classes? *Australian Journal of Learning Disabilities, 5, 3*, 24–35.

Whiting, P., Robinson, G.L. and Parrot, C. (1994) Irlen coloured filters for reading: A six-year follow-up. *Australian Journal of Remedial Education, 26, 3*, 13–19.

Wiener, J. (2002) Friendship and social adjustment of children with learning disabilities. In B.Y.L. Wong and M. Donahue (eds) *The Social Dimensions of Learning Disabilities* (pp. 93–114). Mahwah, NJ: Erlbaum.

Wigfield, A. and Eccles, J.S. (2000) Expectancy-value theory of achievement motivation. *Contemporary Educational Psychology, 25*, 68–81.

Wiig, E.H. (2001) Multi-perspective, clinical-educational assessments of language disorders. In A.S. Kaufman and N.L. Kaufman (eds) *Specific Learning Disabilities and Difficulties in Children and Adolescents* (pp. 247–279). New York: Cambridge University Press.

Wilen, W., Ishler, M., Hutchison, J. and Kindsvatter, R. (2000) *Dynamics of Effective Teaching* (4th edn). New York: Longman.

Williams, J.M., Watts, F.N., MacLeod, C. and Mathews, A. (1997) *Cognitive Psychology and Emotional Disorders* (2nd edn). New York: Wiley.

Williams, S.C. (2002) How speech-feedback and word-prediction software can help students write. *Teaching Exceptional Children, 34, 3*, 72–78.

Wilson, V. (2002) *Does Small Really Make a Difference? A Review of the Literature on the Effects of Class Size*. Edinburgh: The Scottish Council for Research in Education.

Wing, A.M. (2000) Motor control: Mechanisms of motor equivalence in handwriting. *Current Biology, 10, 6*, R245–R248.

Wing. L. (1996) *The Autistic Spectrum*. London: Constable.

Wise, B.W. and Snyder, L. (2002) Clinical judgments in identifying and teaching children with language-based reading difficulties. In R. Bradley, L. Danielson and D.P. Hallahan (eds) *Identification of Learning Disabilities: Research to Practice* (pp. 653–692). Mahwah, NJ: Erlbaum.

Wolf, M. and Bowers, P.G. (1999) The double-deficit hypothesis for the developmental dyslexias. *Journal of Educational Psychology, 91*, 415–438.

Wolf, M. and Kennedy, R. (2003) How the origins of written language instruct us to teach: A response to Steven Strauss. *Educational Researcher, 32, 2*, 26–30.

Wong, B.Y.L., Butler, D.L., Ficzere, S.A. and Kuperis, S. (1997) Teaching adolescents with learning disabilities and low achievers to plan, write, and revise compare and contrast essays. *Learning Disabilities Research and Practice, 12*, 2–15.

Wong, B.Y.L. and Donahue, M.L. (2002) *The Social Dimensions of Learning Disabilities*. Mahwah, NJ: Erlbaum.

Wong, Y.Y. and Westwood, P.S. (2002) The teaching and management of children with autism. *Hong Kong Special Education Forum, 5, 1*, 46–72.

Workman, E.A. and Katz, A.M. (1995) *Teaching Behavioral Self-control to Students* (2nd edn). Austin, TX: ProEd.

World Health Organization (1992) *The ICD-10 Classification of Mental and Behavioural Disorders*. Geneva: World Health Organization.

Wynn, K. (1998) Numerical competence in infants. In C. Donlan (ed.) *The Development of Mathematical Skills* (pp. 3–26). Hove: Psychology Press.

Xin, Y.P. and Jitendra, A.K. (1999) The effects of instruction in solving mathematical word problems for students with learning problems: A meta-analysis. *Journal of Special Education, 32, 4*, 207–225.

Yates, G. (1988) Classroom research into effective teaching. *Australian Journal of Remedial Education, 20, 1*, 4–9.

Ysseldyke, J., Algozzine, B. and Thurlow, M. (2000) *Critical Issues in Special Education* (3rd edn). Boston: Houghton Mifflin.

Zaslavsky, C. (1994) *Fear of Math*. New Brunswick, NJ: Rutgers University Press.

Zeffiro, T. and Eden, G. (2000) The neural basis of developmental dyslexia. *Annals of Dyslexia, 50*, 3–30.

Index

collaborative learning (*continued*)
  group work 22, 118, 130, 144
communities of learners 23
comprehension (*see* reading: comprehension)
computational skills 120, **127**
computer-assisted learning 18, 57, 82, 113, 129
concept development 4, 85, 87, 122, 123, 127, 141
confidence:
  as a factor in learning 1, 49, 54, 56, 97, 121
  learners' loss of 55–56, 61, **63**, 88, 119, 121, 128
congenital wordblindness 76
constructivist theory of learning: 5, 20, 118
  basic principles **22–23**, 24, 58
  criticisms of **23–24**, 56
  influence on curricula 20, 23
  students with difficulties and **24–25**, 56, 58
contexual cues: in reading 86, 88, 96
controlled attention 68
Corrective Spelling through Morphographs 19
creative intelligence (Sternberg) 49
cueing 18, 45, 139, 144
curriculum:
  planning 1, 3, 57
  relevance of 58, 144
  as a source of learning failure **57–58**, 120
  special school 83, 138, 142, **143–144**
'curriculum-disabled' students 57, 72

D

deaf students 65
declarative knowledge **5**, 20, 100
dendrites 36, 37, 38
depression 91, 141
descriptive praise 29
developmental delay 134, 137, **142**
Diagnostic and Statistical Manual of Mental Disorders (DSM 4) 71, 106, 122
diagnostic assessment: 78, **79**, 96
  in mathematics **124**, **127–128**
diagnostic-prescriptive teaching **94**
differential diagnosis: 92, 93
  from WISC profile 79–80
differentiation:
  of curriculum 134, 138
  of teaching method 59, **94**, 96, 106, 110
direct instruction 19, **56**, 82, 143, 144
  (*see also* direct teaching)
direct teaching 4, 5, 6, 13, 19, **24**, 55, 117, 143
discovery learning 25, 108, 117, 118
discrepancy formula 78
discrimination learning 4, 92
double deficit hypothesis: in dyslexia **95**
Down's syndrome 135, 137

dynamic assessment 127
dyscalculia 73, **121–122**, 123
dysgraphia 73–74, **106–107**
dyslexia 72, 73, 74, 76, **80–81**, **92–95**, 98, 105, 122
dysnomia 73
dysorthographia 73, 106
dyspedagogia 78

E

effect size: in meta-analysis 82, 112
electronic spellcheckers 115
emergent writing 101
emotional and behavioural disorders 54, 59, **63–64**, 72, 74, 91, 141, 143
epilepsy 61, 135
episodic memory 41, **42**
error analysis: in mathematics 74, **124**, 127
executive processes **7**, **42**, 49, 68, 100, 140
expectancy-value theory **32–33**
explanatory style **28**
explicit teaching 24, 25, 55, **83–84**, 87, 88, **89**, **96**, 98, **99–100**, 104, 108
externalised behaviours 64
extrinsic motivation **31–32**
extrinsic rewards 18, 32, 113, 141

F

fading cues 18
failure:
  causes of 1, 56 (*see also* learning difficulties: causes)
  fear of 19, 26, 29, **32**
  impact on motivation **26**, **27**, 56, 58, 61, 63, **78**, 84, 104, **119**, **121**, 139, 141
  self-worth and 1, 26, 63, 104
feedback 56, 90, 96, 98, **99**, 108, 114, 119, 127
fetal alcohol syndrome 134
fluency: 12, 13, 90
  in performance 88, 90
  as a stage in learning **12–13**
forgetting 10, 14, **41**, 43, **43–44**, 58
formative assessment 82, 83, 97, 126
Fragile X syndrome 135, 137
frontal lobes 37, 41, 47
Frostig, M. 67
functional magnetic resonance imaging (fMRI) **39**, 76

G

'garden-variety' learning difficulties 53, 72, **74**, 76, 95
generalisation:
  in learning 6, 7, 12, **14**, 115, 131, 140, 142
  problems with 110, 123
  in students with intellectual disability **140**, 142

long-term potentiation (LTP) **39**
look-say-cover-write-check spelling strategy **105**, **114**
low-achieving students 71, 72, 73, 80, 95, 105, 118, 119, 121
low vision 66

M
maintenance of learned behaviours 12, 131
malnutrition **38**, 137
mastery learning **12**
mathematics:
    anxiety 119, 121, 128
    assessment in **126–128**
    dyscalculia 73, **121–122**, 123
    learning difficulties in 74, 77, **117–127**
Matthew effect 56
meaning-based approach in reading **86**
meaningful learning 10–11
mediated learning (Feuerstein) 51, 143
memorisation **10–11**, 44, 118, 130, 140
memory 9, 17, 35, 38, **39**, **40–45**, 64, **70**, 100, 119, 125, **139–140**
    decay 14, 44
    forgetting 10, 14, 41, **43–44**, 58
    interference 14, **44**
    long-term 11, 14, **20**, **42–43**, 45, 70, 92, 100, 114, **139**
    meta-memory **43**, 45
    neurological correlates 35, 39
    recall, 43, **104**
    recognition **44–45**, **104**
    remembering 9, 40, 44, **44–45**
    retrieval 35, 40, 42, **44–45**, 70, **77**, 92, 124, **125**, **139**
    short-term 20, **40–41**, 80, 91
    traces 43, 44
    working memory 5, **20**, **41–42**, 47, 88, 100, 103, 121, 125, 138
mental retardation (*see* intellectual disability)
meta-analysis 57, 80, 81, 131
metacognition 7, 29, 103
    deficits in 66
    defined 7
    role in learning 7, 29, 68, 86, 100, 103, 104
metacognitive training **7–8**, **29**, 78, 111, 112, 139, 145
milieu approach to language development **142**
mnemonics:
    teaching of 43, 45, 112, 130
    value of 45, 82, 130
mobility 135
    in vision impaired students 66
modelling 4, 7, 9, **13**, 19, 25, **57**, 96, **98**, 99, 110

motivation: 1, **30–32**, 51, 58, 88, 102, 126, **140–141**
    in the classroom 2, 30, 33, 119
    expectancy-value theory **32–33**
    extrinsic **31–32**
    importance of 30, 33, 126
    intrinsic 1, **31–32**, 56, 102
    motivational style 33
    types of **31–32**
motor skills learning **4–5**
multiple handicaps 136, 142, 143
multiple intelligences (Gardner) 49–50
multisensory teaching 44, 114, **115**
myelination **36**

N
neobehavioural theories of learning 10, **25–26**
neural networks 21, 35, 36, 38, 39, 40, 45, 47
neurological development 35–39, 76, 123
neurons **36–39**, 40, 128
neurotransmitters 36, 37, 69
noise in classrooms 58
number:
    facts 6, 118, 123, 124, **125**, 126, 127
    number sense 120
    skills 120, 122
nutrition:
    and development 38
    and learning 62, 82

O
observational learning **9–10**, 25, 66
on-task behaviour 58, 64
operant conditioning **18–19**
orientation in vision impaired students 66
orthographic units **88**, 92, 93, 114
overlearning 11, **45**

P
parents:
    involvement in reading 90, 97
    poverty and 60
    support from 57, 60, 61, 64, 88, 90, 145
pedagogical content knowledge 2
peer assistance 61, 83, 97, 113, 129
peer group pressure 90
perception 67, 119 (*see also* auditory perception and visual perception)
perceptual-motor difficulties 67–68, 82, 83, 143
petit mal epilepsy 61
phonic skills 85, **87–88**, 102, 105 (see also reading: decoding)
phonological awareness 68, 76, **77**, 80, **87–88**, 91, **94–95**, 101, **105**, 125
physical disability 5, 61, 65
Piaget, J. 21, 22, 137

specific learning disability (SpLD) 27, 42, 48, 54, **71–84**, **92–95**, 121
    causes **75–78**
    definition 71, **72–73**, 81
    identification of **78–80**
    prevalence 54, **74–75**, 77
    types of 72, **73**, 80
speech therapy 142
spellcheckers **115**
spelling 88, **101–106**
    by analogy 105, 114
    difficulties 77, **104–106**
    and handwriting 108
    interventions for **113–115**
    invented 97, 101
    stages in learning 101
    visual perception and **105**
stages in learning **12–14**, 24, 129
strategy training 51, 57, **82**, 86, 103, 106, 110, **112–113**, 114, **130–131**
stress 38, 41, 70
    in the home 64, 90
    related to failure 27, 61, 70, 90, 93
structure of intellect (Guilford) 47
student-centred approach 19, 21, 22, 25, 56, 81, 117, 144
student-teacher relationship **18–19**, 54, **60–61**, 83, 100, 128
subtypes:
    of dyscalculia **126**
    of dyslexia 80, **92–93**
    of learning disability 80
Success for All 97
support for learning 60, **89**, 104, 145
    in-class 89, 97, 130
    students' attitude toward 63, 90, 97
    withdrawal groups 63, 89, 97
surface dyslexia 93
synapse **37**, **38**, 39, 48

T

task analysis **12**, 19, 127, 129, 143
task-approach strategies 29, **112**, **130**
teacher expectancy 54, 55, **60**, 63, 91, **141**, **145**
teaching methods:
    activity-based 13, 21, 23, 24, 56, 118, **119**
    behavioural approach **18**, 19, **83**, 133, 135, 141, **144–145**
    as a cause of failure 54, 55, 72, 78, 88, **89**, 95, 105, **106**, 107, **119**
    child-centred 9, 21, 22, 24
    direct 4, 5, 6, 9, 13, 19, **24**, 55, **56**, **83**, 117, 143
    explicit 24, 25, 55, **83–84**, 87, 88, **89**, 96, 98, **99–100**, 104, 108

theories of learning **17–29**
    behavioural **17–19**
    cognitive **19–25**
    neobehavioural 10, **25–26**
    social-cognitive theory 10
Think Sheets 111
thinking aloud 7, 99, 112
    as demonstration 7, 30
transcription 100, 103, 108, 112
    problems with 103, **104**
transfer of learning 6, 7, 14
traumatic brain injury 68
triarchic theory of intelligence (Sternberg) 49
tutoring 128
types of learning **3–11**

U

underachievement 64, 71

V

verbal association 4
verbal self-instruction 29, 30, 121, **130**, 142
vicarious punishment 26
vicarious reinforcement 26
vision impairment 66
visual dyslexia 77, **92**
visual functioning 66–67
visual imagery 101, 102, **105**, 114
visual images 92, 105, 115
visual perception 67–68, **77**, 82, 85, 91, **125**
visuo-spatial ability 124, 125, 126
Vygotsky, L. 22, 23

W

whole language approach: reading 8–9, 86
WISC III and WISC-R 80
word building 98, 115
word concept 87
word families 106, 114
word-processing 103, 110, 115
word recognition 6, 24, 76, 80, **87–88**, 91, 92
working memory 5, **20**, **41–42**, 44, 45, 47, 66, 68, 88, 100, 103, 121, **125**, 138
writing 96, **99–115**
    assessment of **108–109**
    developmental aspects of **100–101**, 102
    difficulties 74, **103–104**, **107**, 108
    skills involved in **100**, 115
    strategies for 102, **111–113**, 115
    teaching of 97, **99–100**, **109–113**

Z

zone of proximal development **23**